Contemporary Kazakh
Proverb Research

International Folkloristics

Alan Dundes
Founding Editor

Wolfgang Mieder
General Editor

Vol. 18

The International Folkloristics series is part of the Peter Lang Humanities list.
Every volume is peer reviewed and meets
the highest quality standards for content and production.

PETER LANG
New York • Berlin • Brussels • Lausanne • Oxford

Contemporary Kazakh Proverb Research

Digital, Cognitive, Literary, and Ecological Approaches

Edited by Gulnara Omarbekova
and Erik Aasland

PETER LANG
New York • Berlin • Brussels • Lausanne • Oxford

Library of Congress Cataloging-in-Publication Control Number: 2022032198

Bibliographic information published by **Die Deutsche Nationalbibliothek**.
Die Deutsche Nationalbibliothek lists this publication in the "Deutsche
Nationalbibliografie"; detailed bibliographic data are available
on the Internet at http://dnb.d-nb.de/.

ISSN 1528-6533
ISBN 978-1-4331-9588-4 (paperback)
ISBN 978-1-4331-9589-1 (ebook pdf)
ISBN 978-1-4331-9590-7 (epub)
DOI 10.3726/b19538

Peter Lang Publishing, Inc., New York
80 Broad Street, 5th floor, New York, NY 10004

www.peterlang.com

Table of Contents

List of Figures

List of Tables

Foreword

This book is intended for anyone interested in paremiology, especially the study of proverbs of Kazakh-speaking linguists, philologists, anthropologists, folklorists, and students of linguistic specialties. Kazakh proverbs are not only a literary expression of Kazakh people's spiritual wealth and centuries-old culture, but they are also a vivid chronicle of the level of consciousness, intelligence, and wisdom of the Kazakh people. A proverb—*maqal* in Kazakh(from Arabic)—is a short, simple, and traditional saying or phrase that gives advice and embodies a common truth based on practical experience or common sense (G. Mamırbekova 2017). A proverb may have an allegorical message behind its appearance. For instance, *Azǧa qanaǧat qylmasaŋ, köpten qür qalasyŋ* could be translated into English as (Grasp all, lose all). It addresses the human issue of greed, encouraging the interlocutor to be satisfied with small things instead.

Many Kazakh collectors have contributed to the enrichment and accumulation, making them a wonderful heritage of the Kazakh people. Since the second half of the nineteenth century, Kazakh proverbs have been collected and published. Among the first collectors of Kazakh proverbs were Sh. Ualikhanov, Y. Altynsarin, A. Divayev, and M. Zh. Kopeev and Russian scientists A.A. Vasiliev, F. Plotnikov, P.A. Melioransky, V.V. Katarinsky, and V. Radlov, who presented to the public treasures of folklore. Proverbs in the Kazakh language were published for the first time in 1914 in Kazan, with subsequent publication of *A Thousand and One Proverbs* in 1923 in Moscow, *Kazakh Proverbs* (compiled by A. Divayev) in 1927 in Tashkent, and *Kazakh Proverbs and Sayings* (O. Turmanzhanov) in 1935 in Almaty (Makhat 2019).

In the late twentieth and early twenty-first centuries, the proverbs of the Kazakh language became an object of study in the field of colloquial speech, fiction, and journalistic and other discourses. During this period, Kazakh linguistics began to consider proverbs in an anthropocentric direction, paying attention to the communicative and pragmatic possibilities of paremic units. However, in the era of globalization, proverbs should be studied as an integral part of the paremiological discourse on the Internet, media and artistic discourse, communication, conflict management, and environmental discourse. The formation of the corpus of the national Kazakh language in paremiological studies is relevant today.

The present collection contains articles by Kazakh authors. These works focus on the structure and semantics of proverbs and their cognitive, lingua-cultural characteristics, pragmatics, and variability/changeability. It was determined that one of the most important issues is the scholarly analysis of the cognitive structure and conceptual models of the human image in proverbs within the framework of an anthropocentric approach, such as "recognition of a person through his/her language" in modern linguistics. Therefore, the pragmatic and communicative function of proverbs is the main focus of the works included in the collection. Attention is drawn to the essence, pragmatic and cognitive aspects, and structural features of proverbs, along with the ethnolinguistic and cognitive foundations of the logical-semantic grouping of proverbs in the Kazakh language.

The first chapter of the first part, "*Contemporary Issues of Proverb Use*," has four papers. Proverbs and sayings are an ancient genre of folk art. As time and social conditions change, proverbs and sayings will also be adapted and supplemented or fall out of use among the people. Kazakh proverbs and sayings are valued and, in turn, are subject to modifications based on modern realities. G. Omarbekova in her paper "*Perspectives on Proverb Use Among Kazakhs: Ecological Issues*" presents the results of recent fieldwork on contemporary use of Kazakh proverbs. We found proverb competency uneven among students and determined that senior scholars use the same set of proverbs. The author will try to answer what this means for the ongoing vitality of proverb use among Kazakhs. The American scholar E. Aasland in his paper "*Contrasting Two Kazakh Proverbial Calls to Action: Using Discourse Ecologies to Understand Proverb Meaning-making*" utilizes an approach called discourse ecologies to explore how two comparable proverbs operate in terms of representative and frame-aligning discourse for contemporary Kazakhs. In the era of modern globalization, one of the ways to learn proverbs and sayings for young people is to use the achievements of information technology, to make them available to young people and the general public. Currently, accessibility is aided by the creation of a database of proverbs and sayings on mobile phones, in social networks, and the creation of a corpus of proverbs for the convenience of the user. In the paper "*Content and Software Structure of the Kazakh Proverb Corpus*," A. Zhanabekova considers theoretical and practical issues in creating a corpus of Kazakh proverbs and sayings. The corpus is a tool for automatically receiving information or texts of a large volume on national character, not only for linguists and educators, but also for the public. The authors of the paper: "*A Modernized Tradition in*

Kazakhstan: Kindik Sheshe" F. Guven and A. Amalbekova investigated the term *Kindiksheshe* that in some Turkic languages refers to the woman who acts as a midwife during the delivery of the baby and plays a special role in the life of the newborn baby later. The author argues that the modernization of the tradition affects the use of proverbs concerning this institution in Kazakh and Turkish languages, considering that Kazakh society highly values this institution today.

The aim of the second chapter, "*Common Problems of Paremiology*" is to systematize and monitor the use of Kazakh proverbs in various communicative situations by focusing on ontological, social, and axiological types of cognitive accumulation. The authors of the paper "*Kazakh Proverbs from the Perspective of Cultural Cognition and Communication*" F. Orazbayeva and E. Orazaliyeva describe Kazakh proverbs from the perspective of cultural cognition and communication. The authors of the paper "*Story of the Use and Study of Kazakh Proverbs in the Soviet Period: The Use of Proverbs in the Works of the Writer M. Auezov,*" G. Pirali and A. Kurmanbayeva, studied the works of a prominent representative of Kazakh literature, writer M. Auezov, and conduct a comprehensive analysis of the use of proverbs and sayings in his prose texts based on the stylistic features of the writer. The authors investigate the transformation of proverbs and sayings and their semantic function. The article also examines the expressions and words of the author, which have become widespread among the people and entered the form of proverbs and sayings. The author of the paper "*National Cognitive Activity of Proverbs in the Language of Fiction,*" Zh. Abdigapbarova, examines the use of proverbs and sayings in the works of the famous Kazakh writer Mukhtar Magauin. Proverbs not only decorate the language of works but also serve to deepen reflection on the knowledge of the nation. They are often found in the writers' narrative tools and in the language of their characters. Writers use proverbs and sayings to reveal the literary image of the hero, express ideological purposes, and provide the author's positions.

The third chapter "*Proverbs as a Part of the Culture*" consists of three papers. D. Nurgaliyeva and B. Arinova, in the paper "*Analysis of Kazakh Proverbs in Writing (Notes) of Mashkhur-Zhusip Kopeiuly,*" provide the semantic analysis of Mashkhur-Zhusip Kopeiuly's several proverbs that have fallen out of use in our time and are now exposed to the ecology of language. G. Shokym et al., in the paper "*Gender Linguistic Picture of the World in Kazakh Proverbs,*" provide insight into how women and men are represented in Kazakh proverbs. The article is devoted to the study of the problem of the relationship of language as a means of building and maintaining a certain picture of the world and gender as a system of interpersonal interaction.

In G. Abdimaulen's paper *"Linguistic Characteristics of the Images of 'Kyz-Kelin-Ana' in the Concept of 'Woman'"* the concept of "girl" is described by phraseological phrases and proverbs in the context of "Language-Culture-Society" in the traditional Kazakh worldview. The article reflects the special meanings of proverbs, sayings and phraseological phrases about Kazakh girls. The latter chapter discusses changes in proverbs relating to girlhood, womanhood, and marriage from the early twentieth century to current usage.

The fourth chapter is devoted to *"The Role of Proverbs in Pedagogy."* G. Bekkozhanova et al., in the paper *"Cognitive and linguo-cultural Aspects of Transference of English Proverbs and Sayings into Kazakh Language,"* compare Y. S. Kengesbayev's, L. P. Smith's, and S.G. Akhmetova's dictionaries, and reveal linguo-cultural and cognitive peculiarities of proverbs while transferring them from Kazakh into English. The research distinguishes the adequate transference of different types of proverbs and determines suitable forms of cognitive and linguo-cultural transference. In the paper *"Case Study of Teaching Paremiological Units in Digital Education to Multilingual Students"* the authors R. Zhussupova and A. Tolegen collected examples of proverbs and sayings in electronic format and classified them into certain semantic groups. It analyzes the peculiarities of using applications in teaching and learning proverbs. A system of exercises was modeled for working with proverbs and sayings to examine the use of select English, Kazakh, and Russian paremiological units in digital learning. The results show that using proverbs in teaching English through digital tools improved Multilingual Pre-service teachers' vocabulary skills, spoken language, and written essays, as well as their cultural awareness.

In the second part of the volume, transformed proverbs are recognized as "anti-proverbs" in the Kazakh language and considered a separate genre. At present, there are frequent transformations reflecting new realities from the sociopolitical sphere: medicine *El bolamyn deseŋ, maskaŋdy tuze* (If you want to be a country, wear the mask); *Sau bolamyn deseŋ, shekaraŋdy zhap* (If you want to be healthy, close the border), education *Kitap—ğalym, tilsiz müğalim* (The book is a scientist, a teacher without a language); *Bilim bazarda satylmas* (Knowledge is not sold in the market), policy and government *Ukimetke khalyktan salyk kymbat* (For the state the taxes are more precious than people); *Ysh ret deputat bolsaŋ da, khalyktyŋ qaryzynan qutyla almaysyŋ* (Even if you became a deputy three times, you still cannot get rid of people's debts), time *Qaltasyna qaray—toqaly, zamanyna say—maqaly* (Depending on the pocket—the younger wife, according to the time—the proverb); *Qazirgi bala men brynğy zamannyŋ balasynyŋ arasy zher men köktei* (The difference between today's child and the child of the past is like a distance between heaven and earth), crime and law enforcement *Dostastyq qazhet, tauelsizdik qymbat* (Concord is needed, independence is dear), the economic sphere *Önimiŋdi ötkizu de— bir öner* (Selling product is an art); *Bank basynan shiridi* (The bank is destroyed from the top); sport *Sport—beybitshilik elshisi* (Sport is an ambassador of peace), alcohol *Araq iship, temeki shekken, densaulyqtyŋ tybine zhetedi* (Who drinks vodka and smokes reaches the bottom of health); spheres of leisure *Zhaŋa zheŋedi, eski øledi* (The new wins, the old dies); *Eki kjïnnen keyin zhaŋa qumuranyŋ suy da suyp ketedi* (After two days, even the water in the new jar has cooled down). These lexemes are the cultural realities of modern times; these units are nationally determined linguistic signs that reflect the phenomena of today's social spheres.

As Walter and Mokienko point out, W. Mieder characterizes anti-proverbs figuratively as twisted or distorted wisdom (German, verdrehteWeisheiten) (2005, 8). Modifications to existing proverbs that challenge or contradict the former proverbs are classified as anti-proverbs. Thus, the proverb *Adam qanaty—at* (a person's wings—a horse) as part of a governmental posting should be considered as a variant of the traditional *Yer qanaty—at* (a man's wings—horse) since there is no intent in formulating the variation to critique the traditional proverb (Aasland 2018). According to the definition of O.N. Antonova, an anti-proverb is "speech formation of a wide range; these are modified paremias that undergo changes at the lexical, morphological and syntactic levels" (Antonova 2010, 98). The anti-proverb has not yet become an object of close attention of linguists of the Kazakh language; even now the term itself has not been accepted. Linguists call transformed, reworked proverbs "invariants" (Qaidar 2004), "occasional" (Rssalieva et al., 2014), or "proverbial transformations" (Dyussembina 2016). Thus, the widespread dissemination of anti-proverbs on the one hand, and the low level of knowledge about them on the other, leads to the fact that one of the urgent tasks of modern paremiology of the Kazakh language is not only the registration of traditional and new proverbs, but also the fixation and functional-stylistic interpretation of their transformations.

As we worked on this volume, we committed to not violating the original contributions of the authors. We see this book as a meeting of Kazakh and Western scholarship. It has been a stretching experience for us to be faithful to this vision. Western scholars may be surprised by two aspects of the chapters: (1) the long introductory paragraphs extolling the virtues of proverbs, and (2) the literature review sections having a long list of the names of key scholars.

If you traveled to Kazakhstan and enjoyed some traditional Kazakh food served by your hosts, you might hear the following description: "For

Kazakhs, we are the leaves, and our ancestors are the tree." In a similar way, Kazakh scholars may see themselves as the leaves and the great poets who have gone before them as the tree. As a result, their writing is a celebration of the connection with and continuation of a rich tradition. Part of this abiding is expressed by sharing one Kazakh proverb after another.

Such a sense of attachment stands in stark contrast to the Western tradition. Consider the German for an argument: Auseinandersetzung (literally to place separately). Even in our current era that acknowledges that objectivity is impracticable, the process of self-reflection involves recognition of the distance between self and others.

Then there are the literature reviews. Our Kazakh colleagues list name after name of key scholars. Here we would draw a parallel to a foundational Kazakh practice. When Kazakhs are young, they are taught to recite their last seven generations of fathers. This is called the *jeti ata* (seven fathers). When youth are in the process of finding a spouse, they will share their *jeti ata*. This process serves two purposes: (1) It ensures that close relatives don't marry/ maintains the tradition of distant marriage, and (2) it serves as an indication of those who were raised properly. In a comparable way, the Kazakh scholar offering a chain of scholars' names is proof of their having been trained uprightly in their discipline. Here the basis for the scholars' activities is likely comparable to the second reason.

Well, that is our attempt at explaining two of the stretching experiences involved in bringing this volume together. I hope you enjoy this journey into contemporary research on Kazakh proverbs.

I would like to express our gratitude to all authors who contributed to this volume. Special thanks to my Co-PI of this project to Dr. Erik Aasland for his commitment to developing the paremiological study of the Kazakh language.

This book marks the culmination of the three-year grant provided by Nazarbayev University. In the chapter about discourse ecologies and Kazakh proverbs, the authors report on the field research they carried out under the grant. I would like to express our appreciation for Nazarbayev University as this publication was financially supported by Nazarbayev UniversityFaculty Development Competitive Research Grant No 110119FD4509. Permission is gratefully acknowledged to reprint the following essay in this volume: Aasland, Erik. "Contrasting Two Kazakh Proverbial Calls to Action: Using Discourse Ecologies to Understand Prover Meaning-Making." *Proverbium: Yearbook of International Proverb Scholarship*, 35 (2018), 1–14.

All translations are the authors' unless otherwise noted.

Gulnara Omarbekova
Nazarbayev University
Nur-Sultan, Kazakhstan

Bibliography

Aasland, E. 2018. "Contrasting Two Kazakh Proverbial Calls to Action: Using Discourse Ecologies to Understand Proverb Meaning–making." *Proverbium: Yearbook of International Proverb Scholarship* 35: 1–14.

Antonova, O. N. 2010. "Antiproverbs as a Means of Functional Modification of Media Discourse (Based on the Material of the British and American Press)." *Bulletin of SamGU.#3* (77): 96–98.

Dyussembina, G. Y. 2016. *Merzimdi baspasözdegi ğalamnıñ aksïologïyalıq beynesi.* Axiological image of the universe in periodicals. PhD thesis for the degree of Doctor of Philosophy, Almaty.

Makhat, D. A. 2019. "Proverbs and Sayings Are a Source of Data of the Kazakh History." *Journal of History* № 2 (93): 192–199. file:///C:/Users/gulnara.omarbekova/Downloads/459-1-956-1-10-20190621.pdf

Mamırbekova, G. 2017. *Qazaq tilindegi arab, parsı sözderiniñ tüsindirme sözdigi (An explanatory dictionary of Arabic and Persian words in the Kazakh language)*, Almaty: State Institute of Language Development.

Qaidar, A. 2004. *Khalyq danalygy.* [Folk wisdom]. Almaty: Toganay T.

Rssalieva, A. M., and Smagulova Zh. G. 2014. "*Kazak maqal-mətelderinin uzualdy qoldanysy.* Usual use of Kazakh proverbs." *MolodoiUtcheni* 4.1 (63.1): 67–68. https://moluch.ru/archive/63/10022/ (20.07.2020).

Walter, H., and V. M. Mokienko. 2005. *Antiproverbs of the Russian People.* St. Petersburg: Neva.

Part I The Current Paremiological
Studies of the Kazakh Language

Chapter 1 Contemporary Issues
of Proverb Use

Perspectives on Proverb Use Among Kazakhs: Ecological Issues

GULNARA OMARBEKOVA
Nazarbayev University, Nur-Sultan

Introduction

In this article, we view proverbs as part of contemporary spoken language in everyday modern colloquial speech and context in the Kazakh language environment. The article offers insights into the proverbs of colloquial Kazakh in everyday life. The Kazakh people have a vast number of proverbs and aphorisms. They include all fields of life: birth and death, wealth and poverty, friendship and enmity, love for the Motherland, family values, human relations, gender relations, attitude to work, peculiarities of education of children, and many other topics.

A proverb *maqal* in Kazakh (from Arabic) is a short, simple, and traditional saying, or a phrase that gives advice and embodies a commonplace truth based on practical experience or common sense. A proverb may have an allegorical message behind its odd appearance. For instance, *Azǧa qanaǧat qylmasaŋ, köpten qür qalasyŋ*, English equivalent will be (Grasp all, lose all). In the course of work, we use different language units: traditional proverbs, aphorism, and modern adaptation of old proverbs, called "anti-proverbs." *Traditional proverbs* are inherited from the old generation as the eloquence of spoken language as classic, natural, and pure proverbs. *Aphoristic statements* are quoted in writings and our daily speech and have a particular author. *A modern adaptation of old proverbs* is a language phenomenon based on a traditional proverb that gives a humorous effect or current view on a situation in the form of a statement. It usually consists of two short sentences: one keeps the structure of old proverbs, and another part may be replaced by determinant words borrowed from Internet languages, such as *Blogs, Facebook, YouTube, Follower's page or files*, mostly *English loan words*.

This phenomenon is currently in the process of development in the Kazakh language. The correct inclusion of proverbs in speech makes the language more vivid and expressive and emphasizes the speaker's wit. Proverbs of the Kazakh language reflect the wisdom of the nation, its experience, history, and ideals. When translating proverbs literally, one cannot correctly understand their meaning, as they can be presented as metaphors. Eloquence has always been valued among Kazakhs. Usually, a literal translation of proverbs from the Kazakh language, for example, into English, will appear absurd. Sometimes, to understand the meaning of proverbs, it is necessary to know certain customs and traditions of the people, as they permeate the whole life of a person and their values.

Research Questions

The project's main aim is arranged by considering the key trends and the leading worldwide conclusions in discourse ecologies and Kazakhstani science on the stated problem. In our research, we gathered evidence for the proverbial discourse analysis in the contemporary Kazakh language. This process involved unpacking, evaluating, and realizing the resources in forms such as proverbs that can be used to address contemporary issues more effectively. We investigated the reasons and cases through the proverb usage of the ecological problems of the Kazakh language, which has over 11 million speakers around the world.

Does the younger generation know proverbs well? How well are the proverbs transmitted to the young generation? If their proverb competency is adequate, is it an indication that cultural embeddedness provides a strong moral character in a globalized world. If their competence is weak, does it show the *"deverbalization"* of society (Karasik 2010, 113), which leads to poor development of discursive competence in the use of proverbs by some Kazakh speakers? "If the circle of people who understand and appreciate such words narrows in society, their transition from a living vocabulary to the area of a passive dictionary inevitably occurs," write L.A. Brusenskaya and E.G. Kulikov. In their opinion, "through the efforts of modern masters of the word, this vocabulary can again return to the 'bright field of consciousness'" (2018, 22). The discursive ecology approach looks at how this can be achieved at the community/media level and in close personal interactions. Our research examines the question of how past proverbs can gain new meaning in modern Kazakhstan. This research will open new realities to overcome the linguistic ecology and effectively postulate possible future directions and solutions.

Methodology

Proverbs are a cultural treasure for the Kazakh people and continue to be relevant. Many Kazakh proverbs are still old fashioned, although now they are often used in a new context with a new meaning. Under the influence of globalization, some transform into new ones, new anti-proverbs, and other new proverbial units. This study explores some unique uses of contemporary proverbs in the Kazakh language under the concept of "the ecological discourse". Proverbs are living, mobile organisms that absorb like a sponge all the realities of the modern world and the changes in society's life and reflect on them in their many variations and transformations. With the widespread and diverse implementation of Kazakh proverbs, they serve as a crucial part of the ecological features of the contemporary Kazakh language. The contemporarily used proverbs from the linguistic point of view create a language violation, creating language ecology cases, the composition of traditional proverbs changes, the components are replaced with other words, or they are shortened, etc.

The success of a proverb's performance as such must depend ultimately on the listener's ability to perceive that he or she is being addressed in traditional, i.e., proverbial, terms (Aasland 2018). Studying proverbs means participating in an ongoing discourse in culture since proverbs are considered the linguistic heritage of any nation. It serves as a hypothesis of the study, which was to study the ecological discourse of the proverbs of the Kazakh language.

The study is an initial report on the language ecology of Kazakh proverbs. The Kazakh folklore is rich in proverbs covering all fields of life. Erik Aasland explores two proverbs using an approach called discourse ecologies as a methodology. Consideration is also given to whether anti-proverbs have emerged for the proverb in question and will provide the content for discussing the discourse ecologies of the two proverbs (Aasland 2018), which fits this technique's consideration of both genre transmission and cultural embeddedness.

The acclaimed American paremiologist Wolfgang Mieder points out the empirical identification of the "familiarity" or "recognizability" of the proverb among the speakers of the language. The present study strives to assess the results of a survey among university students of different majors in different cities of Kazakhstan. The purpose of this survey was to find out whether the native speakers were "familiar with the particular types of proverbs, and whether the youth use a mostly particular type of proverbs, old or new transformed ones, and their preferences and reasons for proverb usage." The survey was carried out among a group of 418 students in five universities. The locations for conducting the survey were chosen purposefully in different geographically located cities. The participating students were of both genders, aged between 20 and 23. During the fieldwork, we also interviewed 45 senior scholars who teach in five universities in Kazakhstan. Using an approach called card sort, we had participants group eighteen sentences into the categories of the traditional proverbs, aphorisms (winged words), and contemporary sayings (Qaidar 2009, 14–23). Questions for students focused on their familiarity with Kazakh proverbs, their knowledge of the meaning, their personal use of these proverbs, and attitudes towards the modern adaptation of old proverbs that incorporate borrowed online terminology. Semi-structured interviews were one of the most used qualitative methods (Kitchen and Tate 2000). Interviews with scholars focused on their use of Kazakh proverbs and their ability to distinguish between traditional proverbs, aphorisms (i.e., sayings with known authors), and a modern adaptation of old proverbs.

We found that students use proverbs daily and continue to place a high value on traditional Kazakh proverbs. A significant percentage of students surveyed (66%) insisted that only traditional proverbs should be used. However, our interview of scholars indicated that they could not consistently distinguish between traditional proverbs and those created by known authors. The emergence of a modern adaptation of familiar Kazakh proverb structures shows the value of tradition and globalization and the potential of the two to work together in the meaning-making process. The correlation and use of proverbs and anti-proverbs in modern discourse is an interesting topic for further research.

Literature Review

The work aims to study the current state of proverbs to identify environmental problems of the paremiological units of the Kazakh language. Indeed, with the increasing importance of ecology in the life of modern society, the role of environmental discourse increases. What is meant by the term "ecology"? How is it expressed in language, in speech, and the linguistic environment of the speakers of the Kazakh society?

Language knowledge of ecologization promoted environmental laws of application, rules, and axioms in linguistics, which encouraged the formation of a new branch of science—ecolinguistics. The ecology of language is a framework for studying language as conceptualized primarily in Einar Haugen's 1972 work, where he defines *language ecology* as "the study of interactions between any given language and its environment." Another inspiration was the work of Michael Agar. He published an article on institutional culture in which he draws from Foucault and Habermas in proposing "discourse ecologies" as a new approach. Agar (1985) considers the research done at that time by scholars, such as Gumperz and West, who compare everyday discourse with what occurs in institutional contexts, especially medical and legal settings.

In modern linguistics, the eco-linguistic approach emphasizes the study of various linguistic phenomena in terms of interaction between the language and the environment. The problem of language purity and colloquial culture enhancement of native speakers is one of the issues in linguistics today. Many scientists who investigate problems of language ecology believe that the ecological crisis is growing and expect an ecological catastrophe. According to A.I. Subetto (2013), in the conditions of globalization oriented towards the market unification of cultural models, the tendency "towards unification of cultures" intensifies correspondingly. Ever-increasing jargonization, "macaronization", and vulgarization of speech are becoming a threat to language purity. The interlingual aspect of the study of language ecology problems has helped identify competitive and uncompetitive languages that are potentially in danger of extinction (Bernatskaya 2003, 32–38).

Using "ecology" as a metaphor, we will look at issues relevant to language purity, usage, and contact. In the Kazakhstani multicultural community, the subject of linguistic ecology is the sociolinguistic study of the state of the language as a complex semiotic system due to the quality of its environment and functioning and the linguistic consciousness of its speakers. N. Ualiev introduced linguistic ecology in Kazakh linguistics. The linguist defines Kazakh speech culture from normative, communicative, pragmatic, cognitive, linguo-cultural, and lingua-ecological aspects and defines its conceptual bases as a theoretical discipline. He also presents the scientific basis for objectively evaluating communicative qualities of speech and codification of linguistic norms (Ualiev 1984).

Cultural information about norms of behavior is passed from one generation to another in the form of traditional stereotypes (habits, rites, customs, and rituals) and language stereotypes (proverbs) represented in a simplified form and patterns of behavior. "Facts about the language—this is the history of the people who speak that language. That is why we must first look for the history and ethnographic richness of the ethnos in that language" (Balaqaev 1965). Omarbekova (2015) states "The connection with previous generations and the interdependence of alive and dead are reflected in the Kazakh proverbs: *Aruak riza bolmai, tiri baiymaidy* (If you do not satisfy (with the sacrifices) the spirits of the ancestors, the living one will not get rich), *Oli risa bolmai, tiri baiymaidy* (while the dead are not satisfied, the living person will not get rich)". All the world's images are seen in the language because this is the only phenomenon of human knowledge. The ecology of language in Kazakh linguistics was discussed within the linguistic (speech) culture, and the history of linguistic (speech) culture appears much later than the other areas of linguistic sciences. This requirement appeared on the agenda as the language, especially its written literary and national form, developed and its sphere in social services expanded. This problem does not appear from the point of view of the general use of a particular language but its correct use in a particular society. Therefore, the Kazakh linguistic (speech) culture soon became the subject of consideration (Syzdykova 2014a).

The "ecology" of the modern Kazakh language, in the sphere of inter-communication, in translation, its usage in business, and in everyday life causes indignation of specialists, as well as of everyone who loves and appreciates their native tongue. Kazakh linguists Syzdykova (2014a) and Iskakuly (2014, 2020) are concerned about the state of the language and its role in modern society, as well as grammatical and stylistic changes in the modern Kazakh language. They state that journalists often make mistakes in punctuation and that TV and radio journalists do not follow spelling rules. All these feature "discourse ecologies" of the language. In its most general form, linguistic ecology serves to analyze the objective picture of language development, identify factors that have a negative impact on its development and application, search for ways and means of enriching the language, improve the practice of direct speech communication, and preserve language as a unique means of communication (Syzdykova 2014a, 91).

The article examines the ecological discourse of the language in general and its influence on proverbs; according to A. Potebnya, "the real life of a word ... takes place in speech ... words in speech each time corresponds to one act of thought. This thought also applies to proverb transformations". They infiltrate into all spheres of human life and demonstrate semantic variability in various types of discourse (2012). In the modern linguistic world, the new figurative expressions, everyday occurrences (Mieder 1982) are created from old, original proverbs. There are different notations for modified proverbs: transformation, quasi-sayings, and anti-proverbs. Modifications to existing proverbs that challenge or contradict the former proverbs are classified as anti-proverbs (Aasland 2018).

As a novelty of the research, we state that proverbs do not lose their relevance in our times. In everyday discourse, they are often found in the form of traditional proverbs and aphorisms (winged words). They are quoted in our everyday speech, and there is a specific author. Modern adaptations of old proverbs are a linguistic phenomenon based on a traditional proverb. They reflect and evaluate the recent past and modern realities. Modern adaptations of old proverbs are called anti-proverbs. The term "anti-proverb" is a calque of the German "Anti-Sprichwort," created by W. Mieder, famous modern paremiologist. In the Kazakh language, A. Qaidar (2004) names them "invariants," G.Y. Dyussembina (2016) calls them "occasional proverbs," "occasional occurrences." She states that these new modified expressions will exist just for a short time, as such expressions do not live long in a language. O. Antonova uses the term "paremiological transformation" to understand it as a transformed version of a common proverb, enduring changes at the lexical, morphological, and syntactic levels and preserving an associative connection with the common prototype of the proverb." Anti-proverbs as a phenomenon of the proverbial modification are increasingly studied by experts in different countries. Although many new occurrences exist, this term has not yet found widespread use in Kazakhstani linguistics as a prototype of a classic proverb easily recognized by native speakers.

Interesting material for our study is represented by paremiological transformations found on the Internet. Computer technology has recently begun to define the life of a modern person. A computer is used as a work tool and a tool for solving various communicative tasks. Thus, proverbs are the basis for creating proverb-like transformations, which become the "linguistic mirror" of the national experience and worldview of the people; they express the most important, relevant facts of culture and contribute to the stereotyping of ideas, assessments, and actions that are significant for ethnic culture and ethnic, linguistic consciousness. Paremiological transformations result from a contextual (discourse) rethinking of the prototype proverbs but are based on this close relationship. They can be included in the paremiological space of the language. For example, *Bilegi kýshti birdi jiǵady, bloǵy kýshti myńdy jyǵady* (If you are strong, you will defeat one, but if you are strong, you will surpass 1,000). Originally this proverb sounded like this: *Bilegi kýshti birdi jiǵady, bilimi kýshti myńdy jyǵady* (If you are strong, you will defeat one, but if you are educated, you will surpass 1,000). The determinant word "blogy" is used instead of the Kazakh word "bilim"/education, knowledge/. "Traffic," "site," "blogger," "post," "hosting," "like," "comment," "Facebook," "SMS," and other loan computer vocabulary are used as the markers in new proverbial discourse. Of course, not all Internet users own all the wealth of the new vocabulary subsystem in the Kazakh language, but the very fact of borrowing and assimilating such immense paremiological layers for about a decade has no analogues in the history of discourse ecologies.

Results and Discussion

Over the period of five weeks, I and my colleague Erik Aasland carried out proverb field research. We worked with two different groups in five key cities, among students and senior university professors. The students were given the following tasks: to find the next part of certain proverbs and to expand the meaning of proverbs. The students were asked if they use proverbs in everyday life. Based on feedback from students and senior scholars, we have compiled a rating of the most frequently used proverbs. The attitude of respondents to the modification of proverbs was studied among all respondents during personal interviews.

Scholars

Senior scholars, 45 in number, were given labeled cards in *the card sorting session* and were asked to place them into groups. This task aimed to divide followed proverbial units into three groups: traditional proverbs, aphorisms, and modern adaptation of origin proverbs. More than 90% of the responders quickly identified the modifications to existing proverbs in a card sorting session. About 82.87% of the responders correctly distributed old proverbs, and in contrast, 17.13% of them could not recognize the original proverbs. 50.46% of respondents found aphorisms. Ultimately, the respondents could not accurately determine the type of proverbs or could not distinguish old proverbs from aphorisms. However, they could quickly identify modern adaptation of origin proverbs, as the modified proverbs had indicators or determinant loan words such as *blogger, Facebook, YouTube, file, dollar, blog, site,* and others. Word determinants served as a clue to the recognition of modified proverbs. Furthermore, the traditional proverb *Atyń barda jer tany, jelip júrip, asyń barda el tany berip júrip,* which has the meaning (Explore the world while you have the opportunity) was attributed by respondents to the aphorisms. The aphorism by Kazakh writer M. Auezov *El bolam deseń, besigińdi túze* (Childhood development should be in the spirit of national traditions) was complex enough for scholars to distinguish between an aphorism and a traditional proverb. Respondents confused proverbs and aphorisms. It should be noted that 47% of scholars separated aphorisms from proverbs, and the remaining 53% could not correctly distribute aphorisms.

According to card sorting results, it is evident that 78% of scholars recognized proverbs with modern aspects due to the new Internet terms such as a blog "blogy" in *Bilegi kúshti birdi jiǵady, blogy kúshti myńdy jyǵady,* a newly adopted version of *Bilegi jýan birdi jyǵady, bilimdi jýan myńdy jyǵady* (If you are strong, you will defeat one, but if you are educated, you will surpass thousands*)*. Nevertheless, 69% coped with the task of separating proverbs from aphorisms and modified proverbs.

Students

Proverb completion questions. To analyze the first task *"to find the next part of certain proverbs,"* for instance: *Balalı üy bazar* which means (The home with a child is a bazaar), and 95% of respondents correctly completed this section. However, 4% of respondents could not find the correct part of the proverb; only 1% of respondents mixed the meanings of proverbs and indicated another option.

Expanding the meaning of proverbs. According to the results of the second task, students were asked to expand the meaning of proverbs: *Üy artında kisi bar* which means (be careful or be safe), English equivalent "Fields have eyes, and woods have ears/ Walls have ears," about 57.18% of respondents revealed the meaning of the proverb, 21.77% could not fully indicate the meaning, and 21.05% respondents moved away from the primary meaning and indicated another option.

Students were asked to answer the following question: "Do you use proverbs in your daily life?" According to the results, we can conclude that 60.7% of students sometimes use proverbs, 22.4% use proverbs in colloquial speech, and 16.9% do not use proverbs at all. This report draws attention that proverbs are used less often, and for some of the participants, it was difficult to recognize the meaning of some proverbs.

While investigating the given research theme, we have analyzed *the most frequently used proverbs.* According to the questionnaires, we found out that most of the respondents mentioned proverbs that concern friendship and family, morality and wisdom, poverty and wealth, dignity, courage, education, and negligence. The highest point of the data axis is determined by proverb knowledge of topical areas such as "Good breeding," "Health," "Fault." Furthermore, the lowest point is fixed on the topics of "Compliment," "Poverty and Wealth," "Negligence." During the interview, we found out that scholars and students know and name the same proverbs, for example, friendship and family, morality. The shortness of proverb usage and proportions of proverbs grouped by semantic groups by users indicate a narrowing of the proverb knowledge among users.

The respondents' attitude towards the modification of proverbs. Around 64% (268 participants) gave negative answers and did not agree with changes or modifications of the proverb, although they understand the meaning and significance of these modified proverbs in modern life. Around 29% (120 people) of them agree with the changes and claim that "some *traditional proverbs have lost their relevance to modern realities.*" Therefore, new proverbs that reflect contemporary society are created instead. This group of respondents supported changes in favor of modernized proverbs, and they hold this idea as an impulse in the developing technological world. Listed below are the arguments and reasons for the transformation of proverbs as given by the respondents:

Why do respondents support changes?

- *Some traditional proverbs have lost their relevance to modern realities. Therefore, new proverbs that reflect contemporary society are created instead.*
- *Easily applied by youth.*
- *Modern adaptations of old proverbs—modern language indicator.*
- *If the modern aspect of the proverb carries the semantic value, it is possible to be guided by it in our daily lives.*

Why do respondents not support changes?

- *Proverbs are a part of the spiritual heritage that we have inherited from our ancestors. No need to change proverbs*
- *Correct and appropriate use of proverbs gives the speech unique originality and particular expressiveness.*
- *Modified proverbs lost the true meaning of the old proverb*
- *Modern proverbs which have no value do not enrich the language.*

Overall, we see that respondents readily joined in finding and sharing their ideas about the role of proverbs and their ecological issues in the modern Kazakh language.

Conclusion

Proverbs are part of the culture of contemporary Kazakh people; they have been and remain relevant. Proverbs are relevant and understood by any class of citizens, which is especially important and valuable for their existence and application. "The circulation of proverbs in our everyday lives reminds us that folklore is, indeed, a truly dynamic process. The vitality of proverbs—the constant emergence of new proverbs, together with their continual expression in new contexts—captures how folklore draws together our gravest concerns and our strongest commitments, our most precious values, and our wisest perspectives. At times, even our coarsest humor and our meanest beliefs, thereby structuring the world around us" (Lau et al. 2004).

In our updated research on proverbiality, we interviewed 45 senior scholars teaching in five universities in Kazakhstan. Using an approach called card sort, we had participants group 18 sentences into the categories of the traditional proverb, aphorism (winged words), and contemporary saying (Qaidar 2009, 14–23). Each sentence is in circulation, so we were not working with any pseudo-proverbs made up by us. None of the participants successfully classified all 18 sentences. The discourse ecological crisis state of the Kazakh lingua-culture was revealed:

- This report draws attention to the fact that proverbs Are used less often, and for some of the participants, it was difficult to recognize the meaning of some proverbs.
- During the interview, we found that scholars and students know and name the same proverbs, for example, friendship and family, and morality. The shortness of proverb usage and proportions of proverbs grouped by semantic groups by users indicate a narrowing of the proverb knowledge among users.
- There is a decrease in Kazakh proverbs in the lexicon of young people, which contributes to the weakening of transmission between generations.
- Undoubtedly, the emergence of modern proverbs that meet the spirit of the time reflect the mood of modernity due to the emergence of modern technologies.

The processes taking place in the language require the attention of specialists and the state and the adoption of measures to strengthen the state language. For this, it is necessary to take measures to determine the ecological profile of consumers of the Kazakh language, their quantity and quality, and the level of proficiency in oral and written forms of the literary language.

Even though computational linguistics is one of the most dynamically developing areas of modern linguistics, the study of the Kazakh language in this area lags. For this purpose, the Kazakh Corpus can be used as part of our efforts to analyze the ecology of proverbial discourse.

Bibliography

Aasland, E. 2018. "Contrasting Two Kazakh Proverbial Calls to Action: Using Discourse Ecologies to Understand Proverb Meaning–making." *Proverbium: Yearbook of International Proverb Scholarship* 35: 1–14.

Agar, M. 1985. "Institutional Discourse." *Text* 5, no. 3: 147–168.

Arora, Shirley L. 1984. "The Perception of Proverbiality." *Proverbium* 1: 1–38.

Balakaev, M.1965. *Kazakh tili medenietinin meseleleri* [Problems of Kazakh language culture]. Almaty: Kazakhstan.

Bernatskaya, A. A. 2003. "On three Aspects of the Ecology of Language." *Bulletin of Krasnoyarsk State University. "Humanities" series.* # 4: 32–38.

Brusenskaya, L., and E. Kulikova. 2018. *Ecologicheskaia lingvistika* [Environmental linguistics]. Moscow: Flinta.

Dyussembina, G. Y. 2016. *Merzimdi baspasözdegi ğalamnıñ aksïologïyalıq beynesi* [Axiological image of the universe in periodicals]. *PhD thesis for the degree of Doctor of Philosophy*, Almaty.

Iskakuly, D. 2014. *Mäñgilik maydan nemese tilder toğısındağı türki älemi* [The Türkic World on the Eternal Front or at the Crossroads of Languages]. Monograph. Almaty: Tamgaly Publishing House.

Iskakuly, D. 2020. *Til épopeyası nemese rwxanï jañğırwdağı qazaq tiliniñ tarïxï mïssïyasi* [The linguistic epic or the historical mission of the Kazakh language in spiritual revival]. Almaty: LLP RPBK.Epoha.

Karasik, V. I. 2010. *Lingvisticheskaya kristallizatsiya smysl.* [Linguistic crystallization of meaning]. Moscow: Gnozis.

Kimberly, J. Lau, Peter Tokofsky, and Stephen D. Winick. 2004. *What Goes Around Comes Around: The Circulation of Proverbs in Contemporary Life.* Logan: Utah State University Press.

Kitchen, R., and N. J. Tate. 2000. *Conducting Research into Human Geography.* Edinburgh Gate: Pearson.

Mieder, W. 1982. *Antisprichwörter.* [Anti-proverbs] *T. 1.* Wiesbaden: Verlag für deutsche Sprache (Beihefte zur Muttersprache).

Omarbekova, G. 2013. "Cultural Background Knowledge about the National Character of the Kazakh and English People." *Philology, Theory and Practice. Tambov. Diploma.* # 6. Ch 2: 142–147.

Omarbekova, G. 2015. "linguo-cultural Practices and Their Associative Field." *International Journal of Multidisciplinary Thought*, CD-ROM. ISSN: 2156-6992: 05(04): 17–24.

Potebnya, A. A. 1993 [1926]. *Mysl' i yazy.* [Thought and Language]. Kiev: Nauka.

Proverbs. Source: https://www.soyle.kz/proverbs/index/page/2?cat=11

Qaidar, A. 1998. *Kazak tilinin ozekti masselerii* [Topical issues of Kazakh linguistics]. Almaty: Ana Tili.

Qaidar, A. 2004. *Khalyq danalygy.* [Folk wisdom]. Almaty: Toganay T.

Qaidar, A. 2009. *Kazaktar ana tili aleminde: etnolingvistikalyk sozdik.* [Kazakhs in the world of the native tongue: Ethnolinguistic dictionary]. Vol. 1. Almaty: Daik-Press.

Shaikhyuly, E. *The Proverb Is the Word Mayonnaise. There Are New Modern Proverbs.* Source: https://kaz.zakon.kz/4983086-ma-al-s-zd-mayo nez-zaman-a-say-zha-a-ma.html

Subetto, A. I. 2013. *Man, Science and Economics in the Epoch of the Great Evolutionary Fracture: Noospheric Imperative.* Monograph. Saint Petersburg: Asterion.

Syzdykova, R. 2014a. *Tildik norma jäne onıñ qalıptanwı (kodïfïkacïyası).* Linguistic norm, and its formation (codification). Collection of multivolume works. Almaty: El-Shezhire.

Syzdykova, R. 2014b. *Sozder suyleidi. Sozderdin ķoldanylu tarikhynan. Kazakh tilindegi eskilikter men zhagalyktar. Words spea.* [From the history of the use of words. Antiquities and novelties in the Kazakh language]. Scientific and educational research: Collection of multivolume works. Vol. 4. Almaty: El-Shezhire.

Ualiev, N.1984. *Til madenieti* [Language culture]. Almaty: Ğılım.

What proverbs of the 21st Century do you know? https://surak.baribar.kz/618367/

Contrasting Two Kazakh Proverbial Calls to Action: Using Discourse Ecologies to Understand Proverb Meaning-Making

ERIK AASLAND
Fuller School of Intercultural Studies
Pasadena, California

Two proverbs from the same society can operate in different spheres of circulation even if one encounters them on the same list. I will consider an example from Kazakhstan of two contrasting calls to action. One operates in the mass-media whereas the other is limited to private discussions or online chat sessions. They also vary in their intertextual relationships. I explore the two proverbs using an approach called *discourse ecologies* (Agar 1985; Shoaps 2009).

Kazakhs consider their proverbs as an entrustment from their ancestors. Kazakh scholars praise their proverbs as a prized resource for defining problems, making moral judgments, and suggesting remedies (Arğınbayev 1996, 94; Gabdullın [1958] 1996, 5; Tabıldıyev 2001, 17–18). Teachers are expected not only to cover Kazakh proverbs as content, but to also use these same proverbs on a daily basis in their classes. The Kazakhstani government mandated instruction in Kazakh proverbs for all students (Ministry of Culture 2004). They trusted this process to establish a moral compass for the new nation—a means to getting people on the right track in terms of roles, relationships, and values. In part, this is the self-presentation of national culture (Herzfeld 2016) as it relates to proverbs. A discourse ecologies approach may help us gain a more nuanced understanding of contemporary proverb use in Kazakhstan.

At the outset, we will consider discourse ecologies as a methodology. Then, I will provide a brief summary of each proverb with variants. The discussion will include categorization, meaning, and related metaphorical themes.[1] Next, I will present information concerning internet usage for each proverb along with search results from work with the Kazakh corpus (Makhambetov et al. 2013). Consideration will also be given as to whether anti-proverbs have emerged for the proverb in question. This will provide the content for the discussion of the discourse ecologies of the two proverbs.

Framework

I first came across the term *discourse ecologies* when reading Quayson's intriguing comparison of advertisements posted on taxis and billboards in the same general location of Accra. He argues that even though they are in the same context, they represent two distinct communicative milieus in terms of both content and intertextual connections (Quayson 2010). What captivated me was the thought that something comparable could be true of proverbs in the same proverb collection. You see two proverbs on the same page and assume that they are similar in some way, but perhaps they have different ecologies.

I will consider two other anthropologists' independently developed approaches. Considering both studies will provide the detail we need to utilize discourse ecologies analysis with the proverbs in question.

Michael Agar published an article on institutional culture in which he draws from Foucault and Habermas in proposing "discourse ecologies" as a new approach (Agar 1985). He considers the multitude of research done at that time by such scholars as Gumperz and West comparing everyday discourse with what occurs in institutional contexts, especially medical and legal settings. Agar attributes some of the dynamics of interaction between doctor and client to systemic factors of efficiency, economy, time pressure, and background knowledge. Agar points out that these factors are outside of the control of both parties. Foucault's discussion of limitations on discourse (Foucault [1970] 1984) informs much of what Agar presents in terms of set systemic processes of diagnosis, report, and directive. Finally, Agar utilizes

---

[1] I would like to give special thanks to my colleagues Talant Aktanzhanov, Ulan Bigozhin, and Gulnara Omarbekova. They assisted with or checked translations, provided their perspective on meaning-making using the two proverbs, and interacted with the thesis of the article. Robin Shoaps also provided valuable input on the Framework section. Any remaining errors of translation or summation are solely the author's.

Habermas ([1976] 1979) to describe opportunities that doctors have to work around these scripted institutional expectations.

More recently, Shoaps presented what she terms "communicative ecologies"[2] as an approach to get beyond an idea of context which she describes as too static (Shoaps 2009, 265). She shifts the focus to the discourse interaction. Elements that can be considered in this approach are lexical factors, grammar, participant frameworks, and genre. At the heart of her analysis is the contrast of two folk catholic rituals, *pixab'* (advice for those about to wed) and the Testament of Judas (an immoral approach to address community immorality). The focus is on how material and symbolic linguistic resources produce idealized "voices" with which ritual participants can either side or counter. Key influences include Bakhtin, Baumann, and Briggs (Bakhtin 1981, 1986; Bauman 1977; Briggs and Bauman 1992).

The idea of discourse ecologies is that within a given society there are multiple milieus. Each is distinct in terms of the players, dynamics, genres, values, and procedures that are realized. Agar and Shoaps contexts of analysis are quite different. Still, I would argue that if we step back we can see similar patterns. Each explores the contrasts between more public scripted behaviors and an alternative, more private communicative option. The one that is offered more publicly serves as self-presentation. Herzfeld presents something comparable in exploring the discourse of the state contrasted with that of the people (Herzfeld 2016, 8–9). We will see what we encounter in a similar relationship between two Kazakh proverbs.

The Two Proverbs in Question

In my initial plan for this article, I was interested in working with Kazakh social media and the Kazakh corpus. Thus, I decided to work with two commonly known proverbs with comparable purposes rather than selecting two Kazakh proverbs from the same category based on one collection.

The "Work" Proverb

A small group of Kazakh graduate students attending the Central Asian New Year (Nauruz) celebration in Los Angeles' Griffith Park suggested the

---

[2] Shoaps' article uses both terms "communicative" and "discourse" extensively, so I am describing her focus as "discourse ecologies." Also the author did not raise an issue with my using this term for her approach (Shoaps 2018, pers. comm.).

first proverb. Upon hearing that I specialize in Kazakh proverbs, they asked whether I was aware of this common Kazakh proverb:

Еңбек етсең емерсің.
Eŋbek etseŋ emersiŋ.
(If you work, you will nurse.)

Proverbs related to this one call upon maternal and agricultural symbolism:

Еңбек—адамның екінші анасы.
Eŋbek—adamnıŋ ekinshi anası.
(Work—a person's second mother.)
Еңбек етпесең, елге өкпелеме, Егін екпесең, жерге өкпелеме.
Eŋbek etpeseŋ, elge ökpeleme, Egin ekpeseŋ, jerge ökpeleme.
(If you do not work, the people will take offense; if you don't plant, the ground will take offense.) (Qaidar 2004, 284).

The proverb posits a causal relationship "if a, then b" that is seen as mirrored in nature. A stronger causal statement would have the logical structure "if not a, then not b" (Aasland 2009, 12–13). For example: "No pain, no gain" which Talant Aktanzhanov suggested as a cognate proverb to the Kazakh proverb in question. The Kazakh "work" proverb leaves the possibility open that someone could garner their food by means other than honest[3] work.

The first proverb with its direct linkage of working and receiving sustenance is reminiscent of this Soviet era poster from the 1920s that proclaims: With guns we will defeat the enemy, with hard work we will have bread. Everyone to work, comrades! (King 2016, 138).

One might argue that the concept of work presented in the "work" proverb is Soviet. The poster Figure 2.1 above could be considered as evidence of this link. However, this option actually cuts our investigation short and grants undue weight to this one poster. Rather than assume that the work proverb is Soviet in origin, it is better to explore earlier considerations of the importance of "work."

Abai Kunanbayulı wrote during the classic period of Kazakh literature from the 1850s to the beginning of the twentieth century. Trained as an orator and leader, he was familiar with Turkish, Persian, Kazakh, Russian and Western literature. In his writings, he frequently quotes or adapts proverbs. Kazakhs consider him as their poet laureate based on his songs, poems, and essays (Paltore, Zhubatova, and Mustafayeva 2012). He was concerned about how the Kazakhs lived their lives, especially desiring that they avoid laziness.

---

[3] I slipped in the adjective "honest" here. Kazakhs also consider work to be virtuous or honest (Kazakh *адал*).

Figure 2.1. Poster by Nikolai Kogout in Vkhutemas, Moscow (1920).

In his 29th Word of his *Black Words* he critiques a proverb about angels and gold in this regard (Kunanbayulı 1918). He counted work among five worthy activities as presented in his song "Ғалым таппай мақтанба" [*Ğalım tappay maqtanba*] (don't brag about science without evidence):

> Demanding goals, diligence, deep thought,
> Contentment, and compassion—commit to memory
> Five worthy actions, if I can persuade you. (Kunanbayev 1994, 47)[4]

---

[4] Thanks to Talant Aktanzhanov for his assistance in translating this section of Abai's song.

Internet Presence

A Google search using google.kz showed 3,660 hits for the "work" proverb. A number of these were for personal interest stories in the news media highlighting productive work in society. A YouTube search came up with twenty-seven similar news reports. The proverb lends itself to presenting work as productive and rewarding.

The corpus search did not turn up as much. The Oktöbe Gazette (Articles) had ten hits for ("if you work"), one for the proverb itself, and one for the well-known aphorism by Abai. The corpus is still in development and could be further expanded which would be a boon to future research.

I was also looking for adaptations that challenged the meaning of the original proverb. In societies that are more skeptical concerning the veracity of proverbs, adaptations of given proverbs emerge that serve as a critique to the original proverb. Wolfgang Mieder coined the term anti-proverbs to describe such occurrences (Mieder 1982). He and other scholars have documented anti-proverbs in a significant number and wide variety of cultural contexts. One such culture is Russia (Reznikov 2009, 2012) that has a centuries long relationship with the Kazakh people. I will follow Mieder's definitions of variant (Mieder 2004, 5) and anti-proverb (Litovkina and Mieder 2006, 2–3; Mieder 2004, 26). Modifications to existing proverbs that challenge or contradict the former proverbs are classified as anti-proverbs. Thus, the proverb *Adam qanatı—At* (a person's wings—a horse) as part of a governmental posting should be considered as a variant of the traditional *Er qanatı—At* (a man's wings—horse) since there is no intent in formulating the variation to critique the traditional proverb.

Neither in a search for the specific Kazakh "work" proverb nor when I put simply "Еңбек етпесең" (if you don't work) into google.kz did I come across even one instance of an anti-proverb. A larger corpus may certainly have an anti-proverb.

The absence of any anti-proverbs is especially surprising given that Russian has a cognate proverb and an anti-proverb:

Кто не работает, тот не ест.
(He who does not work shall not eat.)

As Reznikov points out, this proverb is originally biblical (II Thessalonians 3:10) (Reznikov 2012, 241–2). This particular Russian proverb also has an anti-proverb:

Кто не работает, тот ест.
(He who does not work shall eat.)

The "work" proverb has numerous related proverbs and can be connected to a long history of Kazakh thought on the topic. It lends itself to mass media messages about the merits of honest labor. This is attested to in literature, art, and the internet.

The Hound Proverb

I asked two Kazakhstani colleagues, one from northern Kazakhstan and one from the south to provide me with a short list of commonly used Kazakh proverbs. Since there is considerable linguistic and cultural difference between these regions of Kazakhstan, I was especially interested to see which proverbs would be on both their lists. They each attested to the frequent use of the following proverb:

> Заман тулкі болса тазы бол.
> *Zaman tulki bolsa tazı bol.*
> (If (your) era is a fox, then be a hound.)
> Variant: заман тулкі болса таз боп шал
> *Zaman tuli bolsa taz bop shal.*
> (If (your) era is a fox, then try to be a hound.)

One of the first things one notices with this proverb is the central role of animals. There are numerous Kazakh animal stories about the fox and his encounters with other animals including lions, cranes, and snow leopards (Esmen 2000). In each case, the one creature pits their own strengths against the cunning of the fox. Animal stories are considered to be the oldest forms of tales among the Kazakhs (Gabdullın [1958] 1996, 124).

Animal proverbs also deserve special consideration because their symbolism is culture-specific (Talebinejad and Dastjerdi 2005). Thus, I interviewed Gulnara Omarbekova to more closely determine the meaning of the proverb. In particular, I asked about replacing "hound" with "dog." This contrast question (Spradley 1979, 155–73) was intended to tease out the distinctive meaning of the proverb. Omarbekova promptly replied that one could certainly not make that replacement. In Kazakh proverbs, dogs' service is acknowledged but they are symbolically used to express deficiency. Take for example, "Иттің мойнына алтын қарғы тақсаң да, боқ жеуін қоймайды"[*Ittiñ moynına altın qarğı taqsañ da, boq jewin qoymaydı]* (even if you put a gold collar on a dog, he won't stop eating turds). (Qaidar 2004, 347) In contrast, the "hound" proverb is classified as "human characteristics" because it encourages the listener to be fast and flexible like a hound (Omarbekova 2018, pers. comm.). The one difficulty is that the type of action called for is unclear from this proverb on its own. The meaning ranges from just doing something to giving way to immorality and doing whatever it takes.

Internet Presence

The "hound" proverb has considerably less internet presence than the "work" proverb. A google.kz search came up with just seventy-eight hits and a YouTube search came up with zero. There were also no hits in the Kazakh corpus. What is significant is the contested status of the proverb on social media. Unlike in the case of the "work" proverb, I found an anti-proverb based on the "hound" proverb in my internet search (Jumbayev 1922).

When situations are not a fit for the "work" proverb, then Kazakhs will use the fox proverb. However, some Kazakhs insist categorically that there should be no deviation from the standard of the "work" proverb. One Kazakh posted in response to the "hound" proverb, "Qay zamanda ömir sürseñ de ötirikşi, qw bolğannan da adal bolğan durıs qoy" (regardless of the age in which one lives, it is always better to be honorable rather than deceptive or cunning) (VKontakte 2015). What followed were a number of others exhorting the original poster to be gentle and kind.

References to "communism" and "capitalism" that are common in Kazakh discussion of different eras are used to refer to the Soviet and post-Soviet eras respectively. In one education site the question about the meaning of the "hound" proverb was asked. One responder stressed the contrast between the two eras (Baribar 2015). During the first ten years after independence, Kazakhstanis depicted outsiders whether foreigners or those outside their respective region as *khitryi* (cunning) (Nazpary 2002, 127–30, 69–70). These same foreigners were bringing in *dikii kapitalism* (wild capitalism) (Nazpary 2002, 2–3, 9). Kazakhstanis developed a cynicism that was not limited to foreigners, but rather assumed that Kazakhstanis who had wealth were involved in illegal activities (Nazpary 2002, 2, 81). It has been over twenty years since Kazakhstan's independence, however the contrast between the era of communism and the cunning age of capitalism continues to color Kazakhstanis' perspectives.

In contrast to the cunning capitalists, Kazakhs have a long history of presenting themselves and being represented as a "gentle" people emphasizing their nomadic heritage (Kudaibergenova 2013, 843). Kazibek Bi in the seventeenth century made a statement about the Kazakhs to the ruler Tzewang Rabtan, who was the Zünghars' lead commander in their attack on the Kazakhs (Attwood 2004, 294). The statement starts out *"Qazaq degen mal baqqan elmiz "* (We, the Kazakhs, are a sheep-herding people ...). The statement is both factual and indexical. It uses one of their societal roles as a metaphor for their gentleness. Kazibek Bi continues to describe the Kazakhs going from metaphors to direct statements about their ability to live peaceably and in harmony with others. Although the contemporary fit of this traditional saying has been challenged (Qayratulı 2011), it continues to be referenced by individuals and institutions as the quintessential description of Kazakh identity.

The "hound" proverb is connected to animal stories that are prized as the oldest stories among the Kazakhs. For Kazakhs the characteristics of being fast and flexible are things people should emulate. The proverb shows neither the internet nor press media presence of the proverb addressing "work." Whether online or in person the proverb is used as part of interpersonal communication. Compared to the other proverb reception of the "hound" proverb is considerably more contested. This is likely for two reasons: (1) Ambiguity of the type(s) of action being called for; (2) proximity of the "hound" to the "fox" which triggers the concept of "cunning," a key term in Kazakh's description of others as compared to themselves.

Analysis

Tradition provides the resources for understanding experience and addressing societal and personal issues. Roger Abrahams asserts that proverbs colorfully represent both recurrent situations and methods of recourse for the given society (Abrahams 1971). The work of adapting and applying proverbs to current situations is an example of what Elliott Oring calls "cultural reproduction" and presents as the process and production of tradition (Oring 2012).

Both the work proverb and the hound proverb appropriate tradition. Where they differ is their discursive function which we saw earlier in the framework section in Herzfeld's distinction between the discourse of the nation and that of the people (2016). The limitation with Herzfeld's distinction is that it remains unclear how the two discourses relate to each other. Another approach would be to look at seminal as contrasted with frame aligning discourse (Snow et al. 1986). We considered that the work proverb is the more public and the hound proverb the more private option of addressing what type of effort to put forth. Some Kazakh proverbs are treated as seminal discourse. These more public proverbs are employed to delineate national character. The "work" proverb seems to enjoy such status. The hound proverb could be considered frame aligning discourse, one employed in more private contexts. It is used to get buy-in, to shape the understanding, representation, and interaction in contemporary society (Johnston 2002). In societies with a higher incidence of anti-proverbs, they may function as frame aligning resources. Thus they have the potential for challenging or reshaping the contrasting seminal discourse.

The "work" proverb posits a causal relationship that encourages hope that (honest) work will pay off. As such, it serves to provide something to which the public can give ascent. Swinehart presented this in an analysis of discourse in Norway as a "mass-mediated chronotope" (2008). Going back to Agar's work, this proverb would express the institutional perspective. On the other hand, the proverb calling the listener to be a hound relating to a crafty age is a piece of personal advice directly addressing the nuances of contemporary life. It is a workaround for situations where the standard reliance on work is not enough. It provides a line of reasoning to which individuals and groups can align themselves (Agha 2007, 96–103).

Conclusion

This inquiry marks an initial attempt to consider differing discourse ecologies amongst the overall set of Kazakh proverbs. The proverb revival that Kazakhstan has undergone offers Kazakhs resources to situate themselves. As I have demonstrated in the case of proverbial calls to act, this leads to the contrasting use of two proverbs with distinct discourse ecologies. In comparing the two proverbs, we have seen that there are two distinct discursive contexts, mass media and private discourse. On the one hand, there is the ongoing need to be assured of the promise of one's work. The "work" proverb provides a propositional/causal position with which the public may align through mass media. The "work" proverb posits a generalized hope in productivity paying off while leaving open that there may be more than one way to get one's bread. On the other hand, there is an accompanying necessity of understanding the times in which one lives. These are not mutually exclusive positions; individuals need not give ascent to one position in public and the alternative in private. Still, some Kazakhs reject the "hound" advice categorically. Such a position is most likely shaped because the theme sources are colored by historical experiences and perspectives. Meaning making does not happen in a vacuum thus the need to consider a discourse ecologies approach to proverb research focusing on intertextual relationships, semantics, circulation, and usage of proverbs.

Bibliography

Aasland, Erik. 2009. "Two Heads Are Better Than One: Using Conceptual Mapping to Analyze Proverb Meaning." *Proverbium: Yearbook of International Proverb Scholarship*: 1–18.

Abrahams, Roger D. 1971. "Personal Power and Social Restraint in the Definition of Folklore." *Journal of American Folklore*: 16–30.

Agar, Michael. 1985. "Institutional Discourse." *Text* 5: 147–68.

Agha, Asif. 2007. *Language and Social Relations*. New York: Cambridge University Press.

Arġınbayev, Halel. 1996. *Qazaq Otbası* [the kazakh family]. Almaty: Qaynar.

Attwood, C. P. 2004. "Tsewang-Rabtan Khung-Taiji." In *Encyclopedia of Mongolia and the Mongol Empire*, edited by C. P. Attwood, 550. New York: Facts on File.

Bakhtin, Mikahail Mikhallovich. 1981. *The Dialogic Imagination: Four Essays*. Austin: University of Texas Press.

———. 1986. *Speech Genres and Other Late Essays*. Austin: University of Texas Press.

Baribar. 2015. 'Заманың түлкі болса, тазы болып шал деген сөздердің мағынасы қандай? [what does it mean if your era is a fox tne try to be a hound]', Accessed March 7. https://surak.baribar.kz/570169/.

Bauman, Richard. 1977. *Verbal Art as Performance*. Prospect Heights, IL: Waveland Press, Inc.

Briggs, Charles, and Richard Bauman. 1992. "Genre, Intertexuality and Social Power." *Journal of Linguistic Anthropology* 2: 131–72.

Esmen, A. 2000. *Qazaq Ertegeleri [kazakh folktales]*. Almaty: Jazushı.

Foucault, Michel. 1984 [1970]. "The Order of Discourse." In *Language and Politics*, edited by Michael Shapiro. Oxford: Basil Blackwell.

Ġabdullıyn, Mälik 1996 [1958]. *Qazaq Halqınıŋ Ayız Ädebıyeti* [oral literature of the kazakh people]. Almaty: Sanat.

Habermas, Jurgen. 1979 [1976]. "What Is Universal Pragmatics." In *Commiunication and the Evolution of Society*, edited and translated by Thomas McCarthy. Boston: Beacon Press:.

Herzfeld, Michael. 2016. *Cultural Intimacy: Social Poetics and the Real Life of States, Societies, and Institutions* (version Third edition.) Third ed. Routledge Classic Texts in Anthropology. Abingdon, Oxon: Routledge.

Johnston, Hank. 2002. "Verification and Proof in Frame and Discourse Analysis." In *Methods of Social Movement Research*, edited by Bert Klandermans and Suzanne Staggenborg. Minneapolis: University of Minnesota Press.

Jumbayev, Maġjan. 2018 [1922]. 'Қазағым (my kazakh)', Accessed March 8, 2018. http://bilim-all.kz/olen/1320-Qazagym.

Kazakhstan, Ministry of Culture and Information. 2004. ' "Mädeni Mura" Memlekettik Baġdarlaması ["cultural heritage" societal goals]', Accessed April 16, 2017. http://www.madenimura.kz.

King, David. 2016. *Red Star Over Russia: A Visual History of the Soviet Union from the Revolution to the Death of Stalin.* New York, NY: Tate Publishing.

Kudaibergenova, Diana T. 2013. "'Imagining Community' in Soviet Kazakhstan. An Historical Analysis of Narrative on Nationalism in Kazakh-Soviet Literature." *Nationalities Papers: The Journal of Nationalism and Ethnicity* 41: 839–54.

Kunanbayev, Abai. 1994. *Шығакмалар* [compositions]. Almaty: мөр.

Kunanbayulı, Abai. 1918. "Qara Sözderi [black words]." http://www.abay.nabrk.kz/index.php?page=content&id=115.

Litovkina, Anna T. and Wolfgang Mieder. 2006. *Old Never Die, They just Diversify.* Burlington, VM: The University of Vermont.

Makhambetov, O., et al., 2013 "Assembling the Kazakh Language Corpus." In *2013 Conference on Empirical Methods in Natural Language Processing,* 1022–31. Seattle, Washington: Association of Computational Linguistics.

Mieder, Wolfgang. 1982. *Antisprchwörter.* Wiesbaden: Gesellschaft für Deutsche Sprache.

———. 2004. *Proverbs: A Handbook.* Westport, CT: Greenwood Press.

Nazpary, Joma. 2002. *Post-Soviet Chaos: Violence and Dispossesion in Kazakhstan.* Sterling, VA: Pluto Press.

Omarbekova, Gulnara. 2018. *Global discourse as a result of cultural expansion and acculturation,* Norwegian Journal of development of the International Science, #25, Vol. 4: 23–38.

Oring, Elliott. 2012. "Thinking Through Tradition." In *Just Folklore: Analysis, Interpretation, Critique,* edited by Elliott Oring. Los Angeles: Cantilever Press.

Paltore, Y. M., B. N. Zhubatova, and A. A. Mustafayeva. 2012. "Abai Kunanbayev's Role in Enrichment of the Kazakh Language." *International Science Index* 67: 1142–45.

Qaidar, Äbdüäli 2004. *Halıq Danalığı* [Wisdom of the people]. Almaty: Toğaniy T.

Qayratulı, Beken. 2011. '*Qazibek Bidiŋ Sözi nemese Qazaq Qanday Halıq edi* [kazibek bi's words or what kind of people are the kazakhs]', Accessed February 9. http://www.namys.kz/?p=4384.

Quayson, Ato. 2010. "Signs of the Times: Discourse Ecologies and Street Life on Oxford St., Accra." *City & Society* 22: 72–96.

Reznikov, Andrey. 2009. *Old Wine in New Bottles: Modern Russian Anti-proverbs.* Burlington, VT: The University of Vermont.

———. 2012. *Russian Anti-proverbs of the 21st Century: A Sociolinguistic Dictionary.* Burlington, VT: The University of Vermont.

Shoaps, Robin Ann. 2009. "Ritual and (Im)moral Voices: Locating the Testament of Judas in Sakapultek Communicative Ecology." *American Ethnologist* 36: 459–77.

Snow, David A., E. Burke Rochford, Jr., Steven K. Worden, and Robert D. Benford. 1986. "Frame Alignment Processes, Micromobilization, and Movement Participation." American Sociological Review 51: 464–81.

Spradley, James P. 1979. *The Ethnographic Interview.* Belmont, CA: Wadsworth Group / Thomas Learning.

Swinehart, Karl F. 2008. "The Mass-Mediated Chronotope, Radical Counterpublics, and Dialect in 1970s Norway." *Journal of Linguistic Anthropology* 18: 290–301.

Tabıldıyev, Ädibay. 2001. *Qazaq Etnopedagogıykacı [Kazakh ethnopedagogy]*. Almaty: Sanat.

Talebinejad, M. Reza and H. Vahid Dastjerdi. 2005. "A Cross-Cultural Study of Animal Metaphors: When Owls are Not Wise!." *Metaphor and Symbol* 20: 133–50.

VKontakte. 2015. "Әйел кұпиясы [woman's fault]", Accessed March 5. https://vk.com/wall-68927058_1919376.

Content and Software Structure of the Kazakh Proverb Corpus

AIMAN ZHANABEKOVA
Institute of Linguistics Named after A. Baitursynuly, Almaty

What are your sources for the corpus? The source of the corpus of proverbs is the works of academician Abduali Qaidar, who studied proverbs from an ethnolinguistic point of view in Kazakh linguistics. The method of the scientist who discovered the ethnolinguistic semantic meaning of proverbs was guided as a methodological basis, and the concepts and circumstances that led to the emergence of each proverb are given as interpretational explanations. This ethnolinguistic method also includes *The Words of The Ancestors*, a collection of proverbs in the Kazakh language as a source.

Why have you chosen these sources? A proverbial corpus is not merely a list of proverbs but a search engine that provides explanations of proverbs and translates them into English.

What are the sources of the corpus? The source of the corpus of proverbs is collected in the Kazakh language, taken from materials published in books. After all, proverbs are preserved linguistic units that have been formed in our language since ancient times in the form of set regular expressions. Thus, the corpus article will focus on its work.

How many proverbs are you planning to have in the corpus? Currently, 1,800 proverbs and sayings have been collected. It is planned to reach 2,000.

What type of corpus is this going to be? There is a search system for words and word forms and thematic groups of proverbs. A person using proverbs for different purposes can quickly find them in the search box, including proverbs and sayings with Kazakh interpretation and English translation, which contain the words they need or belong to a thematic group. The article deals with the content and search for programs embedded in the corpus of proverbs.

Proverbs are a treasure of the national language, folk wisdom, and a spiritual heritage formed in every national language for centuries. They are preserved in the language of the culture and religion, and they are passed down from generation to generation. Proverbs are born with the purpose of summarizing ideas, wisdom, and experiences that come from a deep understanding of the various relationships between people that have been formulated over a long time. Therefore, proverbs are a living phenomenon that is constantly being created and renewed in accordance with modern requirements. Because it is a philosophy that is embodied in the life experience of the people, its conceptual ideas are inherent in human nature and activities. There is no doubt that the only way to educate future generations is to teach proverbs, especially among young people with little life experience.

In this regard, it is important for young people to memorize proverbs and use them effectively in their vocabulary and to know the motives for the emergence of proverbs. In today's globalized world, information technology can make proverbs accessible to young people and the general public. They are accessible through the creation of a database of proverbs on mobile phones and social networks.

Today, the corpus is a computer language resource as an indispensable innovative informational tool that allows us to obtain information easily and quickly on the research of linguists, teachers, and students (Qaidar 2004). According to computer linguists, computer language resources offer the ability for a scientist to look at his research object in a new way (Qaidar 1998; Kydyrbekuly 1993).

The larger the language corpus is, the deeper the secrets of language structure and the wider the range of concepts about the object of study are. In the same way, the potential of the researcher increases more and more, and the sources of creative energy open. These new opportunities will undoubtedly be used to improve the system of the Kazakh language and the understanding of the language corpus. At the same time, the issue of language process automation should not stagnate but should be constantly improved (Mitrofanova, Grachkova, and Shimorina 2010).

In today's era of globalization, the automation of all areas of science and education has become an urgent issue. The need for automation of language materials has allowed the development of the field of computer linguistics. Corpus linguistics is a new branch of computer linguistics. Corpus linguistics studies the general principles of design and use of linguistic corpora (text corpora) using computer technology. The subject of research in the field of corpus linguistics is the theoretical basis and practical mechanisms for the creation and use of a wide range of linguistic data for language research by users in various fields (Grishina and Savchuk 2008)

The body of texts is a set of linguistic data that is unified, structured, marked (with symbols), and philologically competent, which can be read by a large machine (computer) for finding solutions to specific linguistic problems. In other words, the corpus of the Kazakh language texts is a large-scale systematically arranged linguistic data set for specific linguistic problems. It is structured with the introduction of appropriate linguistic and extralinguistic (meta-text) notations (Ufimtseva 1974).

In the process of text selection and input to the electronic base, there are issues of representativeness (representability) and balance (tendency) in relation to the language materials collected. This issue is especially important in the formation of the national corpus. The representativeness of the corpus is subject to the condition of satisfaction of the theory of probabilities in terms of the textual material volume and variety.

At the same time, the formation of a fully annotated national corpus with linguistic information, covering various functional styles (fiction, drama, scientific and technical texts, journalistic texts) in the Kazakh literary language, is a very important issue today.

The corpus is divided into sub-corpora: *poetry language, prose language, newspaper texts, scientific and technical texts, national corpus,* and similar.

The task of the authors of the corpus is to collect as many texts as possible from the areas corresponding to the purpose of the corpus. The case can be considered a large-scale model of that language. The concept of representation is sufficient, and the texts of different periods are divided into genres, styles, authors, and so on. It is relatively proportional to the volume obtained, the volume of the text, which reveals the scope of linguistic research (Mitrofanova, Grachkova, and Shimorina 2010; Mordovin 2009).

According to A.N. Baranov, the simplest way to implement representativeness is to reduce the sample texts obtained by subject areas to the appropriate level. Only in this case, the strategy of conformity will be preserved in the organization of the corpus (Baranov 2003).

Thus, *representativeness* (versatility) is the ability of the case to reflect all the properties of the subject context, i.e. the frequency of occurrence of the phenomenon in the subject context in relation to the type of linguistic research should be such that it can distinguish language units (Atakhanova 2005).

Corpus linguistics deals with at least two different types of objects (text corpora):

1. Universal that covers all areas of language functions.

2. Special purpose, such as a corpus of proverbs or a corpus of political metaphors in the language of the newspaper (Mordovin 2009).

In both cases, the representative criterion is maintained.

The first type of text corpus was created in the 1960s, having a universal character. In the United States, for example, a corpus of texts was built at a satisfactory level for that period. There are between six to eighty simple selected texts representing fifteen genres: (1) periodicals; (2) press: main articles; (3) press: reviews; (4) religious texts; (5) skills, lessons, hobbies; (6) popular science literature; (7) fiction, biographies, essays; (8) various (government documents, enterprise reports, industrial reports, college catalogues); (9) scientific works; (10) science fiction; (11) mystics and detectives; (12) scientific prose; (13) story literature and westerns; (14) novels about love; and (15) humor (Zhubanov 2002).

The purpose of the *second type* of corpus is to reflect the existence of the phenomenon as a criterion of representativeness as objectively as possible. For example, a corpus of English proverbs may have the most representativeness in a certain period of speech practice and geographical area of the English speaker (Orazov 1983; Rykov 2002).

There is a great need not only for the styles of the Kazakh language but also for the creation of corpus of other linguistic units—phrases, idioms, and proverbs that are the vocabulary of the national language. In this regard, within the framework of the research project, "How Kazakhs use proverbs in a globalized world: discursive ecology," we have created a "Corpus of proverbs in the Kazakh language" and put it on the Internet. Figures 3.1 and 3.2 show the main page of the corpus website with a description of the purpose of the project and a menu for key areas of the website.

The source of the corpus of proverbs is collected in the Kazakh language, taken from materials published in books. Proverbs are language units that have been formed in our language since ancient times, formed as ready-made set expressions. Therefore, the corpus is from books, but the corpus is the first corpus of proverbs in the Kazakh language, and this article will talk about its functions.

Currently, there are 2,000 proverbs in the corpus of proverbs with a motivational explanation and an alternative translation into English.

Corpus Manager is a specialized search system that includes statistical data retrieval software, as well as statistical information retrieval and user-friendly presentation of results (Mitrofanova, Grachkova, and Shimorina 2010). According to the corpus, the researcher can find the necessary words,

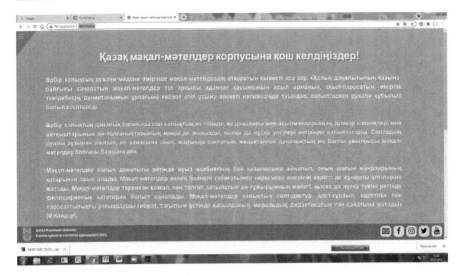

Figure 3.1. Website of the Kazakh proverbs' corpus.

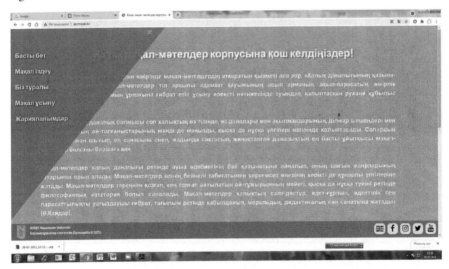

Figure 3.2. Sections (pages) in the corpus of Kazakh proverbs.

phrases, and grammatical forms through a specially designed search system that reveals their meanings (Sirazitdinov et al. 2013).

Most current corpus managers search for several types of information: specific word forms, word forms that correspond to the lemma (all forms of a single lemma found in the text), motivated and unmotivated (set) expressions, or stable and unstable phrases (Markasova 2008, 352).

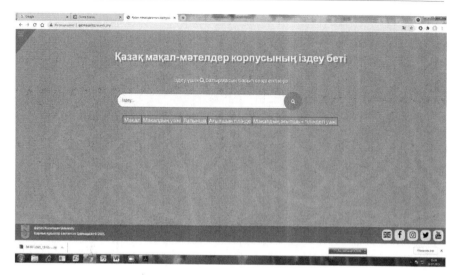

Figure 3.3. Search box of the Kazakh proverbs corpus (search system).

By accessing the *proverb search engine*, the user can find the required stream of proverbs in the proverb's corpus using the keyword. Figure 3.3 shows the search proverb search page.

The corpus of proverbs works on the search system of words, word forms, and thematic groups of proverbs. A lot of research has been done on thematic, lexical, and semantic groupings in the Kazakh language (Baranov 2009; Belyaeva 2004).

A person who uses proverbs for different purposes can quickly find them in the search box by entering in the searched proverbs that contain the necessary words or are related to the topic group with Kazakh expressions and English translations (Atakhanova 2005; Baranov 2009; Dinayeva 2002).

The source of the corpus of proverbs includes the works of academician A. Qaidar, who studied proverbs and sayings from the ethnolinguistic point of view in Kazakh linguistics. The method of the scientist is guided as a methodological basis who reveals the ethnolinguistic semantic meaning of proverbs. The concepts and circumstances that led to the emergence of each proverb are given as motivational explanations (Savchuk 2005; Suleimenova 1992).

The corpus of proverbs is not merely a list of proverbs but a search box that provides explanations of proverbs and translates them into English. Therefore, we take as a source A. Qaidar's works, who made an ethnolinguistic analysis of proverbs. Also, due to the large number of proverbs in the Kazakh language in *Words of the Ancestors* the proverbs collected in *Words*

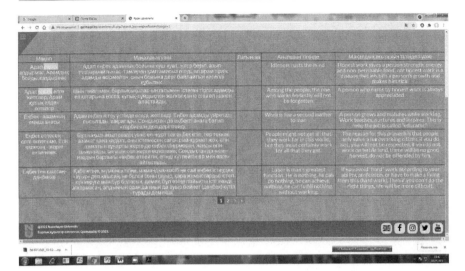

Figure 3.4. Information found by the keyword "labor" in the search program in the Kazakh corpus of proverbs.

of the Ancestors are interpreted by this ethnolinguistic method (Kamshilova 2010; Markasova 2008).

The Figure 3.4 shows a list of proverbs searched for by the keyword "labor." Line 1—a proverb, line 2—explanatory definition of the proverb, line 3—graphics in the new Latin alphabet, line 4—the English equivalent of the proverb, line 5—the English translation of the proverb.

Explanatory notes of Kazakh language proverbs were not created before A. Qaidar's research. Unfortunately, proverbs are seldom used today. It is true that many young people have heard some proverbs but do not understand them. In this regard, we note that A. Qaidar's method of interpreting

Table 3.1. Examples of proverbs.

Baylıq emes, birlik—baylıq.	Wealth is not a life value, there are values in life (health, well-being, spiritual wealth, and etc.) that are higher than wealth. "Where there is unity, there is life" means that in a united country, where there is unity, there are results in joint work.
Intımaq jürgen jerde, Irıs birge jüredi.	It is a blessing to work together. In any case, if there is unity, it means there is prosperity.
Bir kisiniki—maqul. *Eki kisiniki—aqıl.*	In practice, it is better to decide something in consultation with someone else.

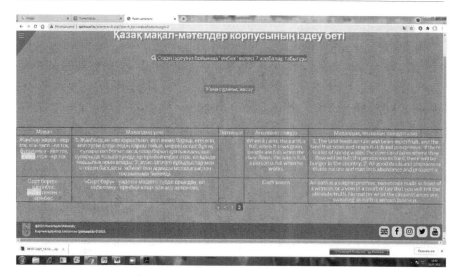

Figure 3.5. Statistics of proverbs found in the Kazakh corpus of proverbs under the keyword "labor."

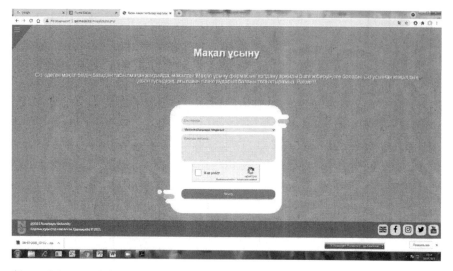

Figure 3.6. Proverb box in the Kazakh proverbs' corpus.

the meaning of proverbs in a cultural and semantic way is the only method that can be used to explain proverbs that are not covered in this corpus.

Table 3.1 provides an example from the explanation of proverbs contained in the corpus of proverbs with selected Kazakh proverbs on the left and explanations in English on the right hand side.

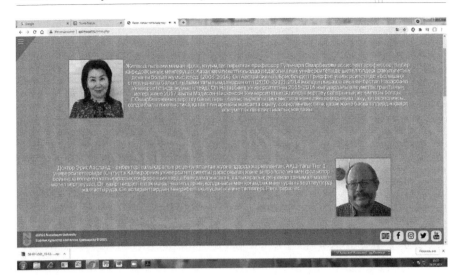

Figure 3.7. Page "About Us" in the Kazakh proverbs' corpus.

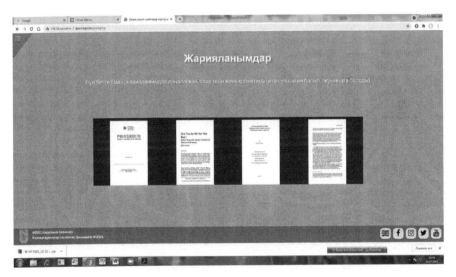

Figure 3.8. Publication's page of the Kazakh proverb's corpus.

Figure 3.5 is the initial results page of a search for proverbs about "labor". It shows the number of proverbs found during the search in Kazakh language followed by a list of proverbs fitting the search criteria.

Figure 3.6 shows the results page after a search that came up with no matches based on the search criteria. Here one can suggest the addition of proverbs that are not included in the corpus of proverbs. In the part of the corpus called "About Us," shown in Figure 3.7 provides information about the investigators of the research project, "How Kazakhs use proverbs in a globalized world: discursive ecology". In the "Publications" page shown in Figure 3.8 one can find articles about this project, works on proverbs, and similar publications.

In our future research, a frequency dictionary of proverbs will be created in the Proverbs Corpus. With this update research can be done concerning which words are frequently used in Kazakh proverbs, which topics are important for Kazakhs in proverbs, among other data.

Bibliography

Atakhanova, R. K. 2005. *Tuıs emes tilderdegi maqal-mätelderdiñ étnolingvistikalıq sïpatı* [Ethnolinguistic nature of proverbs in unrelated languages]. Abstract of Dissertation of the candidate of philological sciences. Almaty: Kazakh Ablai khan University of International Relations and World Languages.

Baranov, A. N. 2003. *Korpusnaya lingvistika: Vvedeniye v prikladnuyu lingvistiku.* [Corpus linguistics: Introduction to Applied Linguistics]. Moscow: Editorial URSS.

Baranov, A. N. 2009. *Vvedeniye v Prikladnuyu Lingvistiku: Uchebnoye Posobiye* [Introduction to Applied Linguistics: Study Guide]. Moscow: Editorial URSS.

Belyaeva, L. N. 2004. *Leksikograficheskiy potentsial parallel'nogo korpusa tekstov* [Lexicographic Potential of the Parallel Corpus of Texts]. In *Proceedings of the International Conference: Corpus Linguistics,* 55–64. St. Petersburg: St. Petersburg University Publishing House.

Dinayeva, B. 2002. *Qazaq tilindegi maqal-mätelderdiñ kognïtïvtik pragmatïkalıq aspek-tileri* [Cognitive pragmatic aspects of proverbs in the Kazakh language]. Abstract of dissertation of candidate of philological sciences. Almaty: Akhmet Baitursynov Institute of Linguistics.

Garabik, R., and V. P. Zakharov. 2006. *Parallel'nyy russko-slovatskiy korpus* [Parallel Russian-Slovak Corpus]. Proceedings of the International Conference. Corpus Linguistics, 81–87. St. Petersburg.

Golovin, B. N. 1970. *Yazyk i statistika.* [Language and statistics]. Moscow: Prosveshcheniye.

Grishina, E. A., and S. O. Savchuk. 2008. *Natsional'nyy korpus russkogo yazyka kak instrument izucheniya variativnosti grammaticheskikh norm* [The National Corpus of the Russian Language as a Tool for Studying the Variability of Grammatical Norms]. Proceedings of the International Conference, Corpus Linguistics, 161–69. St. Petersburg.

Kamshilova, O. N. 2010. *Lingvisticheskiy objekt v interpretatsii korpusnykh tekhnologiy: v pol'zu dokazatel'noy paradigmy. Prikladnaya lingvistika v nauke i obrazovanii. Lingvisticheskiye tekhnologii i innovatsionnaya obrazovatel'naya sreda* [Linguistic Object in the Interpretation of Corpus Technologies: In Favor of the Evidence-based Paradigm. Applied Linguistics in Science and Education. Linguistic Technologies and Innovative Educational Environment] (Collective monograph). 84–96. St. Petersburg: LEMA.

Kydyrbekuly, B. 1993. *Sözdiñ mağınasın bileyik: Tutas sözdiñ tübi bir* [Let us know the Meaning of the Word: The Root of the Whole Word is the same]. Almaty: Kazakh University.

Markasova, E. V. 2008. *Ritoricheskaya enantiosemiya v korpuse russkogo yazyka povsednevnogo obshcheniya "Odin rechevoy den"* [Rhetorical Enantiosemia in the Corpus of the Russian Language of Everyday communication "One Speech Day"]. Materials of the annual international conference "Dialogue". Periodical publication, issue 7 (14), A.E. Kibrik (chief editor), Moscow. 352–355.

Mitrofanova, O. A., M. A. Grachkova, and A. S. Shimorina. 2010. *Avtomaticheskaya klassifikatsiya leksiki v parallel'nykh tekstakh (na osnove russkoyazychnykh tekstov A. S. Grina i ikh perevodov na slovatskiy yazyk).* [Automatic Classification of Vocabulary in Parallel Texts (Based on Russian-Language Texts by A. S. Green and Their Translations into Slovak)]. *Structural and Applied Linguistics* 8: 161–74.

Mordovin, A. Yu. 2009. *K voprosu o zhanrovoy poleznosti sovremennykh nespetsializirovannykh korpusov tekstov* [On the Issue of Genre Usefulness of Modern Non-Specialized Text Corpora]. *Bulletin of ISLU* 2: 48–52.

National corpus of the Russian language. http://ruscorpora.ru

Orazov, M. 1983. *Qazaq etistiginiñ semantikası: Semantikalıq klassifïkacïya täjiribesi* [Semantics of the Kazakh Verb: Experience of Semantic Classification]. Doctoral dissertation. Almaty: Kazakh National University.

Qaidar, A. 1998. *Kazak tilinin ozekti masselerii* [Topical issues of Kazakh linguistics]. Almaty: Ana Tili.

Qaidar, A. 2004. *Khalyq danalygy.* [Folk wisdom]. Almaty: Toganay T.

Rykov, V. V. 2002. *Korpus tekstov kak realizatsiya objektno-oriyentirovannoy paradigmy* [Corpus of Texts as an Implementation of the Object-Oriented Paradigm]. In Proceedings of the International Seminar "Dialogue," 124–29. Moscow: Nauka.

Savchuk, S. O. 2005. *Metatekstovyye oboznacheniya v Natsional'nom korpuse russkogo yazyka: osnovnyye printsipy i osnovnyye funktsii* [Meta-Text Notations in the National Corpus of the Russian Language: Basic Principles and Main Functions]. In *National Corpus of the Russian Language: 2003–2005; Results and Prospects*, 62–88. Moscow: Indrik, 2005. 344.

Sirazitdinov, Z. A., L. A. Buskunbaeva, A. Sh. Ishmukhametova, and A. D. Ibragimova. 2013. *Informatsionnyye sistemy i bazy dannykh bashkirskogo yazyka* [Information systems and databases of the Bashkir language]. Ufa: Book Chamber of the Republic of Bashkortostan.

Suleimenova, E. D. 1992. *Semanticheskiye parametry slova v mezh"yazykovykh issledo-vaniyakh: teoreticheskiye i prikladnyye aspekty sopostavitel'nogo analiza* [Semantic Parameters of a Word in Interlingual Research: Theoretical and Applied Aspects of Contrastive Analysis]. Moscow: Nauka.

Ufimtseva, A. A. 1974. *Vidy slovesnykh znakov* [Types of verbal signs]. Moscow: Nauka.

Zakharov, V. P. 2005. *Korpusnaya lingvistika* [*Corpus linguistics*]. Educational and Methodological Guide. SPD.

Zasorina, L. N. 1977. *Chastotnyy slovar' russkogo yazyka.* [Frequency dictionary of the Russian language]. Moscow: Nauka.

Zubov, A. V., and I. I. Zubova. 2004. *Informatsionnyye tekhnologii v lingvistike* [Information Technology in Linguistics]. Moscow: Academy.

Zhubanov, A. K. 2002. *Osnovnyye printsipy formalizatsii soderzhaniya kazakhskogo teksta* [Basic principles of formalizing the content of the Kazakh text]. Almaty: Arys.

Zhubanov, A. 2008. *Qoldanbalı til biliminiñ mäseleleri.* Questions of applied linguistics. Almaty: Arys.

A Modernized Tradition in Kazakhstan: Kindik Sheshe

FUNDA GUVEN
Nazarbayev University, Nur-Sultan

AIDANA AMALBEKOVA
L.N. Gumilyov Eurasian National University, Nur-Sultan

The Term: *Kindik sheshe* is a spiritual mother of a baby who takes a role in their life from birth to death in Kazakh society. She was the woman who cut the umbilical cord of a newborn baby before the delivery was not modernized in hospitals. In Kazakh, one word, *kindik*, is used to express both the umbilical cord and the belly button (Kuderinova et al. 2011). Although *kindik sheshe* acts like a midwife, she is not a midwife, practitioner, or professional in today's Kazakh society. Today, *"kindik sheshehood"* is losing its functional meaning as a social status, given the woman is highly respected in the society. *Ebe* in Turkish refers to midwifery as a profession and the word grandmother in dialects (Eyüboğlu 1991, 101). The word comes from its old version, *"apa,"* meaning grandmother in old Turkic. We assume that grandmothers also acted as midwives. The word *ebe* as midwife possibly absorbed the second word which was *ana* and became a word for a profession so that midwives kept their importance and dignity in Turkish society. Then, "grandmother," who also functions as a midwife in the society, leaves her esteem to a stranger as a significant person in an individual's life (Ersoy 2007). In Kazakh, the words "grandmother" and "old lady" are interchangeable. Atemova (2016), Musilimkyzy (2017) and Rashatkyzy (2015) all emphasize the importance of choosing a "grandmother" for the role of *kindik sheshe* in relation to her age and experience as a mother and grandmother. It is argued that female shamans, or *kams*, were the initial midwife role later taken by *kindik sheshe*

since they are not only professionals but also have dignity in the communities. Ersoy argues that the lineage of shamans are not from father to son
but among the relatives (Ersoy 2007, 2012). The institution of *kindik sheshe*
as a continuum of women shamans allows society to expand their close ties
among the members.

Godparenthood in Russian Orthodox Society

Though Muslim societies have their own practices such as foster mother/wet
nurse, the tradition of *kindik sheshe* is a similar practice to godparenthood, a
common spiritual kinship practice among Christian communities (Muravyeva
2012). *Kindik sheshe* (*kindik* mother) along with *kindik ake* (*kindik* father) are
akin to godmother and godfather. We will leave this practice of Catholic
and Lutheran societies out and explore whether there are similarities and
differences of both institutions in Russian and Kazakh societies since they
intermingled and are culturally interwoven. Russian Orthodox godparenthood has religious significance, creating strong ties in the community. The
ritual does not start with the birth but during the baptism in the church. The
gender of the infant determines who is going to take a role during the ceremony. Godmothers bring girls, while godfathers bring boys into the church,
although gender of the *kindik* child is not significant, and the religious ceremony is not a rite of passage in Kazakh society. They foster their godchildren
spiritually so that they can be loyal members of the Orthodox Christian community. Mashkova mentions in the Kazakh-Russian dictionary that *kindik
sheshe* is translated as *krestnaya mat,* which means "godmother." She argues
that they are translated this way due to the paraphrastic meaning of two
concepts. She continues to argue that *kindik sheshes* lack the spiritual and
religious role godmothers have in Orthodox Christianity (Mashkova 2014,
228). While it is true that a religious component is absent in the institution of
kindik sheshe in Kazakh society, spiritual ties between child and *kindik sheshe*
are still lifelong and culturally cemented.

Kindik Sheshe *in Kazakh Society*

Choosing a kindik sheshe

The institution of *kindik sheshe* knits Kazakh society by creating substantial
ties among them. In contemporary Kazakh society, a woman, either a relative
or a friend, is then decided to be the *kindik sheshe* of the infant among elderly
members of the family. Since *kindik sheshe* will be considered a spiritual relative

of the entire family, it gives honor to the woman who is offered to be a *kindik sheshe*. Refusing the offer is considered rude and maybe a shame. There were cases when women competed for being given a status of *kindik sheshe*, and candidates quarreled among each other (Atemova 2016, 234). Moreover, for the women who cannot conceive a baby, this institution creates protection and psychological support. We will explain the role of *kindik sheshes* during the pre-birth, laboring, delivery, and after the birth. *Kindik sheshe* is responsible for dressing the baby as soon as they are born. They usually used to sew a snapsuit *it koilek* prior to birth. In the contemporary Kazakh society, they buy clothing for newborns rather than sewing them. The family of the baby prepares gifts for *kindik sheshe* to give after the birth. One way to show appreciation and respect to *kindik sheshe* used to be slaughtering livestock. This is still practiced in some households. *Kindik sheshes* used to be skilled midwives, but in contemporary times, duties of *kindik sheshes* during delivery are performed by medical professionals. The symbolic part of *kindik sheshe's* role remains, although traditional *kindik sheshes* took an active part in the baby's delivery. Great significance is bestowed on cutting the umbilical cord because it enables one to be the first person to touch an infant, even before the birth mother (Atemova 2016, 234). Now, state-appointed midwives and doctors help the mother during labor. Some hospitals do not allow any relatives in the hospital to visit the mother and the baby. *Kindik sheshes* with other relatives, mostly grandparents and father, arrive at the hospital when mother and baby are discharged. Here, she was the person who received the baby from the nurse. They keep the significance of the institution authentic, allowing her to be the first person touching the baby. The baby is believed to resemble the first person to touch him or her. It is expected that *kindik sheshe* assists the pregnant woman after the delivery with rituals, such as the baby's first bath, cutting baby's hair, and putting baby to sleep in the cradle for the first time (Naumova 2018, 98).

Nowadays, *kindik sheshe* brings the baby and mother home from the hospital. She may be asked to give the baby's name. Then, she prays and whispers the baby's name in his/her ear. Then all guests eat together. She is expected to visit the baby daily the first forty days. She gives the baby a bath. Baby's family organizes a feast called a *toy* to celebrate the baby's birth. *Kindik sheshe* is the honorable guest of the ceremony. Guests bring gifts to the baby. Baby's parents give *kindik sheshe* gifts during the celebration. The baby's family and guests give a toast in honor of *kindik sheshe*.

The fortieth day of birth is considered an important passage in a baby's life. The baby's family cleans the house they live in. *Kindik sheshe* gives a bath to the baby in water with 40 pebbles. They pray and sprinkle clean water around the baby's room. The other very important moment is to give the baby a haircut. The ritual is called *qaryn shashyn alu*, where abdomen hair or the baby's hair is cut which it started growing in the mother's womb. *Kindik sheshe* cuts when the baby has his/her first long hair. Baby's mother or other guests share the baby's hair to keep it. All guests bring gifts to the baby, including the *kindik sheshe*. After that, they eat and celebrate the fortieth day.

Kindik sheshe is an important figure at the celebration of a toddler's first steps, which is called *tusau keser* (cutting the shackle). Guests are invited to see the baby's first steps when the baby is one year old. They put a tablet, a comb and/or crayons in front of the baby. Those items may vary based on family's preference. Then, they ask and direct the baby to choose one. Mostly, the mother of the baby helps them to pick one, but the idea is to make the baby choose one of them freely. Guests enjoy this moment to see what proficiency they will adopt in the future. After this ritual, they eat and have fun together. One of the family members manages the order of giving a toast. *Kindik sheshe* as the guest of honor for the ceremony gives the first toast. Then, they give the baby presents.

From now on, the baby is a spiritual daughter or son of the *kindik sheshe* and spends time with her. When the baby grows up, they can visit *kindik sheshe* and her husband, *kindik ake*.[1] They are natural members of the *kindik sheshe's* household, which means, whenever the child wants to visit them, he or she is welcome. During the special days, they call *kindik sheshe* and talk; *kindik sheshe* considers them as her own children. They must be present during the first day of school or graduation ceremonies.

If the child's mother or father passes away, *kindik sheshe* is the one to take care of the child until he or she gets married. The bond strengthens over time. Children develop their personality not only around their biological family but also their *kindik sheshe*. This lifelong relationship is a very special relationship only between *kindik sheshe* and the child that no one can break. Once you are a *kindik sheshe*, forever you are a *kindik sheshe*.

Despite the modernization that changed practices in the society, Kazakhs kept this tradition by adopting it in the new establishment. The poet Kullyash Akhmetova mentions how doctors help women give birth. Yet, she emphasizes that *kindik sheshes* have experience and know how hard labor is in her

---

[1] In some rare cases, *kindik ake* has the same status and privileges of *kindik sheshe*, only if they are the one who cuts the baby's umbilical cord. However, *kindik sheshe's* husband does not automatically become a *kindik ake*. Unlike godparents in Christianity, men are assigned the role of *kindik ake* in extraordinary situations in Kazakh society since *kindik sheshe's* or *kindik ake's* role is performed solitarily and is not subject to sharing, even within a spousal relationship.

poem entitled "Kindik Sheshe". The poem, "Kindik Sheshe," (Akhmetova 2021, 159) takes place in a village, Usharal, where the poet was born and raised. The plot centers around a medical professional named Liza who came to help women alleviate the hardships of giving birth. Lisa, the midwife, arrives at the village in the spring. She helps people maintain or regain health and wellness. People start calling her from remote villages after they learn Lisa practices in Usharal. Even in the stormy winter days, she goes to help people. The poet values her job, saying that there is no other job more valuable than this. Women who are due soon arrive to the village to see Liza the midwife from faraway pastures. The proverb, *Daulet pen bailyq—qol kiri* (Fortune and wealth are dirt on the hands of the man) is mentioned in the poem to emphasize that wealth is irrelevant to pregnant women since all they want is to end the pain. She is compared to Queen Elizabeth twice. Her name, Liza, short for Elizabeth, is emphasized throughout the poem. Even though the poet does not know her family, for her Liza is like the Empress Elizabeth because of her kind personality. During the reign of Russian Empress Elizabeth II, Kazakhs started to become settlers and abandoned the nomadic lifestyle. The plot most likely takes place in the twentieth century since the poet who was born in 1946 and witnessed this herself. She witnessed the changes in this aspect of the village's life. The third person narrator says the village Usharal has become bigger now and there are more midwives now. Those midwives replace *kindik sheshe*s during the delivery. After learning the positive role of midwives, women in the rural area call for Liza to help them during the delivery. The narrator emphasizes the fact that delivering a baby is a matter of life and death because it is a matter of survival for women. In the end of the poem, the narrator says *Bosantu ayel-anani Jer betindegi en uli is!* meaning that assisting women with delivering a baby is the greatest, noblest job in the world. Although she is a medical professional, the narrator inexplicitly adds her to the ranks of *kindik sheshe*. The narrator argues that Liza exceeds Empress Elizabeth in status. At the end of the poem, it is mentioned that more and more medical professionals came to the village. The narrator stresses in the lines "Tolğaqtıñ qiin maydanı, Kindik şeşeler — ayğağı" (Delivering a baby is like a battle ground; *Kindik sheshe*s are proof of it) that *kindik sheshe*s know it better than anyone.

Since the government appoints midwives after modernization, the poet tries to avoid causing a clash between modern and traditional institutions by highlighting the importance of modern medicine. However, bringing the Russian Empress into the poem, presenting Lisa the midwife as a modern image of the Queen, reminds us of the colonial point of view. She explicitly suggests that *kindik sheshe*s should yield their roles to modern midwives.

State-Led Feminism and Ending the Function of Ebe Anne in Turkish Society

The institution of *kindik sheshe* is not common in the contemporary life of Turkish society. Although the institution was common in the rural areas among some Turkic tribes in Turkey, appointed midwives displaced them after governments had followed strict modernization and Westernization policies. The tradition can be seen in old nomadic Turkic people called Turkomans living in mountainous areas, although scholars consider this practice as a Central Asian practice.[2]

There is also a maternity institution among the Ottoman Turkmens of the Ottoman Empire, who lived in the Amanos Mountains in the southeast of the Taurus and settled with the *Fırka-i Islahiye* (Law of reform). Here, too, it is seen that in addition to the practices around childbirth, a multifaceted function is assigned to the institution in question:

> The role of midwives does not end with giving birth; It helps the family with the child in washing the child, treating him when he is sick, and controlling the mother's condition. After birth, she would name the baby's umbilical cord, cut the umbilical cord, wash it, wash the baby, and hand it over to his family. One night he was waiting for his mother at home. If the house of the woman giving birth was close to her house, she would go to her house every day, check her condition, have someone take care of the baby, take a bath, and wrap it in a log. Those children visit them during the holidays and bring gifts to her by addressing her as 'may ebe' 'ebem' (my midwife). (Doğaner 2006, as cited in Ersoy 2007, 62)

Turkish society underwent radical changes after the collapse of the Ottoman Empire and the emergence of the new Republic of Turkey in 1923. The government aimed not only to establish a modern state but also to transform society into a modern Western society. Women became state agents to show to the West and the rest of the Turkish society that they could access higher education and respectable jobs, as well as be visible in the public space. Leaving old traditions and adopting Western values became a trend especially among educated urban classes. The language was standardized by using the Istanbul accent as a model. Thus, a cleavage occurred between urban elites

---

[2] According to the ritual of the child's umbilical cord being taken care of after birth and buried by his or her aunt in a sacred place among the Tahtacis and the Ulashli Turkmen: If, after the birth of a child, the process of dispersal of dried fruits, reminiscent of the ritual of bloodless sacrifice and called *gombet*, can be viewed as phenomenological, it can be said that these practices are a continuation of the Central Asian Turkish tradition (Ersoy 2012, 2007).

and rural people who did not have access to education. "The Republican state determined the characteristics of the ideal woman and set up a monopolistic system to propagate this ideal in a population that held often quite different values and perceptions of ideal women's behavior" (White 2003, 145). Thus, people in rural areas were introduced to the new Republican women appointed as either teachers or midwives. The state used them as the agents of the state's ideology with their uncovered hair and Western dress codes.

By modernizing medicine and sending educated midwives to the rural area, the government targeted to increase the population that suffered after long years in the war. Those educated midwives served for free and replaced the role of the traditional midwives or *ebe ana* in the society. However, those mobile midwives were not able to connect with the children later in their lives. Hence, the tradition has been forgotten in Turkish society. The word *ana* disappeared and *ebe* has become a generic name of midwives in Turkish.

The institution of *kindik sheshe* not only can be seen commonly in Kazakh society or Turkish society rarely but also in other Turkic societies, like Kyrgyz, Tatar, Karakalpak and Uyghur. Here there are more intricate rituals related to the umbilical cord of the baby. Holding on to Islam and living under the colonial policies of Russian imperialism may be the cause of some differences along with modernization. After all, the tradition transformed itself or kept it in the lexical semantics. Being a *kindik sheshe* and following the rituals have an interrelational value embedded in the identity of the society.

Proverbs in Kazakh:

1. *Bala kindik sheshege tartady*
2. *Tumagan balaga kindik sheshe*
3. *Yeshki özi tua almay jatıp, qoyga kindik şeşelikke barıptı*

A commonly used proverb, *bala kindik sheshege tartady*, can be directly translated as (A child will take after his or her *kindik sheshe*). This proverb is usually used to emphasize the importance of carefully assigning the role of *kindik sheshe*. It is never used to blame *kindik sheshe* for a child's undesirable qualities, as this proverb is used only while choosing a *kindik sheshe*.

Another proverb has irony: *tumagan balaga kindik sheshe* can be literally translated as (Being a *kindik sheshe* to an unborn child), which describes someone behaving absurdly. The harshness of this proverb shows that the status of *kindik sheshe* is held in high regard.

The third proverb, *yeshki özi tua almay jatıp, qoyga kindik sheshelikke barıptı* serves a similar purpose. It can be translated as (The goat tried to be *kindik sheshe* to the sheep's child before becoming a mother herself). When one uses this proverb in a conversation, it is implied that one is attempting to manage a situation in a manner that is not acceptable. The status of *kindik sheshe* is elevated in making this point.

Turkish and Kazakh societies followed different processes of modernization. During the colonization period, Kazakh society turned to their tradition to keep their identity alive, whereas modernization of Turkish people meant abandonment of their traditional identity and adaptation of a Westernized identity. Disappearance of the institution of ebe-anne in Turkish culture and modernization of the institution of *kindik sheshe* in Kazakh society shows that language and cultural practices of both societies are proof of their modernization. Kazakh women played a significant role to keep their tradition despite modernization of reproduction methods. Paradoxically, Turkish society underwent a cultural colonialism, while Kazakh society resisted against it.

Bibliography

Atemova, T. K. 2016. Kazak aile terbiyesinin özellikleri ve onun gelişmesine küreselleşme sürecinin etkisi [The characteristics of family upbringing of Kazakhs and effects of globalization on its development]. *Marmara Türkiyat Araştırmaları Dergisi* 2: 229–242.

Akhmetova K. 2021. Collection of works, 2011. Almaty: Dauir.

Doğaner, A. 2006. Osmaniye yöresi'nde yaşayan Ulaşh Türkmenlerinin geçiş törenleri [Parade of Ulash Turkomens living in Osmaniye District]. Unpublished master's thesis, Hacettepe Üniversitesi Sosyal Bilimler Enstitüsü, Ankara.

Ersoy, R. 2007. Kadın kamlar'dan göçerevli Türkmenler'de 'ebelik' kurumu'na dönüşüm [Transformation from the female shamans to the midwifery institution among nomadic Turkmens]. *Türkbilig* 13: 60–71.

Ersoy, R. 2012. Halk bilimi çalışmalarının gelişimine paralel olarak 'alan araştırması' kavramını yeniden düşünmek [Rethinking the concept of "field research" in parallel with the development of folklore]. *Millî Folklor* 24, no. 94: 5–13.

Eyüboğlu, İ. Z. 1991. *Türk dilinin etimoloji sözlüğü* [Etymology dictionary of the Turkish language]. Istanbul: Sosyal Yayınlar.

Kazakhtyn etnografoyalyk kategoriyalar, ugymdar men ataularynyn dasturli juyesi. [The Traditional system of Kazakh ethnographic categories, concepts, and names]. Vol. 3. 2012. Almaty: Slon.

Kuderinova Q., et al., 2011. Kazakh traditional system of ethnographic categories, concepts and names. Encyclopedia. Volume 1. Almaty: DPS, 738.

Mashkova, S. N. 2014. Obogashcheniye russkogo yazyka kazakhskimi frazeologicheskimi obrazami v usloviyakh kazakhsko-russkogo dvuyazychiya [Enrichment of Russian language by Kazakh phraseological images in terms of Russian and Kazakh bilingualism]. *Journal of Historical, Philological, and Cultural Studies* 3: 229.

Muravyeva, M. G. 2012. Godparenthood in the Russian Orthodox Tradition: Custom Versus the Law, 1500–1900." In *Spiritual Kinship in Europe, 1500–1900,* edited by G. Alfani and V. Gourdon, 247–74. London: Palgrave Macmillan.

Musilimkyzy, B. 2017. *Qazaq ultynyn urpaq tarbiesinin tarihi qainary* [Historical sources of upbringing of the Kazakh nation]. *Vestnik KazNU, Seriya istoricheskaya* 86, no. 3: 86–91.

Naumova, Yu. 2018. *Sobach'ja' rubashka dlja rebenka v kazahskih obrjadah mladenchestva i detstva* [Newborn's first bodysuit in Kazakh rituals of infancy and childhood]. *Tradicionnaja kultura* 19, no. 2: 96–104.

Rashatkyzy, M. 2015. *Kazak halkynyn balalarga katysty yrymynyn mani jane tarbiesi.* [The significance and education of superstitions of the Kazakh people about children]. *Vestnik KazNU. Seriya filologicheskaya* 134, no. 4: 337–339.

Temür, Nezir. 2010. *Kırgız Folklorunda Ritüelistik Türler* [Ritual Types in Kyrgyz Folklore] *Gazi Türkiyat Türkoloji Araştırmaları Dergisi* 1, no. 6: 297–317.

White, J. B. 2003. State Feminism, Modernization, and the Turkish Republican Woman. *NWSA Journal* 15, no. 3: 145–59.

Chapter 2 Common Problems
of Paremiology

Kazakh Proverbs from the Perspective of Cultural Cognition and Communication

FAUZIYA ORAZBAYEVA
Abay Kazakh National Pedagogical University, Almaty

ELMIRA ORAZALIYEVA
Nazarbayev University, Nur-Sultan

Introduction

Proverbs in the Kazakh language are the results of spiritual ethnic mentality and historical development. Like all linguistic material, proverbs are objects of interdisciplinary research and unique discoveries in this regard. Kazakh proverbs have absorbed all the values of human relationships in the surrounding reality, the inner world, and literary imaginable perception by being an example of steppe philosophy. As far as we know, proverbs of every nation become the core of their cognitive and communicative formations. Therefore, Kazakh scholars note two main factors that form the basis of these wise sayings as internal and external issues (Qaidar 2014, 389). Studying proverbs as "the collection of folk wisdom" (Qaidar 2014, 389) helps to create the first ethnic factor of "spiritual and cultural life, worldview experience, and centuries-old historical formation" (Qaidar 2014, 389). For example, *Zhuyely soz zhuyesyn tabady, zhuyesyz soz iyesyn tabady,* (Systemic word finds the system, unsystematic finds the owner) *At baspaimyn degen zeryn ush basady, yer kormeimeyn degen zheryn ush koredy* (The horse comes three times to the place that it thinks it will not come, the man returns three times where he thinks he will not return) (Qaidar 2014, 398—399). The external factor is explained as long-term proximity with other ethnic groups and their social relationships. The maxims *Zhyltyragannyng barlygy altyn emes*, (All that glitters is not gold) *Yeshten kesh zhaqsy* (Better late than never) have equivalents in Russian and English languages like "All that glitters is not gold," and "Better late than never." This approach to proverbs and their functional features in communication is also emphasized in the world research practice where such combinations as "social interactions for thousands of years," "everyday experiences," "common observation in succinct" (Mieder 2004, 11) become key details of definitions and theoretical concepts.

The "proverbial repertoire" (Mieder 2004, 11) is the result of the "literary and folklore traditions" (Qaidar 2014, 390) and the "preliterate time" (Mieder 2004, 11) of mankind. It identifies both the content fund and the situational-motivational background of every nation. As objects of informational and cultural values, proverbs preserve not only national identity but also become a transitional inter-linguistic link of mutual influences. Thus, it becomes possible to diachronically-synchronously language model studies by combining the platform of linguistic, social, and cognitive interpretations. Because agreeing with the idea that "every proverb obviously originated from one person once upon a time" (Mieder 2004, 12) implies a number of historical studies in the context of personal and cause-and-effect relationships. So, by referring to the research of literary scholars such as B. Adambayev, M. Alimbaev, N. Torekul, T. Kakishev, the linguist A. Qaidar notes the significant role of individual historical figures as, for example, *Kunanbay* (the father of Abai), his adviser Kaskyrbai *biy* (judge), Zhirenshe *sheshen* (orator). In particular, the scientist gives a number of examples that once came by the resourcefulness of Kazakh famous people. Among such proverbs and maxims, the author cites the following sayings: *otken isten ongai zhok, keshegi kunnen alys zhok, yertengi kunnen zhaqyn zhok* (There is no easier than the past, more distant than yesterday and closer than tomorrow) (Kunanbay); *Tyngdaushysy zhok soz zhetym, korery zhok koz zhetym, yely zhok yer zhetym* (Without a listener the word is an orphan, without the ability to see the eye an orphan and without a country son an orphan) (Kaskyrbai *biy*); *Zhylky—maldyng patshasy, tuye—maldyng kaskasy* (The horse is the king of animal husbandry, the camel is a proud species) (Zhirenshe *sheshen*) (Qaidar 2004, 393–394). Here we need to clarify that two types of proverbs have two different opportunities (ways of being used or translated) to translate or to use:

> on the one hand, there are those proverbs that have the same meaning but different structures, vocabulary, and metaphors, and they consequently have different origins in their respective languages. Whoever needs to translate one of these texts would have to know the quite different equivalent in the target

language or find it in a dictionary. On the other hand, many proverbs are identical ... and these do not present any particular translation problem since they are cognates. (Mieder 2004, 26)

Proverbs of the first position are more specific in their language structure, conceptual comparisons, and ethnic characteristics.

The heritage of our ancestors marks a long way in the linguistic and content unit's formation. Concepts and their meanings are passed from generation to generation, and they preserve valuable and integral elements of ethnic consciousness in the era of globalization. As an example, scholars analyzed the "significance of the hadith of the Prophet Muhammad in Kazakh proverbs and sayings" (Mansurov et al. 2014). By the words "Indeed proverbs and sayings are a historical heritage that never tarnishes. It is an enduring poetic genre that is full of cultural and educational color" (Mansurov et al. 2014, 4899–900), authors give a number of examples demonstrating the historical period in the development of Kazakh society adapting to Islam. For example, "Kazakh nation established the manner of greeting on the basis of Islam" as a greeting can also be observed and discussed in Kazakh proverbs: *Adepty yeldyng balasy alystan salem beredy* (the son of a civilized nation greets people from distance), *Adamdyqtyng belgysy—iyulyp salem bergeny* (the sign of humanity is to greet people). It has to be mentioned that the word "salem" in Kazakh was borrowed from Arabic and used in the same meaning. The role of religion and sacred books among the four main sources of proverbs was noted by W. Mieder who emphasizes the uniqueness of the Bible as "the early wisdom literature" and "classical antiquity" (Mieder 2004, 27).

Thus, this article focuses on the problems of cultural cognition and communication goals in the usage of Kazakh proverbs. The purpose of this work is to identify traditional stereotypes in understanding meanings of proverbs by analyzing communicative frame situations and the formation of the concept sphere in the mind of the speaker. The article sets the following statements: to identify a methodology for studying stereotypes of thinking on the basis of a literature review and theoretical concepts; to classify the main target indicators of using proverbs in communication; to determine the cultural and cognitive background of understanding and perceiving proverbs.

Literature Review

Proverbs as linguistic units have a functional feature in the figurative transmission of life's realities. In that case, their purpose is exactly "to give people's assessment of the objective reality of phenomena as the world's expression" (Syzdykov 2014, 319). Definitions of proverbs include different aspects such as "short, generally known sentence of the folk" (Mieder 1985), "a unit of meaning in a specific context", "a traditional, conversational, didactic genre" (Norrick 1985; Syzdykov 2014, 319; Dabaghi et al. 2010, 807), and, generally, "rhetorical force" (Mieder 2004, 17) in communication with moral, sapient, cultural outlook. We agree with the conclusion of W. Mieder, "Proverb definitions often include the term 'traditional' but proving that a given text has gained tradition is quite another matter" (Mieder 2004, 21). According to figurative nature, five proverb types were investigated by N. Norrick: synecdoche, metaphoric, metonymic, hyperbolic, and paradoxical proverbs (Syzdykov 2014, 808). At that point, paremiology as an independent part of linguistics formed a block of important issues in the proverbs study. Today, problems of "the proverb's history, its universality in comparative analysis, logical correlation, imagery, and its transmission methods" (Qaidar 2014, 425) are related to the objects of paremiology. Indeed, "the paremiologists address such questions as the definition, form, structure, style, content, function, meaning, and value of proverbs" (Mieder 2004, 12). The impressive development of this area is reflected in Mieder's annual bibliographies in *Proverbium: Yearbook of International Proverb Scholarship.*

Proverbs in scientific content are explored in various directions, creating core concepts of anthropological, sociological, ethnographic, cultural, literary, and linguistic topics. In the modern world, they become the object of comparison, translation, knowledge, cognition, and history. Scientists analyze the possibility of using proverbs from friendly chats to political speeches (Mieder 2004, 17) by applying the functional features. For example, a number of scholars have investigated the role of proverbs in the personal formation and development of children in Africa where a comparative cross-cultural study format determined "cultural differences in the ways children from different speech communities are trained to use oral language to display and acquire knowledge" (Penfield and Duru 1988, 119). Proverbs as a necessary element of social interaction between children and caregivers in Igbo Society in southeastern Nigeria described the target of this work. Consequently, "in Igbo society, the content of proverbs conveyed through the association of their vivid imagery with prescribed mores or customary laws of the culture that represent the link between the deceased ancestors or gods and the living" (Penfield and Duru 1988, 119). The authors argue that the purpose of proverbs is to express national identity. There is also an interesting gender fact in the perception of proverbs among boys and girls and among children raised by grandparents and parents (Penfield and Duru 1988, 125). It means proverbs are the most concise instrument of social-oriented upbringing and influential power of ethnic value and wisdom. They outline the rooted mindset of people and save conceptual culture-bounded interpersonal relations in each society because proverbs "address recurrent social situations in a strategic way" (Winick 2003, 595). Thereby, literal functions and applied practical applications synchronize, and researchers resort to sociolinguistic and cognitive methods to measure quantitative and qualitative results in positions of understanding, its perception, saving in memory, using actively or not.

The Kazakh linguist A. Baitursynov (1989h, 225) characterized two aspects of human scrutinizing "the inner world and the outer world. Mind, spirit, and imaginations are the embodiment or personalization of man's inner world where spirituality becomes the main criterion. Other people and material values are results of the external world." Obviously, each product of our mind is a creation of our imagination, spirit, and external conditions. Cognition is the subject of different scientific paradigms. As a tool of thinking and analyzing around, cognition provides the unit of subjective dimension and objective core of explanations. Ultimately, the science of cognition discloses an interaction of social, political, cultural, psychological, and anthropological procedures. For example, *Uldyn uyaty akege, kyzdyn uyaty sheshege* (For the son, shame on the father, for the daughter, shame on the mother) *Annyn zhayin mergennen sura, adamnyn zhayin kurgennen sura* (Ask the shooter about animals, ask the one who has seen a lot about people), *Ozindi osin bilemey, yel bileuge kumartpa* (Not having learned to lead yourself, do not strive to lead the people), and *Zherine karap mal oser, suyna karap tal oser, kataryna karap bala oser* (Livestock's growth depends on land, tree's growth depends on water, a child's growth on an environment) (Sadyrbayuly 2012). This attraction of verity maintains the development of social cognition, psychological cognition, cultural cognition, and language cognition (Orazaliyeva 2018, 79). The cognitive direction in this study is actualized by the need to understand the inner canons of human consciousness.

The cognitive units of the language create the possibility for correct interpretation of the proverb's meanings by activating the inner human memory, perception, and transmission potential. As a result, ready-made comments have deep cognitive and informational meanings, and they help to understand concepts from the point of national code and mentality. The method of "historical and etymological search" (Zhanpeisov 1976, 157) of the twentieth century formed a necessary and important school of ethnographic studies in Kazakh linguistics where a special place is given to oral creativity, "ready-made figurative instruments, combinations, aphorisms, words, and sentences with vivid expression, which have a century-old history, and the observation of our ancestors, the desire to be more effective, the ability to see, notice, and compare" (Zhanpeisov 1976, 18). Scientists argue that "imagination is formed as a result of processing and generalizing of once perceived data." The highest stage of cognition is considered as a thought, which "is based on figurative, sensory details of cognition as a mental process implemented in the human brain" (Sagyndykuly 2003, 6). B. Sagyndykuly explains the transition procedure from thought to a concept through common and distinctive signs because he believes that "a concept, as an image of the world, locates in the consciousness of a person with a distinctive sound" and "a word is their harmonious combination, presented to the judgment of generations" (2003, 6).

By connecting the concepts of spiritual heritage, fertile soil, internal fund, language fund, heritage (Akhanov 1993, 8–18). The Kazakh linguistics carefully treats folklore and ethnographic materials. In search of the answer to the question "How is a concept formed in a person's mind?" (Sagyndykuly 2003, 6), scientists often refer to cognitive categories as consciousness, memory, perception, feeling, knowledge, experience by forming a linguistic platform of interdisciplinary combinations such as linguistic consciousness, linguistic personality, linguistic worldview, concept, and metaphor. The relevance of this metalanguage is characterized by the multidimensionality of the concepts "human mind," "consciousness," which is a key search engine in the study of the proverbs of the Kazakh language as an object of cognitive and communicative acts. In the Kazakh language, it is generally accepted that the "beauty of a word" lies in imagery, resourcefulness, and deep philosophy of life. In the Kazakh language, great importance is attached to the art of words therefore, among the proverbs and sayings, there are a lot of examples about the power of the word. For example, *Oi—sozdin sandygy* (Thought is the key element of the word), *Makal—sozdin atasy* (Proverb is the ancestor of the word), *Otyz tisten shykkan soz, otyz ruly elge zhete* (The word that came out of thirty teeth will reach thirty nationalities), *Ashu oidin bulty, akyl sozdin kilty* (Anger obscures the mind, the mind gives the key to the word) (Sadyrbayuly 2012). Close conjunction with origins, religion, traditions, cultural values, mythological images, and folklore heritage, on the one hand, creates a coin of stereotypical situations. On the other hand, it characterizes the content of the communicative acts. Therefore, Kazakh proverbs have their own "national-cultural genesis, ethno-psychology, and biosphere," from where such concepts as "folk breath," "ethnic feeling," "folk psychology" originate (Mankeeva 1997, 71). It can be possible to clarify with the help of proverbs such as *Korshi akysy—Tanir akysy* (Obligations to a neighbor are tantamount to obligations to the God). *Aueli Tanir zherge beredi, zherge berse, elge beredi* (In the beginning, God gives to the earth, if the earth receives, then the people will receive). *Batyrdyn omiri kyska, danky uzak* (The life of a *batyr* (hero) is short, but his glory is long) (Sadyrbayuly 2012). In the last proverb, the word *batyr* means a hero, which has a folklore origin from an epic genre. In the modern interpretation, it denotes a person who is strong both spiritually and physically. Obviously, the concepts of "image," "background," and "associative image comparison" started in Kazakh linguistics as elements of contact between a person's brain activity and his feelings, which are based on the philosophy of thought, the logic of reason, and the spiritual heritage (Satenova 1997, 119). As a result, the image is considered as "the figurative visualization of individual subjects, the belief of phenomena in the human mind" (Satenova 1997, 120).

Researchers search for the possibility of a comparative analysis of proverbs in different languages by measuring linguistic facts through cognitive tools. According to W. Mieder, nowadays, comparative collections of proverbs include "indices, frequency analyses, sources, geographical distribution, and so on" (Mieder 2004, 17). He also mentioned that this kind of research information helps to develop structural, semantic, and semiotic studies like works about international types of Grigorii L'vovich Permiakov (1970/1979) and Matti Kuusi (1972) (Mieder 2004, 18). By understanding proverbs as "a ubiquitous literary genre" with "rich communicative function" (Dabaghi and Noshadi 2015, 2582), scholars summarize that "the culture-specific attribute of proverbs manifests most when two languages are compared with each other." In this case, the authors compare the conception of time in English and Persian with the focus on a conceptual metaphor. As an example of cross-cultural analysis, they observe the features of the horizontal and vertical understandings of time in the Mandarin and English languages. The question of how it can be possible to get into the mind of a person and to find various ways of conceptualization that have a logical connection with the viewpoint of Kimeny who claimed that "it is possible to get insight into people's world view by investigating their vocabulary and especially proverbs" (Dabaghi and Noshadi 2015, 2583). Metaphor as "the dynamic appearance of logical operations in cognitive consciousness as a model that generates a thought" (Amirbekova 2006, 25) and the process of "changing the meaning of a word" (Syzdyk 2004, 13) has a significant role in the language system. Linguists emphasize that cognitive metaphors are the result of a person's ability to find similarities, associations between different objects and structure them (Arutyunova 1990, 15). In the modern science of language, this term is considered as a way of conscious perception of abstract conclusions or as a mechanism that makes it possible to think abstractly (Lakoff 1993, 249). Consequently, G. Lakoff and M. Johnson underlined that metaphor penetrates everyday life and not only into language but also into thinking and action since our everyday conceptual system is metaphorical (Lakoff and

Johnson 1980, 3). The following functional features of metaphors are distinguished in the literature: cognitive, nominative, communicative, pragmatic, pictorial, instrumental, hypothetical, modeling, euphemistic, popularizing (Chudinov 2001, 49).

Methodology and Methods

E.V. Dzyuba notes that "a method is a way, a way of cognition and practical transformation of reality, a system of techniques and principles that regulate human cognitive activity" (Dzyuba 2018, 73). The methodology, from this position, is considered as, firstly, a system of methods and techniques used in a particular field of activity (in science, politics, art); secondly, the doctrine of this system, the general theory of the methods, the theory in action (Dzyuba 2018, 76). In this paper, the research methodology is presented in connection with cognitive and communicative principles. Cognitive data analysis is based on the classic research methods of comparative analysis, deduction, and induction, explanation, empirical research, experiment, scientific observation. Cognitive methods also involve methods of prototypical analysis based on the works of E. Rosch (1983), cognitive-taxonomic analysis: the works of E. Kubryakova (1994), N. Boldyrev (2007), B. Berlin (1992), the method of crypto class systems in language picture of the world according to the teachings of E. Sapir and B. Whorf (Sapir 1949; Whorf [1956] 2012a), psycholinguistic analysis on the works of A. Leontiev (2003). In our case, we concentrate on methods frame analysis and analysis of blends or conceptually integrated spaces. The communicative method is focused on the characteristics of the transmitter and the recipient, communicative units and stages, and target indicators of speech actions of the speakers.

Language-communication is "the basis of human relationships, which means understanding each other through speaking, exchanging opinions through the necessary fund of public information, through a thought directed to someone" (Orazbayeva 2019, 74). Language-communication has its structural basis as a transmitter—a person transmitting information; recipient—receiving information and units, which make up the linguistic, semantic, and conceptual characteristics of communication. According to E. Passov, language communication like any process has its stages of implementation: the correct transfer of information, the correct transfer of content, and the correct understanding as a result (1991, 8). If in the first case, the speaker's acoustic-articulatory features, pronunciation, tone are taken into account; then, in the second case, semantic characteristics and content of information are important. F. Orazbayeva broadens this series by adding the necessary procedural aspects of communication like the appearance of information inside, information output outside, the transmission of information, its acceptance, and reply (Orazbayeva 2019, 82–83).

Firstly, the stage of "information's appearance inside" in the consciousness of a person identifies his cognitive background, which constitutes the summary of cognition, knowledge, experience, and memory, and it builds the speaker's personal language picture of the world. This concept is the centerline in the language, and it is a "combination of national history, culture, character, and consciousness, professional characteristics, and traditions, cognition, and the ability to choose what is important, what is needed" (Mankeeva 2021, 28). According to the framework of the Faculty Development Competitive Research Grant project "How Kazakhs use proverbs to define themselves in a globalized world: a discourse ecologies approach" of Nazarbayev University for 2019—2021 years, the research experiment was conducted. The participants from Nur-Sultan (55), Almaty (71), Atyrau (86), Semey (80), Taraz (108), and Kaskelen (18) were represented. The questionnaire survey was managed among 418 participants: the gender composition was 49 boys and 216 girls (marked), 179 participants wrote they grew up in the countryside, 131 are from urban areas. First, the monitoring is based on textual material with its linguistic characteristics. In this analysis, elements such as text, subtext, situational basis, association, experience, and comparative characteristics are important. If the text becomes an object of the linguistic search, including lexical, grammatical, and semantic units of the language; then, the subtext forms a metaphorical feature with the assistance of frame and blend components. Thus, using methods of frame analysis, a blend analysis lingua-cognitive picture of cultural concepts is formed.

This connection becomes the rationale for the use of proverbs in certain contexts. For example, the proverb *Zhigittin kuny zhyz zhylky, ary—myn zhylky* (The price of a man is 100 horses; The price of his conscience is 1,000 horses) is based on a frame situation taken from the legal system *Zheti zhargy* (Seven Laws) in the Kazakh steppe. This comparison is based on a set of laws adopted in the Kazakh Khanate (a country ruled by a khan) under Khan Tauke, where the cost of a person's life was measured by the number of cattle (a horse, a camel, a ram). Such an approach in the legal system of the steppe is explained by the attitude of the people to cattle breeding as a source of life and value in everyday life. The Kazakhs moved around the area, fed, raised grain, learned professional crafts, healed, and gained strength with the help of cattle. Also, in the ethnographic studies of the Kazakh language, elements of the cultural heritage are presented through the analysis of national traditions and concepts. One of them is the concept of *Jeti kazyna*, (Seven values).

Zhuirik at (fast horse) is noted at the first place and symbolized human blood and wings (Qaidar 2014, 515). In this proverb, the key comparison is the second part, which determines the significance of the word *ar* (conscience). For a Kazakh, this concept is tantamount to the price of life. It is important not to lose yourself and your conscience as a source of pride and shame. Since, according to C. Fillmore, the theory of frames is important in the study of lexical, grammatical semantics, and semantics of the text (1982, 53). The mental space and the theory of conceptual blending by G. Fauconnier and M. Turner (2002) and M. Turner (1995) helped coordinate the interaction of mental integrations in the analysis of both ready-made proverbs and the appearance of options in communication.

Secondly, the directions of the speech act were identified guided by the principles of the communicative method where the personal characteristics of the speakers, the environment, speaking skills, and functional characteristics are classified (Passov 1991). In the methodological studies of F. Orazbayeva, the communicative method in learning the Kazakh language has the following list of principles: direct communication, types of work, personal abilities of a person, teaching conversational skills, gradual development, dynamic changes, and relevance (2019, 369). As a result, target indicators of the use of Kazakh proverbs in the communicative act are determined, among which educational (with upbringing), patriotic, social, emotional-expressive, cognitive, and contact-establishing goals can be specially noted. These indicators contributed to the identification of the most common lexical and semantic groups of proverbs in the Kazakh language by defining the hierarchy of modern communicative directions in society with their intended use of proverbs. This approach in the study helps to characterize the current actual topics of social institutions today, including the frequency in a percentage of topics such as upbringing, language and the power of words, human character, education, morality, parents, homeland, etc. Additionally, the list of personal characteristics of the participants, which can be represented by gender, age, and social characteristics is one of the interesting details during monitoring. This projection will help to characterize the cultural and cognitive background of the participants and to determine the frequency of the use of certain vocabulary-semantic groups in everyday and purposeful communication.

Thirdly, the methods of description and argumentation have coordinated by the following research actions and conclusions: to understand the modern cultural and cognitive background of the consciousness of young people in society; monitor the actual target indicators of communicative directions and stereotypical situations; define active vocabulary-semantic and conceptual groups of proverbs; to recognize the role and functional feature of proverbs in the period of globalization and make recommendations for increasing activity among the population.

Discussion of the Results

In the works of Kazakh researchers, language and knowledge create a background of certain concepts as "a social picture of modernity," "the world of beauty" (Dabaghi and Noshadi 2015, 66, 74), "the world of language" (Qaidar 1998, 11) and therefore, actualizing the principles of *Adamtanu* (human cognition), *Kogamtanu* (social cognition), and *Tabigattanu* (nature studies). In this regard, the focus of attention on human consciousness' principles contributes to the formation of the world's image, its reflection by being the main part of daily and targeted communication. This approach to the object of research strikes its own set of results, which help, first, to understand the meanings of proverbs; secondly, to provide the frequency of their use in everyday life; thirdly, to pass them from generation to generation with or without changes. As a result, the monitoring data determined a number of cognitive features and the list of communicative characteristics.

By analyzing the frequency groups and types of proverbs in the Kazakh language, the following features were correlated to the cognitive details:

– The basic character of proverbs, which determines the basic concepts in the minds of speakers. So, for example, among the first were noted proverbs from lexical-semantic groups such as "about upbringing"— 18% of respondents in the amount of 50 people; "about the power of words, about language"—9% (25 participants); "about human qualities"—7% (23 participants).
– The frame character of proverbs, created already on familiar details and associations in memory, for example: "about education"—8% (noted by 24 questionnaire participants), "about human qualities and moral issues"—6% (21 participants), "about the role of mother and father"— 6% (21 participants).
– The stereotypical character of proverbs, based on traditional, logical, or antonym associations, which they needed to find. The first task was concentrated on searching the second parts of proverbs and sayings like *Balaly uy bazar* . . . (A house with children is like a bazaar . . .) *Akege karap ul oser* . . . (The son grows up, looking at his father . . .) *Ozge elde sultan bolgansha* . . . Rather than being a sultan in a foreign land . . .). It was concluded that the students correctly noted those stereotyped proverbs that were familiar to them from childhood. The samples used

less often in society were supplemented either by their form, similar in meaning or were marked as an incorrect option. Among such proverbs, we can note such as *Shyn bir soz* ... (True word is one ...) and *Kadirindi bilgin kelse* ... (If you want to know how you are respected ...). As a result, the number of correct answers was 74.69%, which indicates a high level of traditional cognitive background and literacy among young people.

The blend or "conceptually integrated" (Dzyuba 2018, 90) characteristic of proverbs, which combines and associates different life situations or subjects, thereby forming a new concept at the junction of two different elements and helping to understand the figurative meaning, for example: *Asyl pyshak қap tybinde zhatpaidy* (A valuable knife will not remain at the bottom of the bag)—in this case, a person is compared to a valuable knife, which will always be respected and demanded; *Bir yeli auyzga eki yeli kakpak* (Two closing mechanisms are needed for one mouth)—in this context, the human ability to keep his mouth shut or keep silent questioned; *Eki koyandy bir okpen atu* (To kill two birds with one shot)—which means to complete two necessary, important things; achieve two goals. According to the second task, students had to determine the semantic meaning of proverbs in the Kazakh language. The questionnaire included both widely used conceptual integrations and less familiar examples. As a result, the correct answer was given by 64.61% of the students, and the wrong answer was given by 13.67%; the variability was noticed in 21.72% of the respondents. More complex were proverbs with a deep conceptual meaning, for example, *Yel ishi altyn besik* (The nation is a treasure). Here the concept of "treasure" is conveyed through the combination of "golden cradle," which implies history, traditions, and cultural heritage.

The communicative part of the analysis is marked by the following functional features of proverbs in communication:

– By emphasizing the role of social institutions in society, we would like to note the informative-educational function of proverbs. If the older generation uses proverbs to convey thoughts automatically, then young people are limited to educational models that they are taught at home or at school. In this regard, when asked how often you use proverbs in your daily life, 190 students answered "sometimes" and only 52 students answered "always."
– The phatic or contacting function is explained by the desire of students to communicate with dignity not only with their peers, but also with

the older generation. Therefore, in the cognitive baggage of knowledge, the percentage of students who prefer proverbs from the group of social relations, such as parents, morality, upbringing, balance is marked by almost the same number of votes of respondents, on average 7–9%, or about 20 students.

– The emotive function is aimed at the emotional and evaluative impact of the transmitter to the recipient. In this regard, students note the knowledge of patriotic topics as proverbs about the Motherland, about language, about morality, and about values. For example, the meanings of proverbs in the Kazakh language about the Motherland and the country have a deep meaning and emotionality: *Otansiz adam ormansiz bulbul* (A man without a homeland is like a nightingale without a forest), *Otynyn basyn korgai almagan, Otanyn da korgai almaidy* (He who was unable to defend his hearth will not be able to defend his homeland either), *Ottyn basy* among Kazakhs means by the fire / at home / in the family. *Otan ushin kures—erge tigen ules* (Struggle for the homeland is contribution of men). Among students, this indicator has 5.5% (19 students). This small percentage is due to the variety and number of semantic groups chosen by students (22 groups).

Conclusion

Scrutinizing cognitive cognition "as cultural cognition's 'collective memory bank' of a speech community, language is deemed as storing and communicating cultural cognition, i.e. language is a tool to (re)transmit cultural conceptualizations" and by the words "cultural cognition could be addressed systematically, not abstractly" the scholars emphasize "the following analytical tools, which are collectively called 'cultural conceptualizations': cultural schema, cultural category, and cultural metaphor" (Dabaghi 2016, 5). This proves the need for collective consciousness in the formation of a cognitive scheme of cognition, in the ability to share experiences and pass them on to other members of society during communication. Also, cognitive schema as part of cognitive structures includes "knowledge for face-to-face interactions in one's cultural environment. Cultural schema lets us negotiate and re-negotiate meaning and communicate culturally mediated knowledge and experiences" (Dabaghi 2016, 6). Therefore, emphasizing the role of the student's cognitive background in understanding or misunderstanding meanings of proverbs was one of the significant points in explaining the cultural schema. Frame situations, which are reflecting the mutual influence of language and cognition as tools of the national-cultural code, also can determine the knowledge of speakers, their anthropological and physiological characteristics, intellectual abilities, and communication capabilities. Conceptual integration of objects and phenomena in memory has already become the basis for understanding the meanings of proverbs thanks to the background of metaphorical associations and comparisons. In our opinion, understanding and perceiving forms the principles of the language consciousness of individuals today for demonstrating their abilities as members of society. The block of phatic, emotive, and informative characteristics of the communicative acts creates a reliable platform for cultural cognition, and it values traditional thinking and experiences. Frames as "types of cognitive models representing knowledge and opinions associated with specific, often repetitive situations" (Boldyrev 2000, 37) become the basis of blends and the integration of mental spaces.

In conclusion, the frequency of Kazakh proverbs in use is determined by several factors. Firstly, proverbs are anchored in memory through active consumption in the family, school, or in the media. For example, *Kasyktap jinaganyndy shomishtep tokpe* (What was gained with struggle should not be scattered) or *Atadan zhaksy ul tusa, esiktegi basyndy torge suireidi, atadan zhaman ul tusa, tordegi basyndy esikke suireidi* (A good son will bring honor to his father, a bad son will be a disgrace). The key words here are *tor* and *esik*, each of which visually symbolizes among the Kazakh people the honored place at the table and the less respected place near the door. Secondly, some proverbs and sayings have an easy lexical and syntactic form, and they are quickly remembered. For example, *As yesimen tatti* (The food is tasty to the owner), *Ulyk bolsan, kishik bol* (The higher the rank, the more modest one must be), and *Adepti bala—arly bala* (A well-bred boy is well-mannered) (Sadyrbayuly 2012). Thirdly, some proverbs and sayings have a clear frame characteristic, so the description or association embedded in the content is understandable and is easy to imagine visually. Such as, *Adil bilik—altyn tarazy* (Fair governance is the golden scale), *Adam korky shuberek, ahash korky zhapyrak* (A person is decorated by a thing, a tree is decorated by leaves), and *Ananyn suti bal, balanyn tili bal* (Mother's milk is honey, baby's tongue is honey). Fourthly, the number of proverbs in some vocabulary-semantic groups is widely used by their functional capabilities in communication. These include the topics of upbringing, morality, ethics, human qualities, parents. Obviously, it is important to underline the proverb's useful continuity and novelty as a tool of knowledge, cognition, and communication.

The modern approach of understanding proverbs as laconic elements of a meaningful context and a culminating conclusion sometimes has a new characteristic among young people due to changes or impacts of the environment, other languages, and the broadening the horizons of life. As a result, sometimes young generations use modern translations of proverbs instead of already existing ones. In nowadays, some proverbs have translated variants as *Bir bastan eky bas zhaqsy* (Two heads are better than one) instead of *Kelisip pishken ton kelte bolmas* (The fur coat stitched together will not be small / a fur coat cut with counsel won't come up short) (second translation is by E. Aasland (2019, 7)). However, the importance of maintaining basic concepts remains relevant. First of all, this is explained by the need to personify ethnic values through linguistic material, which is the guarantor of cultural and traditional relationships in society, and it is a key to mutual understanding between generations. Secondly, language as a mirror shows the canons and losses in a society by the principles of linguistic (language) ecology. Proverbs as "verbal strategies" (Mieder 2004, 14) with veiled meaningful content have been and will be the basis of diplomatic and competent ways of figuratively solving problems, and here the communicative and emotional needs in society are significant.

Thus, for the frequency integration of proverbs into the daily needs of communicators "as an important resource for self-presentation," and "cultural intimacy" (Aasland 2019, 7), it is necessary to pay attention to the following points:

- Considering the peculiarities of cognitive cognition, it is necessary to pay attention to the cognitive scheme as a detail of the cognitive structure of collective thinking. Obviously, the frequency of use of proverbs depends on the level of cultural intelligence of the members of a society, which means deeply rooted in traditions and values.
- The functional feature of proverbs creates a matrix of its frequency, which assumes a competent balance of categories such as affirmation and communication. Scientists note that today people "are less willing to be told what to do or not to do. In other words, the obvious didactic nature of many traditional proverbs appears to be on the decline" (Dabbagh 2016, 3). In this case, the target of using proverbs among young people is important as a piece of advice, not an order. This will be a guarantee of the desire to use proverbs.
- Linguistic analysis and syntax structures are one of the important components of the study of proverbs. It is based on identifying both semantic and structural features of proverbs. In our case, it becomes obvious that simplicity, conciseness, economy, formulaic structures are integral parts of modern society, where the young generation strives

to put clear and concrete proverbs into their speech with frame background, conceptual space, and familiar parallels for the blend.

Bibliography

Aasland, E. 2019. "A Call for a Digital Turn in Kazakh Proverb Research." Paper presented at the International Conference of Instructors of Kazakh Language, Nazarbayev University, Nur-Sultan, Kazakhstan, June 16, 2019.

Akhanov, K. 1993. *Til biliminin negizderi* [Foundations of linguistics]. Almaty: Sanat.

Amirbekova, A. B. 2006. *"Konseptilik kurylymdardyn poetikalyk matindegi verbaldanu ereksheligi (M.Makatayev öleñderi boyinsha)"* [Verbal features of conceptual structures in poetic texts (based on the poetry of M. Makatayev)]. Abstract for the degree of candidate of philological sciences. Institute of Linguistics named after A. Baitursynov, Almaty.

Arutyunova, N. D. 1990. "Metafora i diskurs" [Metaphor and discourse]. In *Teoriya metafory* [The theory of metaphor]. 5–32. Moscow: Progress.

Baytursynov, A. 1989. *Shygarmalar. Olender, Audarmalar, Zertteuler* [Essays, poems, translations, research]. Almaty: Zhazushy. 320.

Berlin, B. 1992. *Ethnobiological Classification: Principles of Categorization of Plants and Animals in Traditional Societies.* Princeton: Princeton University Press.

Boldyrev, N. 2000. "Freymovaya semantika kak metod kognitivnogo analiza yazykovykh yedinits" [Frame semantics as a method of cognitive analysis of linguistic units]. *Problems of Modern Philology: Interuniversity Collection of Scientific Papers* 1: 36–45.

Boldyrev, N. 2007. "Problemy issledovaniya yazykovogo soznaniya" [Problems of the study of linguistic consciousness]. *Conceptual Analysis of Language,* 95–108. Modern Directions of Research. Moscow: Eydos.

Chudinov, A. P. 2001. *Rossiya v metaforicheskom zerkale: kognitivnoye issledovaniye politicheskoy metafory (1991–2000)* [Russia in a metaphorical mirror: a cognitive study of political metaphor (1991–2000)]. Yekaterinburg: Ural State Pedagogical University.

Dabaghi, A. 2016. "Introducing Cultural Linguistics as an Investigative Framework to Analyze Proverbs." Conference papers of the 4th International on Applied Research in Language Studies, Tehran.

Dabaghi, A., Noshadi M. 2015. *"An Interpretation of the Significance of 'Time': The Case of English and Persian Proverbs."* *Theory and Practice in Language Studies* 5(12) (December, 2015): 2581–90.

Dabaghi, A., Pishbin, E., Niknasab L. 2010. "Proverbs from the Viewpoint of Translation." *Journal of Language Teaching and Research* 1(6) (November 2010): 807–14.

Dzyuba, E. V. 2018. *Kognitivnaya lingvistika: Uchebnoye posobiye* [Cognitive linguistics: Study guide]. Yekaterinburg: Ural State Pedagogical University.

Fauconnier, G., Turner M. 2002. *The Way We Think: Conceptual Blending and the Mind's Hidden Complexities.* New York: Basic Books.

Fillmore, C. J. 1982. "Frame Semantics." In *Linguistics in the Morning Calm: Selected Papers from the SICOL,* edited by the Linguistic Society of Korea. 111–37. Seoul: Hanshin.

Kubryakova, E. S. 1994. "Paradigmy nauchnogo znaniya v lingvistike i yeye sovremennyy status" [Paradigms of scientific knowledge in linguistics and its current status]. *Izvestiya RAN: Series of literature and language* 53(2): 3–16.

Lakoff, G. 1993. "The Contemporary Theory of Metaphor." In *Metaphor and Thought.* 2nd ed., edited by A. Ortony, 202–51. New York: Cambridge University Press.

Lakoff, G., and M. Johnson. 1980. *Metaphor We Live By.* Chicago: University of Chicago Press.

Leontiev, A. A. 2003. *Osnovy psikholingvistiki: uchebnik* [Fundamentals of psycholinguistics: a textbook]. Moscow: Smysl.

Mankeeva, J. 1997. *Madeni lexicanyn ulttyk sipaty* [National characteristics of cultural vocabulary]. Almaty: Gylym.

Mankeeva, Zh. A. 2021. *Qazaq sozinin synergiesy* [Synergy of the Kazakh word]. Almaty: Kazakh National University.

Mansurov, B., B. R. Kulzhanova, S. U. Abzhalov, and R. S. Mukhitdinov. 2014. "Significance of the Hadith of the Prophet Muhammad in Kazakh Proverbs and Sayings." *Procedia - Social and Behavioral Sciences,* 116: 4899–904.

Mieder, W. 2004. *Proverbs: A Handbook.* Westport, CT: Greenwood.

Mieder, W. 1985. Popular Views of the Proverb. Proverbium: Yearbook of International Proverb Scholarship, 2, 109-143.

Norrick, N. 1985. *How proverbs mean: Semantic studies in English proverbs.* Berlin: Mouton, 1985. P. 213.

Orazaliyeva, E., 2018. "Ethno-Cultural Cognition in Teaching the Kazakh Language: Spatial Relations." *Journal of Foreign Language Teaching and Applied Linguistics (J-FLTAL)* 5(2): 73–83.

Orazbayeva, F. Sh. 2019. *Tildik katynas: Gylymi monographiya* [Language communication: Scientific monograph]. Almaty: Arys.

Passov, E. I. 1991. *Kommunikativnyy metod obucheniya inostrannomu govoreniyu* [A communicative method of teaching foreign speaking]. Moscow: Prosvechenie.

Penfield, J., and M. Duru. 1988. "Proverbs: Metaphors that Teach." *Anthropological Quarterly* 61(3) (Fall): 119–28.

Qaidar, A. 1998. *Kazak tilinin ozekti masselerii* [Topical issues of Kazakh linguistics]. Almaty: Ana Tili.

Qaidar, A. 2004. *Khalyq danalygy.* [Folk wisdom]. Almaty: Toganay T.

Qaidar, A. 2014. *Gylymdagy gumyr: Makalalar, bayandamalar zhinagy* [Life in science: Collection of articles, reports.]. Almaty: Sardar.

Qazaq khalkynyn makaldary men matelderi [Proverbs and sayings of the Kazakh people]. 2012, edited by S. Sadyrbayuly. Almaty: Kazakh University.

Rosch, E. 1983. "Prototype Classification and Logical Classification: The Two Systems." *New Trends in Conceptual Representation: Challenges to Piaget's Theory?* edited by E. K. Scholnick, 73–86. Hillsdale: Lawrence Erlbaum Associates.

Sagyndykuly, B. 2003. *Kazirgi Kazakh tili: Lexicology* [Modern Kazakh language: Lexicology]. Almaty: Kazakh University.

Sapir, E. 1949. *Selected Writings of Edward Sapir in Language, Culture and Personality*, edited by David G. Mandelbaum. Berkeley: University of California Press.

Satenova, S. K. 1997. *Kazakh tilindegi kos tagandy phraseologizmderdin tildik zhune poeticalyk tabigaty* [Linguistic and poetic nature of phraseological units in the Kazakh language]. Almaty: Gylym.

Syzdyk, R. 2004. *Abaydin soz ornegi* [Abai's word ornaments]. Almaty: Arys.

Syzdykov, K. 2014. "Contrastive Studies on Proverbs." *Procedia-Social and Behavioral Sciences* 136: 318–21.

Turner, M. 1995. "Conceptual Integration and Formal Expression." *Metaphor and Symbolic Activity* 10(3): 183–204.

Winick, S. 2003. "Intertextuality and Innovation in a Definition of the Proverb Genre." In *Cognition, Comprehension, and Communication: A Decade of North American Proverb Studies*, edited by W. Mieder, 571–601. Baltmannsweiler: Schneider.

Whorf, B. L. (1956) 2012a. "Relation of Habitual Thought and Behavior to Language (1939)." In *Language, Thought, and Reality: Selected Writings*, edited by John B. Carroll, Stuart Chase, and Penny Lee, 173–204. Cambridge, MA: MIT Press.

Zhanpeisov, M. 1976. *Auezovtin "Abai Zholy" epic tili* [The language of M. Auezov's epic "Abai's path"]. Almaty: Gylym.

Story of the Use and Study of Kazakh Proverbs in the Soviet Period: The Use of Proverbs in the Works of the Writer M. Auezov

GULZIA PIRALI, AIZHAN KURMANBAYEVA
Institute of Literature and Art named after M.O.Auezov, Almaty

Introduction

The soul of the nation, the voice of the spirit, the golden storehouse of the most precious world—the language, proverbs. Educator A. Baitursynov says: "Both the vast land and the rich language belong to the Kazakhs" (2003, 34). Kazakhs must have their own land and language. Kazakh language is one of the most melodic, lively, and rich languages in the world. The tasks of mastering the vocabulary and rich treasures of the native language, preserving the essence, and meaning of the language of genealogy and rhetoric, passed down from ancestor to child, and understanding them correctly, are fruitful uses of these proverbs effectively and competently. It is also true that the establishment of language communication through proverbs leads the younger generation to love, respect and develop the native language, and only then the individual's respect and love for the country, the land, the motherland, the nation, humanity will increase.

It is a well-known fact that for the Kazakh people, who grew up in the poetry of antiquity, uttered heroic poems, epics, proverbs, and sayings, there is no greater wealth and life than language. Proverbs, sayings, etiquette can be used to learn the culture of communication of the nation. In the study of geography, based on linguistic communication, there are studies in sociology, geology, etc. It is also natural that national values are studied. Proverbs can also be used to identify people's speech and communication skills. "The

Kazakh people, who have been wandering the Sahara for centuries in search of happiness, could not leave us the monuments of architecture, sculpture and art. But he left us the most precious heritage. The poetic people, the poetic people, use their poetic wisdom from time immemorial and express their spirit in unforgettable epic epics, in a variety of songs," says Mukhtar Auezov (2011, 135). He goes on to say, proverbs are one of the great values we have inherited from generation to generation. Sacred proverbs, which for centuries have gone through many stages of history, do not violate their originality and pattern show the spiritual necessity, expand the field of speech, and show the eternal vitality of our national values. This is evidenced by the fact that proverbs and sayings, which philosophically express the meaning and value of our daily lives, despite the turbulent times, are supplemented, modified, and reinterpreted every year in terms of genre, theme, and art. There is no need to prove that the proverbs are the eternal heritage of the nation, the immortal noble art of the Kazakhs. Famous travelers, scientists, Orientalists, Decembrists, political prisoners, etc., who visited the Kazakh steppes, told the world that talented historians do not speak without proverbs. It's known through records that proverbs, which have a special place in the national art of speech, are a vital principle in the steppe civilization.

In small genres and proverbs, the issue of love for the country and the man, seen from all angles, ranged from patriotic upbringing to patriotic ideas, Folk art, which is the pearl of centuries-old folk wisdom, is characterized by the multifunctionality of folk wisdom and proverbs, and has played an educational, cognitive, and aesthetic function. The artistic features of the proverbs, in accordance with the nature of the genre, also play an important role in the intellectual education of humanity.

The proverbs reflect the worldview and understanding of our ancestors and the social, cognitive, educational, and aesthetic tasks they perform at different times. There is also the unexpected nature of proverbs in debates, in everyday life, in dance councils, in Chechen conflicts, and in improvisational national events.

A proverb is a stable word that conveys a certain idea in a concise, rational, sharp and concise way. In this regard, one example is the *Frequency Dictionary of Mukhtar Auezov's Epic, The Way of Abai*:

> It is not a lie that we are proud of the fact that the number of individual nouns in 4 volumes has reached 16,983. In all of Shakespeare's works there are 18,000, and the famous poet A.S.Pushkin's entire academic collection contains 22,000 individual words, the richness of our native language has proved to the world that the *Frequency Dictionary of Mukhtar Auezov's Epic, The Way of Abai* is another real scientific and literary achievement. If we add that in this dictionary

8,698 out of 16,983 words appear only once or twice, the most frequently used word is also a verb (9,828 times), in the fourth place is Abai's personal name (6,747 times). The richness of the language means the sea (Syzdyk 2005, 88). And what if the Institute of Linguistics publishes *Explanatory Dictionary of Auezov's Language* and *Dictionary of Phraseology in Auezov's Language*? The author's book, *Auezov M.*, published from 1997 to 2011, is a 50-volume complete edition of his works (Auezov 2011, 56).

Given that the work for this purpose will continue in the future on the topics of the writer's work in the history of the Kazakh literary language, the linguistic and stylistic phenomenon of the pen, the imagination about the richness of the Kazakh language in general limits the infinity. If so, it is important to look up the definition of a proverb that is common in the vocabulary of every poet and writer, even an ordinary person.

The literal meaning of the proverb is a connection, a conclusion, born of a real-life situation, and the possibility of referring to other life phenomena like that situation expands its figurative, variable meaning. For example, proverbs such as *Soqyr tauyqqa bari bıdaı* (Everything is wheat for a blind hen), *Shaban ıırek buryn ushar* (a slow duck flies early), are related to human life. Proverbs are valuable for conveying ideas in a way that is rational, mobile, articulate, and appropriate. Sometimes a proverb instructive. For example, *Kulme dosqa, keler basqa* (Don't laugh at a friend; similar things will happen to you); *Oinap soileseń de oilap soile* (Even if you play, speak thoughtfully). The proverb covers a wide range of phenomena of public life. The theme is the richest and most comprehensive. The most important social ideas, such as morality, justice, freedom, diligence, appreciation of art, education, mother tongue, the interests, aspirations of the people, are clearly reflected in the proverb. The proverb has a great educational and cognitive value. Proverbs are easy to remember and say because they are concise, meaningful, expressive, figurative, and simple. The rhythm of the words in the article is consistent, often in line with the poetic expressions. Properly used, the proverb reinforces the meaning of the words and clarifies the point being made. *Sozdin korki—maqal* (The beauty of the word is a proverb) (Tasmagambetov 2005, 356).

Literature Review

In order to study the proverbs, their structural features and, as well as the peculiarities of their use in fiction, the following works were taken into account: *Soz qudireti* (The power of words) (Syzdyk 2005), *Babalar sozi: jüz tomdyq* (Words of the ancestors: one hundred volumes) (Alpysbaeva, Alibekov, and Qosan 2010), *Tauelsizdik jane folklor* (Independence and folklore) (Kirabaev 2012), *Eski türki jazba eskertkishteri: Eski turki halyqtarynyn ataly sozderi men maqal-matelderi jane korkem adebiet shygarmalarynan alyngan uzindiler* (Ancient Turkic written monuments: Proverbs and sayings of the ancient Turkic peoples and excerpts from works of fiction) (Kuryshzhanuly 2001); "Contrastive Studies on Proverbs" (Syzdykov 2014).

Methodology

The study used the methods of summarization, analysis, descriptive analysis, narration.

Discussion of Results

Proverbs describe the centuries-old work and life experience of the people in just a few words, so there is no need to talk too much. Every epoch has its own concept of proverb.

There are many proverbs on Kazakh traditions, customs, and behavior. From them you can see the customs of the people in different epochs, attitudes to society, religion, the way of growth of the people's consciousness. Some proverbs have their roots in fairy tales, songs, and parables. For example, when you need to be modest and humble, people say, *Aıaz, alindi bil, qumyrsqa jolyndy bil* (literally, Aıaz, know your way, ant, know your way). It is known that this word refers to historical legend, that is, it came from the fairy tale *Aiaz Bi* and became a proverb. And what is the history of such proverbs in Kazakh history? Although proverbs cover a variety of topics, depending on the method of creation, they all have a characteristic feature—they reveal the essence of life phenomena, draw conclusions, depict them artistically.

"Proverbs are born in different ways. Depending on the situation, a clever, well-articulated word can be passed on by word of mouth and become a proverb. Such words are first associated with the name of the speaker, and then the name of the publisher is forgotten, and these words are tested, refined, sharpened, and become a proverb" (Kaskabasov 2008, 234).

The proverb uses a variety of metaphors, and metonymy to sculpt and embellish the saying. For example, in proverbs such as *Jaqsy jigit—jagadagy qundyz, jaqsy qyz-koktegi juldyz* (A good son is a hope, a good daughter is a joy), two things, complement each other and create a figurative sculpture by appropriate, logical comparison and alignment. The same method of exaggeration is used, in *Aıdagany bes eshki, ysqyrygy jer jarady* (Only five goats are chasing, and whistle so that the earth cracks).

Now, by contrasting two phenomena, they express thoughts: *Jaqsynyn basyna is tusse ashynar da ashylar, jamannyn basyna is tusse, bir tular da basylar* (A good person becomes brave when he is in trouble, a bad person comes into depression when he is in trouble) and *Jaqsy atqa—bir qamshy, jaman atqa—myn qamshy* (A good horse needs one whip, a bad needs thousand). Sometimes a proverb is created by juxtaposing two similar things, that is, by making parallels between them. For example, *Qoi kormegen qoi korse, qualap jurip oltirer* (A person who has not been a shepherd will kill sheep by chasing). *Ydysyn kor de, asyn ish, anasyn kor de, qyzyn al* (See the owner and eat, see the mother and marry the daughter), etc. There is also a proverb in the form of a sermon, for example an example: *Otken iske okinbe* (Do not regret about the past), *Oinap soilesen de, oilap soile* (Even if you joke, speak thoughtfully).

Proverbs are used for didactic purposes in both life and speech and perform several functions. First, the proverb has an educational and cognitive function. Second, it is said to protect a person against something, that is, it is in a form of prohibition, and to some extent it is associated with magic. Third, it will be a call to take care of nature. It directs a person to something and tries to influence his behavior and actions, in other words, it is a sign of regulation of human life. All this, on the one hand, reflects the applied nature of the proverb, and therefore the proverb is one of the oldest genres. However, because it is closely connected with reality, it is born, renewed, and revived in every era of society. For example, today the proverbs of the poet Abai replace many proverbs.

And the aesthetic function of the proverb—from the process of transformation of folklore into the art of speech, defines the immortality of the national art of speech to the present day, adorns the text, giving beauty and art to the human mind. It is known that the proverbs of our ancestors, which have become an eternal spiritual and artistic heritage for the child, have become a 'school of mastery' for all Kazakh writers, a link to the development of modern Kazakh prose. It goes without saying that today Kazakh proverbs make a significant contribution to the Kazakh vocabulary of more than 350 thousand people. The fact that the proverb, born from life and experience, is an assessment of the phenomena in society, defines the stylistic and artistic features of this genre. It is natural that the proverb, which summarizes the life concepts of each epoch, has long been glorified for its artistic image, philosophical thought, mobility, ingenuity, and wisdom. The proverb, which is as fast as a bullet, but as sharp as a bullet, has a great meaning for the purpose of the nation. In a small work of folk wisdom, the customs of that time, the essence of the phenomenon of life, the nature of the mystery are embroidered. (Kaskabasov 2008, 365)

The Importance of the Research

As the Kazakh written literature developed and the migration of our literature began to move forward, the role of proverbs in the literary text also increased. One of the ways to increase the artistic power of the work and enrich the language is the use of proverbs. In M.Auezov's works, Kazakh proverbs are widely used to convey the character's thoughts and increase the meaning of the word. Proverbs used by the author can be divided into several thematic categories, depending on their content and scope:

1. Depending on the behavior, personal qualities of a person: *Oli arystannan tiri tyshqan artyq* (A living mouse is better than a dead lion); *Kok etikti kez kelmei, kon etiktini kozge ilmei* (Ignore the poor until you meet the rich); *Urysy juan bolsa, iesi oledi* (If the fight is thick, the owner dies) (Auezov 1998, 45); *Tyshqannyn olgeni—mysyqtyn oinagany* (The death of a mouse is the play of a cat); *Tandagan tazga jolygady* (When you can't make choice, you will meet the bald) (Auezov 1998, 78);
2. Connecting with heroism: *Kop qorqytady, teren batyrady* (Many people frighten, the deep water drowns) (Auezov 1998, 53).
3. Depending on the rulers of the country: *Has jaman qasyndagysyn qaraqtaidy* (The scoundrel robs his neighbor); *Han ádilinen taisa, qarashysy buzylady* (If the king is unfair, the pirate will be spoiled) (Auezov 1998, 67).
4. Depending on the action: *Ui artynda bori bar* (There is a wolf behind the house); *Soqyr korgennen tanbas* (The blind tells always what he sees); *Badyraq sen tımesen, men tımeımin* (If you don't touch me, I won't touch you) (Auezov 1998, 321).
5. Concerning good and evil: *Jaqsy lebiz—jarym yrys* (A good word is half the battle) (Auezov 1998, 129).
6. Depending on the size of the child: *Kari qoidyn jasy ulken, isek qoıdyn basy ulken* (Elder sheep's age is older, ram's head is bigger) (Auezov 2001, 89).
7. In connection with life and death: *Tustik omirin bolsa, kundik mal jı* (If you have a noon life, gather daily livestock); *Qyryq jyl qyrġyndy bolsa da, ajaldy óledi* (Even though there have been plenty of battles, death comes on its time) (Auezov 2001, 182).
8. In connection with unity: *Auyl ıti ala bolsa, bori korse biriger* (When the village dogs see a wolf, they unite) (Auezov 2001, 256).

The writer adds a lot of meaning to a few words, which are used by the writer to express the wisdom of the people, a concise and widely used branch of folklore—a clear and concise version of the proverb. The writer also uses proverbs to reveal the character's inner world, psychology, to express his social status and social status, to describe his life, and to promote traditions and customs of his ancestors.

M. Auezov's eloquent words have become a proverb. Such words of wisdom also expand the field of Kazakh proverbs and increase the richness of the language. For example, *Ar jazasy bar jazadan auyr jaza* (The punishment of conscience is the most severe punishment); *Oi da kop, uaıym kop oılaı bersen, Oı da joq, uaıym da joq oınaı bersen* (If you keep thinking a lot, you will continue to worry, there are no thoughts and worries if you play); *Manyna uryq shashpagan jaqsylyq, japanda jalgyz osken baıterekshe, tul bolady da qalady* (If it doesn't spread seed around, it will become like a poplar in desert); *Onerpaz bolsan, bol* (If you are an artist, be successful); *Jigit qadiri onerimen olshener bolar* (A guy"s dignity can be measured by his art). Proverbs such as *Adilet tilese atańnyń bolsyn aıybyn aıt* (literally, If you want justice, even blame your grandfather) are widespread among the people, and even today among the writers. It is not an exaggeration to say that the old words of folk wisdom, not Auezov's words, have become proverbs.

Each nation has its own character, which is reflected in the art of speech, especially in the proverbs and sayings of that nation. The glorious commander and outstanding writer Baurzhan Momyshuly says: "Proverbs are life experience. Moments of hardship, how you got rid of that difficult time, become a proverb if you express them in your thoughts, embroider them in words, summarize them and summarize them" (2010, 137). Is it not true that the proverbial steppe philosophy, the intellectual wealth of the nation? The proverb has a special place in the spiritual history of the Kazakh people, which preserves centuries—old traditions, ancestral customs, language, mentality, religion, culture, history, literature, and art in one oral text.

The only evidence of this is the rich spiritual heritage of our country. It is known that in the past there was a lot of talk about the cultural diversity of nomads. For example, there are the 100 volume *Words of the Ancestors* (Alpysbaeva, Alibekov, and Qosan 2010) and the 10 volume *History of Kazakh Literature* (Qarataev 1964) and a 50 volume collection of academic works by Mukhtar Auezov (1998, 2001). The five volumes of *Words of the Ancestors* contain only Kazakh proverbs. This is a rich heritage that is not found in the peoples of the world. Even in countries that are giant empires, there are only a few ancient epics and the treasures of the national art of speech of the Kazakh people are great values that can be shamelessly offered to anyone. These facts awaken the right attitude of both us and others to history, to free us from the stereotypes that obscure the truth, to experience the sunny moments of the truth, and to force us to admit it. We are fascinated by the old artifacts of our ancestors, or by the shaking of someone's misconceptions and divination, and thus to the denial of the greatness of our nation, which is full of wisdom. All this will determine the knowledge of the reader, the ability of others to think, whether he has the scientific, historical, psychological readiness to face the distorted history.

Texts of Kazakh proverbs became the basis for several volumes of *Words of the Ancestors*. The first volume of *History of Kazakh Literature* analyzes the genesis, formation, development, and genre features of these proverbs from a scientific and theoretical point of view. Thus, the nature and history of the small genre entered the academic community and reached a new stage of national development. Entering the fertile soil of centuries—old culture, our young generation is nourished and spiritually enriched by the living food of our historical past. Every proverb here teaches *shanyrak*[the smoke opening of a yurt] - each owner of the country to appreciate his family, homeland, country, his descendants, glorifies the upbringing of generations. It is obvious that the younger generation will not be able to preserve the traditions and values of their nation, based on certain country rules and strictly follow them. For the first time in the history of Kazakh literature, the eternal values of the proverbs, which were the main target of these national principles and traditions, were analyzed and fully systematized in the first volume of the *History of Kazakh Literature*. There is a lot of new information, new data, previously unseen in the press, collected from the mouth of the country, our compatriots in other countries, the elderly, various archives, and manuscripts in the library.

Kazakh proverbs summarize and systematize the millennial historical experience of our nation and gems of literature, culture, and wisdom. These proverbs are also the great literary heritage of the great steppe, which aims to cherish the national values of the Kazakh people, to systematically study the path of growth to today's civilization, and to inculcate it in the minds of future generations.

Conclusion

Proverbs that have been passed down from ancient times to today's independent Kazakh literature continue the educational tradition and do not lose the spiritual heritage of an entire nation. The artistic, philosophical, didactic, goals and functions of proverbs in the art of speech are studied in detail in various fields. The history of the genre of proverbs, which is divided into stages and systematically studied, is systematized. After all, the work of art of the independent Turkic people, whose grandfather had established his own law since time immemorial, has always been spiritually free. Now that we have gained our sovereignty and put history in its place, we are trying to reveal some bitter truths and glorify our national history.

The main purpose of the proverb, which educates children to ingenuity, is the future of the generation, the interests of the nation. It is true that all spirituality, which makes a small contribution to the education of the nation and future generations, serves the country and its future. There are many scientific conclusions about the proverb, its educational and artistic activity, which exemplifies the mastery of human language in speech, thought and speech, figurative and eloquent speech. Proverbs that train the language of the younger generation, encourage the development of thought, and eloquence are our eternal national values, which serve the care of future generations. After all, the people who create the language make the proverbs figurative, understandable, sharp, lively. The wisest and most winged words are these proverbs. Therefore, they are the eternal heritage and values of the nation.

Is it not the self-knowledge of humanity itself in the discovery of the essence of proverbs that develop the seeds of their spirituality, folk wisdom and teach them to think? Considering that spiritual consciousness is conveyed through language, religion, customs, traditions, literary and cultural values, proverbs have a special place in it. We will be a perfect country when the future of our nation grows from infancy, absorbing the noble ideas, human qualities, and customs that are the essence of the life of the younger generation from the cradle to the grave. Indeed, the seeds of wisdom accumulated over the centuries in thoughtful, small-genre proverbs are a simple principle, an immortal example that our people can glorify from generation to generation.

Bibliography

Alibekov, T., 2010. Vol. 65. *Kazakh Proverbs*. Astana: Foliant.

Alpysbaeva,Q., Alibekov T., and Qosan S., 2010. *Babalar sözi: Jüz tomdıq*. (Ancestor's) words: Hundred Volumes. Astana: Foliant.

Alter, R. 2010. *The Wisdom Books: Job, Proverbs, and Ecclesiastes; A Translation with Commentary*. New York: Norton.

Auezov, M. 1960. *Kazak adebiyetinin tarihy* [History of Kazakh literature]. Almaty: Ğılım.

Auezov, M. 1961. *Ádebı mura jáne ony zertteý* [Literary heritage and its study]. Almaty: Ğılım.

Auezov, M. 1998a. *Elu bes tomdıq şığarmalar jïnağı. (Complete collection of works in fifty volumes)*. Vol. 2. Almaty: Ğılım.

Auezov, M. 1998b. *Elu bes tomdıq şığarmalar jïnağı. (Complete collection of works in fifty volumes)*. Vol. 5. Almaty: Ğılım.

Auezov, M. 2001. *Elu bes tomdıq şığarmalar jïnağı. (Complete collection of works in fifty volumes)*. Vol. 10. Almaty: Ğılım.

Auezov, M. 2011. Encyclopedia. Almaty: Atamura. 688 p.

Clements, R. E. 2003. "Proverbs." In *Eerdmans Commentary on the Bible*, edited by J. D. G. Dunn and J. W. Rogerson, 437–66. Grand Rapids: Eerdmans.

Contexts of Folklore. 2019. Ed. Simon J. Bronner and Wolfgang Mieder. New York: Oxford.

Encyclopedia of Mukhtar Auezov. 2011. Almaty: Atamura.

Encyclopedic Reference Book of Kazakh Literature. 2005. 356–357. Almaty: Aruna, LLP.

Gabdullin, M. 2018. *Oral Literature of the Kazakh People*. Almaty: Kazakh Pen Club.

Kaskabasov, S. 2008. *Qazaq adebietinin tarihy* [History of Kazakh литerature]. History of Kazakh Folklore, 1. Almaty: KazInform.

Kuryshzhanuly, A. 2001. *Eski türki jazba eskertkishteri: Eski turki halyqtarynyn ataly sozderi men maqal-matelderi jane korkem adebiet shygarmalarynan alyngan uzindiler.* [Ancient Turkic written monuments: proverbs and sayings of the ancient Turkic peoples and excerpts from works of fiction]. 2001. Almaty: Qainar.

Momyshuly, B. 2010. *Balalarga arnalgan suretti albom* [Photo album for children]. Almaty: Yel-shezhire.

Perdue, L. G. 2012. *Proverbs*. Louisville: Westminster John Knox.

Qazaq adebietinin tarihy [*History of Kazakh literature*]. 1964. Edited by M. K. Karatayev. Almaty: USSR Academy of Sciences.

Qazaq adebietinin tarihy [*History of Kazakh literature*].1964. Edited by A. Egeubayev. Complete collection of works in ten volumes. Vol. 5. Almaty: Qazaqparat.

Simon, J. Bronner. 2007. *The Meaning of Folklore: The Analytical Essays of Alan Dundes*. Utah State University Press.

Syzdyk, R. 2005. *Soz Qudireti* [The Power of Words]. Almaty: Atamura.

Syzdykov, K. 2014. "Contrastive Studies on Proverbs." *Procedia-Social and Behavioral Sciences* 136: 318–21.

Tauelsizdik jane folklor [Independence and folklore]. 2012. Edited by S. C. Kirabaev. Almaty: Language.

Tasmagambetov I.N. et al., 2005. *Babalar sözi: Jüz tomdıq* [The words of the ancestors: One hundred volumes]. Astana: Foliant

Tate, Marvin E, Harold Wayne Ballard, and W. Dennis Tucker. 2000. *An Introduction to Wisdom Literature and the Psalms : Festschrift Marvin E. Tate.* Macon, Ga.: Mercer University Press.

Tilepov, Zh. 2010. *Kazak makal-matelderi* [Kazakh proverbs and sayings]. *Babalar sozi: Zhuztomdyk* [Words of the ancestors]. Astana: Foliant

Tucker, W. Dennis. 2000. "Literary Forms in the Wisdom Literature." In *An Introduction to Wisdom Literature and the Psalms,* edited by Marvin E. Tate, Harold Wayne, Ballard and W. Dennis, Tucker. Mercer University Press.

National Cognitive Activity of Proverbs in the Language of Fiction

ZHANAR ABDIGAPBAROVA
Nazarbayev University, Nur-Sultan

Introduction

Proverbs and sayings are the basis of folk art. Proverbs and sayings are wise teachings that summarize the key ideas about life events in a rational, concise, and sharp way. Proverbs and sayings emerge from life. They are the experience and philosophical essence of life struggles, constant efforts, and social contradictions. They are made up of deep insights into life laws, comparisons, and reflections of the truths of human society. Like other branches of oral literature, proverbs and sayings have been sorted out over time, replenished, sharpened, and replaced by concepts that do not satisfy modern requirements, and only the most updated versions have been preserved.

Proverbs and sayings are a small genre of Kazakh oral literature. Nonetheless, they have a special significance in the spiritual life of our nation. They describe both the epoch and history of the ancient people, their customs, knowledge and skills, art and culture, professions, beliefs, and the ways of cultural development. Rakhmankul Berdibay writes, "Labor, profession, pastoralism, farming, livestock, unity, courage, bravery, defense of the country, homeland, social relations, morality, education, art, health, friendship, love, youth, oldness, generosity and honor have become the main topic of proverbs and sayings. There are many comparisons in the proverbs related to the ancient profession of the Kazakh people like herding and livestock, which prove the understanding, wisdom, evaluation of the events and artistic understanding of the nation " (Berdibay 2005, 349).

It can be said that each individual work in this genre has been sorted and systematized in terms of content and transmitted from generation to generation. In ancient times, they carried the same burden as the fables of large genres, such as short stories and novels. Zhumat Tilepov (2010, 8) says, "In general, sayings, which are the source of folk philosophy, have become an impressive phraseological unit due to their unique expressiveness, and are an indicator of the thinking level of our nation. The dynasty of writers, who deeply understood this, has always used proverbs and sayings in their works of art, articles, essays and descriptions." Hence, proverbs and sayings are an encyclopedia that summarize various events that take place in people's lives.

Proverbs and sayings are a "golden bridge" that connect the past and present of the people with their future. They are a guarantee of the continuation of spiritual and cultural traditions in the cognition, social memory, language, and mentality of the nation. Any ethnic community that forgets its spiritual heritage is deprived of its past, and its future is obscure. More detailed studies of individual proverbs and sayings in cultural contexts are necessary. The work so far shows that proverbs as *monumenta humana* contain general wisdom that, in many cases, defy geographical or linguistic boundaries (Kuusi 1985). According to the proverb critic Wolfgang Mieder, it is important to study proverbs and sayings in a cultural context because proverbs and sayings are an expression of human wisdom (Mieder et al., 2019). There is both wisdom that is passed down and insight gained in succeeding generations and expressed through new sayings and proverbs.

A number of research works on Kazakh proverbs and sayings have been written in both linguistics and literary criticism. According to the scholar Abduali Qaidar (2004, 142), proverbs and sayings "have extremely important role in the life of the Kazakh people in understanding the history and present nature of the people in terms of ideological, logical and ethnolinguistic point of view. Proverbs and sayings are related to all events in the world, society and nature. There is a natural order in the nature of the world from the very beginning. This sequence can be seen only by grouping all things and phenomena into three large areas and exploring them by concentrating on their internal system and meaning."

In general, the thinking peculiarities of any nation are reflected in its native language. There are also unique proverbs and sayings in the language of each nation that describe the consciousness, knowledge, customs, traditions, culture, and history of that nation. Therefore, proverbs and sayings are integral parts of the language, which determine the process of development of the national language and the main indicators of culture of the nation.

It is impossible to imagine the richness of the Kazakh language without folklore. For example, the art of oratory and aitys are considered as the spiritual treasure of the nation. They have flourished and developed from the rich vocabulary of phraseological units in our language. The language of fiction was also formed as a continuation of such traditional linguistics.

In works of art, poets and writers use vernacular vocabulary in creating the image of the character or conveying their ideas. M. Sergaliyev (1995, 60) writes, "The language of the Kazakh people is both rich and artistic. A variety of beautiful and wise words, oratory and proverbs are in national use. The expressive and impressive methods are also there."

The use of proverbs and sayings in a work of art requires great skills from the writer. The mastery of the poets and writers is assessed according to the extent to which the noble heritage of the people—proverbs—are appropriately used in their works (Sarsenbayev 1980, 14). The writer uses a variety of visual tools to convey the story to the reader effectively. Also, the author makes a good use of proverbs and sayings to convey ideas. "Here, the writer's ability to appropriately and effectively use the pragmatic function of the language plays an important role. One of the main features of proverbs and sayings is their evaluation. Evaluation is the speaker's assessment of the event, object, action, attitude, and viewpoint" (Momynova 1999, 134).

Intricate evaluation is inherent to proverbs and sayings. In proverbs and sayings, the assessment is given both figuratively and explicitly. They also evaluate any situation in human life, human behavior, actions, and human qualities.

B. Dinayeva claims that "The properties of proverbs and sayings such as emotional expressiveness, evaluation, didactics, and conclusiveness about a particular situation are associated with their natural function. The meaning of the evaluative and descriptive function in proverbs and sayings is primarily related to the positive or negative assessment by the subject. Secondly, the exact situation is not considered as an individual phenomenon. A set of typical situations are often given in a proverbial form. The speaker expresses his opinion and evaluates a particular situation by choosing the proverb and sayings. Emotional tone and evaluative quality are not interchangeable. However, there is a similarity between them, because evaluation is a certain type of utterance in the expression of the emotional relationship" (2013, 70).

The evaluative properties of proverbs and sayings are widely used in works of art to depict the image of the characters, reveal their personality, and evaluate their actions. In this article, we will focus on the proverbs and sayings in Kazakh writer Mukhtar Magauin's works. Mukhtar Magauin is a famous Kazakh writer. He stepped towards literature in the 1960s. The author's work, "Tazynyn olimi" (Death of Tazy), which was written in 1969, criticizes the ideology of the Soviet Era. The main character in the work is a hunting dog / hound. The Kazakh people call a hound *tazy*. The name *tazy* comes from the Persian, meaning "pure, agile, and quick." It is also possible that the word *tazy* means "pure," pure-blooded, and may have been changed to *tazy* due to the laws of reduction. It seems that the Kazakh *tazy* and the Afghan *tazy* came to Central Asia at the same time period as the Persian *tazy*. They were artificially selected and improved by the Sakas and Afghans in accordance with the local natural conditions (Hinayat and Isabekov 2007).

The main storyline of this work begins with the puppet period of *tazy*, and every aspect of life is developed through the eyes of the *tazy*, and the theme is revealed through his death.

The death of the *tazy* is not just the death of a dog. "Tazy is a symbolic image taken from the national tradition. For our nation, where a hound is one of the seven treasures, it is also a continuation of antiquity, a source of our virtue, and a value of our traditions. The death of that *tazy* is a death of our spirit, traditions and people" (Baitursyn 2021). This theme is artistically developed by impressive ideas.

> "Hey, why are you beating my hound?" he shouted.
> "I not only beat it; I will skin it."
> "What? Who are you?"
> "You don't know me yet!" Esenzhol said with a sneer. "You will know me. I will make sure you know me. You will follow your uncle."
> "My uncle is none of your business," said Kazy. The pace has slowed. "You can't do anything to me. It is said that "Aq yilip—bugilmes," "white does not bend." I am a bloodthirsty person. Everyone knows. Here it is!" Kazy leaned over and hit his wooden foot. (Magauin 1990, 23)

Here, the proverb, *Aq yilip—bugilmes* (White does not bend), serves to convey the main idea of the work. In the Kazakh worldview, the color white (aq) is a symbol of purity, honesty and justice. In the explanatory dictionary of the Kazakh language, white is an adjective like the color of snow, milk (the opposite of black). It means honesty, purity, and innocence (Zhanuzakov 2008). Bending means bowing down, bowing of one's head, and inflexibility is a negative to white. It means not to bend, not to lower the head, and not bowing. The general meaning of the proverb is that a pure person does not bow his head, bend or bow down in front of anyone. In the work, the main character, Kazy, is slandered innocently. However, after some time, he was acquitted and released. Injustice is defeated by justice. This proverb is repeated twice in the work. In a broad sense, the main problem raised in the work is the destruction of the centuries old native culture and national values of the Kazakh people by the colonial Soviet Union, assimilating alien, artificial, and cheap cultures into the minds of the people. In the end, the writer suggests that Soviet policy will be exposed at last, justice will triumph, and the Kazakhs will become an independent country. The day will come to revive Kazakh culture and national values. In his work, the author uses this proverb to convey the main idea and his metaphor to the reader. During the Soviet Era, censorship in literature was severe. Control over ideas of national interest was especially strong. The Soviet authorities demanded that the literature be based on Communist Party principles. Kazakh literature developed from the experience of a complex society. This period, which spans more than seventy years, was not the same in terms of the development of society and the exchange of ideological positions and ideas. "The Communist Party led the literary process. Literature was mainly based on the tasks of the epoch set by the party, trying to be the voice of that epoch. However, despite political pressure, literature has become a national category" (Adilkhanova 2014). During this period, when creative people could not express themselves freely, writers used different methods to convey their ideas, such illustrations, parables, etc. Mukhtar Magauin used this proverb in order to deliver his thoughts at that period.

The proverb *Aq yilip—bugilmes* (White does not bend) is sometimes used as *Aq yilip synbaidy* (White does not break) (Alpysbayeva, Alibekov, and Qosan 2010, 147). Here, the word "bend" in the proverb is replaced by the word "break." The proverb, "White does not break," means that an innocent person does not give up; thus, no evil can break an honest person. That is why he does not lower his face in front of anyone. The word "unbreakable" here further expands the meaning of "not bending" in the previous article. Such practices are found in the use of proverbs. Finding and using proverbs differently depends on the writing style. The use of different versions of proverbs in colloquials and literary language is of great stylistic significance. Therefore, its two types usual (according to the language norm) and occasional (deviation from the norm or personal use of the speaker) should not be ignored (Smagulova 1983, 68). Variation is also inherent in the nature of proverbs; it is the result of a living process arising from their usual and occasional use. "Variability is not a rigid phenomenon of proverbs, but a living phenomenon that is suitable for use in any field of language, adaptable to changes as needed, and flexible in wording" (Qaidar 2004, 107–108). The scientist says that in paremiology, variability and invariance is inherent in the nature of proverbs. "Usual comes from the term *use* in English, which describes the proverbs that have become an established tradition, in accordance with the norms of literary language" (Akhmanova 1969). Occasional (variable) proverbs tend to be modified and change constantly. Occasional change is a phenomenon that differs from the established speech skills, depending on the context, and belongs to the individual speech patterns of the speaker.

"The occasional events are often found in proverbs. Non-compliance with the norms is the main property of occasional words. Proverbs are mainly used in oral literature, the language of fiction, journalism, in the traditional form and non-traditional form" (Dinayeva 2013, 30). Occasional use is also called "author's use" in paremiology because the proverb is changed at the will of the author, but the main requirement is to fully preserve the meaning of the proverb.

A. Qaidar divides the changes associated with the occasional use of Kazakh proverbs into four groups:

- The first group: changes in the composition of proverbs due to the replacement of lexemes (components).
- The second group: changes due to the expansion of the structure and lexical structure of proverbs.
- The third group: changes due to the narrowing (reduction) of the structure and lexical structure of proverbs.
- The fourth group: the phenomenon of allusions inherent in the compositional development of proverbs.

In particular, the occasional use of proverbs belonging to the first group is divided into several types. One of them is the use of a structural element in a different way (paraphrasing). The purpose of this method is to slightly change and use the proverbs differently that bother the speaker (Qaidar 2004, 113–114). How to change it is up to the user, but the basic meaning should not be altered.

Mukhtar Magauin has changed the popular saying, "White does not bend," to "White does not break." Proverbs, as mentioned above, can be changed in accordance with the author. The original meaning of the proverb has not changed. It can only be said that the author has adapted the proverb to the content of his work. Kazy, who was a victim of injustice, escaped innocent slander and was released from prison, but his illness worsened in prison, and he died shortly after his release. He was a person who continued the Kazakh traditions and national values. At that time, there were few people like Kazy who preserved ancient heritage. However, the injustice that he saw in society hurt both his soul and his body, and he eventually died. Therefore, M. Magauin may have used the proverb in a form, "White does not break." Also, it is possible that the proverb has changed depending on various situations. In any case, the proverb "White does not bend" corresponds to the author's idea raised in the story. The author has a deep knowledge of the Kazakh literary language.

The language of Mukhtar Magauin's works, who had mastered a sacred heritage of the nation—the art of speech—is extremely rich. There, you can find all the literary elements, methods, and techniques that depict artistic phenomena related to literature, language, grammar, and logic. The readers are especially impressed by the skill of the writer, who treats the language responsibly and uses every word with pleasure to revive the ancient words in his works. "Everyone who studied and read the works of M. Magauin would clearly notice the words he created himself. It is not easy to play with the word, to illuminate, characterize and draw a picture with a word. It also needs a certain amount of accuracy, measurement and weighing. Regular phrases, fables, proverbs and sayings, suitable lines, words-pictures, and landscape-painting are typical only for masters of literary methods. If we could classify and filter the synonymous, ethnographic, exotic, and ancient words used by Magauin, how many wonderful dictionaries and books could we create," writes literary critic Zhanat Elshibek (2010). The language of M. Magauin's works is rich and prolific. He frequently and effectively uses proverbs and sayings in his works. In his story "Kara Kyz" (Black Girl), the writer plays with proverbs and sayings depending on the content of his work.

> "There may be times when I did not satisfy your thoughts, but I'm devoted. I am faithful to you, and you also need to try to be a good husband to me."
>
> "There is no doubt that I am trying to be a good husband, but God knows how faithful you are, thought Bekseyit."
>
> "Who will help us if we do not rely on each other? 'Tuiagy butin tulpar zhoq' (There is no steed with a whole hoof). Is there a perfect human being in this life? Let's not let each other down." (Magauin 1990, 51)

In this short dialogue between the main character Bekseit and his wife Gulzhihan, the author uses the proverb, "There is no steed with a whole hoof" (*Tuiagy butin tulpar zhoq*). The steed here is a horse. The Kazakh people highly valued horses and likened them to the man's wing. In the worldview, mentality, and language of the Kazakh people, there is a different philosophical and cultural system formulated about the horse. Kazakhs viewed man and his horse as a single world. And a *tulpar* (steed) is a racehorse. The Kazakh people divided horses into three groups. Kazakhs call racehorses (a kind of national sport) *tulpar, argymak,* and *saigulik.* Such horses were cared for specially. A horse that can withstand heavy loads and long distances is called *kazanat* and was also considered as a special type of horse. The rest of the horses kept for their meat and milk are called *zhaby* (Torekhanov 2021).

The horse's hoof illustrates its power. In particular, if the hooves are thick and the heels are high, it is considered a strong horse. Such horses are fast. Hence, they usually run the races.

A difficult task in the study of proverbs as an object of ethnolinguistics is to accurately identify the factors of their emergence in the language and the reasons for their development and transition to humans (character, behavior, actions, attitudes, etc.). The proverb "There is no steed with a whole hoof" was originally associated with horses, but over time it has become associated with humans. Paremiologists say that proverbs go through two stages in their semantic development. In the first stage, the proverbs preserve their initial meaning, while in the second stage they develop. "Usually the original meaning of proverbs is forgotten, and the version that is abstract and directed to humans is preserved" (Qaidar 2004, 85).

Literally, the horse's hooves are its most important parts. The whole weight of the body falls on them. When it gallops fast, it can hurt its hooves. Hoof injuries are especially common among racehorses. This is probably the origin of the proverb. As for the figurative meaning, there is no one in the world who is without any worries. Everyone has their own sorrows and problems. It means that no human is perfect. This proverb is abstracted, shifting its direction from the horse to humans. There is a logical-semantic connection between the original meaning and the figurative meaning of the proverb.

Another feature of this proverb is that, in the beginning, it had two parts. After some time, the second part was forgotten. In paremiology, this is also called usual-elliptical (usual-elliptical version) or tight version. The essence of this phenomenon is as follows: one, two, or three of the original elements (components) of these proverbs are included in such a way that they do not affect the general meaning when omitted (Qaidar 2004, 11). The general meaning of proverbs do not change when they are simplified, shortened, and their individual components omitted. The full version of the proverb is *Tuiagy butin tulpar zhoq, Qiyagy butin sunqar zhoq*, in English, "There is no steed with a whole hoof, no falcon with the whole nib." Nib (*qiyaq*) is one feather of the bird's wings (Utemisova 2012, 82). Sunkar is a species of falcon. It belongs to the family of predators. The falcon is distinct due to its greatness, courage, and beauty. We can also call the falcon the fastest bird in the world. It flutters its wings four or five times in a second. The second part of the proverb literally means that the beautiful falcon, which flies high and fast, does not have whole feathers. That is, because it is a bird of prey, it often damages its feathers while hunting, so its feathers and wing fibers are not intact. When this proverb is used for the person, it completes the first part of the proverb. That is, no matter how beautiful and strong a person is, he/she is not flawless. It means that nobody is perfect. Both of the components used in parallel have the same pattern. Although their meanings are different, they are repetitive. Scientists call this phenomenon *syntactic parallelism*. In paremiology, this is called *symmetry*. "Symmetry is usually considered to be the basis of beauty, harmony, and elegance as a phenomenon that represents two identical parts of an object that occur in nature. Symmetrical balance is often found in proverbs consisting of two parts" (Qaidar 2004, 104). The features mentioned by the scientist are clearly visible in this article. It is not uncommon for M. Magauin to use this proverb in his work. The main character in the work is Professor Bekseyit, Doctor of Historical Sciences. He has devoted his life to science and left his wife Aigul and son from a simple family in order to achieve his desired position and marry Gulzhihan. Finally, he achieves his dream career. However, the middle-aged couple is not happy in their family life. Although they looked like happy families with no needs, the couple could not communicate well with each other. The writer tells this proverb through Gulzhikhan, Bekseyit's wife. Noticing that Bekseyit was disgusted with her wife, she tried to console herself by saying this proverb. In Kazakh people's cognition, this proverb is often used to comfort people. For example, it is often used to express condolences to the bereaved. There is a tradition of expressing condolences to the beavered. It is called consolation. Consolation is a ceremony of condolences to the bereaved. It is a type of folk song. It is a long-standing tradition which is expressed by a well known compositional system. There are many verses in consolation songs that have become proverbs and sayings. The core themes are developed through proverbs and sayings, the commandments and life experiences (Auezov 1960, 22).

The proverb "There is no steed with a whole hoof, no falcon with the whole nib" is often used in this case. That is, there is nobody without sorrow, without grief, without any problems. Everyone has their own worries. The writer M. Magauin was able to successfully demonstrate this folklore in his work, "Kara Kyz." Let us look at the author's work:

> "There is only one thing I am not satisfied with. I had my first unprotected doctoral work."
> "Yes ..."
> "Invulnerable topic ..."
> "If the knot is strong, the felt stake goes into the ground," the problem is not in the title, but in the writing. (Magauin 1990, 45)

Here, the author uses the Kazakh proverb, If the hammer is strong, the felt stake is driven into the ground *(Toqpagy myqty bolsa, kiyz qazyq zherge kiredi)*. Taking into account the rich information and valuable contribution of each proverb on the essence of the ethnos, its spiritual and material culture, worldview, customs, traditions, and beliefs, we can conclude that they are making a significant contribution to the study of ethnic identity.

This article reflects the names of things used in the daily life of the Kazakh people. *Toqpaq* here is a thick tool that hits something on the ground. *Qazyq* (a stake) is a strong piece of wood or metal that is used to tie an animal to a rope and to keep it loose. It is easy to hit such a stake with an iron hammer, an ax, or a stick and knock into the ground. Felt (*kiyz*) is a thick, dense material made of animal hair. Stake (*qazyq*) is not made of felt, and even if it is made, it is impossible to knock it into the ground. However, the strength of the hook is so great that it drives the "felt stake" into the ground. Figuratively, if a person has someone to rely on, a strong support, he will be able to achieve his goals regardless of being educated or not. In other words, it means that a person who has a supporter will succeed in any sphere of life (Qaidar 2014, 500).

Proverbs and sayings utilize logical formulas and rules created by each nation. It comes to mind in every event or problem. Thus, they explain in a simple way something that is difficult and requires a lot of thinking and lengthy narration. Bekseyit's dissertation on the proverbs and sayings as a young graduate student failed because the topic of his dissertation did not correspond to the political ideology of that time. Bekseyit, who later took a different topic, successfully defended his dissertation and received a degree and became a professor. He enhanced his financial situation, thanks to a new job, a new position, and a reputation. He intends to use the opportunity to refine his scholarly work, which he wrote at a young age, and publish it as a book. The writer uses the Kazakh proverb that "If the hammer is strong, the felt stake is driven into the ground" *(Toqpagy myqty bolsa, kiyz qazyq zherge kiredi)* because of Bekseit's current situation and actions. Proverbs and sayings in a fiction are often used to create an image and reveal the character, as well as draw conclusions about a particular situation. One of the characteristics of our nation is to figuratively deliver the thoughts with the help of proverbs and sayings.

The features in the work of art, such as the use of proverbs and sayings at different levels, the omission of their pairs, or the change of lexical composition, differ depending on the writer's linguiustic skills. Taking into account that the source of the literary language is the national language, the ability to use the proverbs and sayings in a work of art, which are part of this national language, depends on the level of knowledge and stylistic taste of the writer. We aimed to analyze the purpose of these proverbs and sayings in conveying the author's ideas in the work, their meaning, and the scope of their usage in terms of the Kazakh people's cognition by analyzing the proverbs and sayings in the works of the writer Mukhtar Magauin. Considering the language as a living phenomenon, it is normal that proverbs and sayings constantly evolve and update. It is common that proverbs and sayings come in different versions that are similar to each other. This is due to the fact that orators, who are poetic by nature, sometimes use proverbs and sayings in different forms depending on the situation. However, each of these words passes through the analysis of the nation. After all, only beautiful, sharp, profound proverbs and sayings with a deep meaning stay with the nation. Therefore, in the process of oral literature, the nation accepts not the attenuated proverbs and sayings, but the renewed ones (Tilepov 2010, 15). Kazakh is a nation which values witty words and ingenious minds that can be reflected in proverbs and sayings.

Bibliography

Adilkhanova, Zh. 2014. *XX Gasyrdyn Basyndagy 1960–1990 Zhyldaryndagy Adebiyettanu Gylymy zhane S. Seitov Zertteuleri* [Literary Science and research of S. Seitov in 1960–1990s of the 20th century]. Almaty: Kazakh University.

Akhmanova, O. 1969. *Slovar' Lingvisticheskih Terminov.* [Dictionary of linguistic terms]. Moscow: Sovetskaya Entsiklopediya.

Alpysbayeva, Q., T. Alibekov, and S. Qosan, eds. 2010. *Kazakh Proverbs.* Vol. 65 of *Babalar sozi: Zhuztomdyk* [The Words of the Ancestors: One hundred volumes]. Astana: Foliant.

Auezov, M. 1960. *Kazak adebiyetinin tarihy.* [History of Kazakh literature]. Almaty: Ğılım. 300.

Baitursyn, N. 2021. "Magauinnin 'Olgen tazysy' nemese tymagy tozgan Kazak ali zhalanbas zhur me" [Is Kazakh in Magauin's "Dead Hunting Dog" or a worn malachai is still without a hat?]. The Qazaq Times. December 7, 2021.

Berdibay, R. 2005. *Bes tomdyk shygarmalar zhinagy: Kausar Bulak* [Collection of works in five volumes: Clear spring]. Almaty: Kazygurt.

Dinayeva, B. 2013. *Kazakh makal-matelderinin pragma-cognitivtik aspectisi* [Cognitive and pragmatic aspect in the Kazakh proverbs and sayings]. Astana, Monography.

Elshibek, Zh. 2010. "Kudiretti kazyna" [Mighty treasure]. Egemen Qazaqstan. 20 March.

Hinayat, B. and K. Issabekov. 2007. *Sayatshylyk kazaktyn dasturli angshylygy.* [Hunting with a bird is traditional Kazakh hunting]. Almaty: Almaty Kitap.

Kuusi, Matti. 1985. *Proverbia septentrionalia: 900 Balto-Finnic Proverb Types with Russian, Baltic, German and Scandinavian Parallels.* Helsinki: Suomalainen Tiedeakatemia.

Magauin, M. 1990. *Eki tomdik tandamaly shygarmalar: Hikayattar* [Selected Works in Two Volumes: Stories]. Almaty: Zhazushy

Mieder, W. and S. Bronner. eds. 2019. *Proverbs Are Worth a Thousand Words: The Global Spread of American Proverbs. Contexts of Folklore. Festschrift for Dan Ben-Amos on His Eighty-Fifth Birthday.* New York: Peter Lang, 217–229.

Momynova, B. 1999. *Gazet Leksikasy: zhuyesi men kurylymy* [Newspaper vocabulary: system and structure]. Almaty: Arys

Utemisova, G. 2012. *Kazak tilindegi konergen atalymdar lugaty* [Dictionary of obsolete names in the Kazakh language]. Almaty: Kausar.

Qaidar, A. 2004. *Khalyq danalygy.* [Folk wisdom]. Almaty: Toganay T.

Qaidar, A. 2014. *Gylymdagy gumyr: Makalalar, bayandamalar zhinagy* [Life in science: Collection of articles, reports.]. Almaty: Sardar.

Sarsenbayev, R. M. 1980. Auezovtin *"Abai zholy" romanyndagy maqal-matelderding qoldanylyu. Qazaq tilining maseleleri.* [Use of proverbs in M. Auezov's novel "The Path of Abai." Problems of the Kazakh language]. Almaty. Sanat.

Sergaliyev, M. 1995. *Korkem adebiyet tili* [The language of fiction]. Almaty: Mektep.

Smagulova, K. 1983. *Kazakh tilindegi frazeologizmderdin varianttylygy* [Variation of Phraseology in the Kazakh Language]. Almaty: Sanat.

Tilepov, Zh. 2010. *Kazak makal-matelderi* [Kazakh proverbs and sayings]. *Babalar sozi: Zhuztomdyk* [Words of the ancestors]. Astana: Foliant

Torekhanova, A. 2021. "Zhylky – tort tuliktin toresi" [Horse is a leader of domestic animals]. Dala News.

Zhanuzakov, T. 2008. *Kazak tilinin tusindirme sozdigi* [Explanatory dictionary of the Kazakh language]. Almaty: Daik-Press.

Chapter 3 Proverbs as a Part of the Culture

Analysis of Kazakh Proverbs in Writings (Notes) of Mashkhur-Zhusip Kopeiuly

DOLORES NURGALIYEVA
Al-Farabi Kazakh National University, Almaty

BAKYT ARINOVA
Al-Farabi Kazakh National University, Almaty

Introduction

The spiritual and social needs that determine identity of human nature and national values are reflected in the cultural heritage accumulated over centuries. The philosophical and ideological education of the Kazakh people is reflected in folklore, oral literature, mythology, proverbs, and sayings passed from generation to generation. The paremic nature of Kazakh proverbs and sayings, which are the source of folk wisdom, forms a worldview and develops an ethnocultural language environment. A. Qaidar says "Kazakh proverbs and sayings have a great ideological, logical, ethnolinguistic significance in the knowledge of the past and present realities of the people as all the phenomena that have developed in the world, society, and nature are related to proverbs and sayings. In the very existence of the world, there is a natural sequence formed from the very beginning. This sequence can be seen only by grouping all objects and phenomena into three large areas and concentrating them in accordance with their internal system and meaning." If we consider this opinion, then the cognitive meaning of proverbs, linguistic images, and literary and artistic features determine the proverbs' meaning in human life (Qaıdar 2004, 47).

In terms of content, the proverb, by characterizing people's lives on various topics, describes and interprets relationships in human life in a figurative language, and brightens thought. That is why we call proverbs the figurative art that has a deep logical meaning, uniting with the anchor of the life experience of our ancestors. We support this idea with M. Gabdullın's opinion, "at an early age, our ancestors invented various poems, fairy tales, proverbs and sayings, legends about their way of life, social life, economy and profession, joy and sadness, worldview views. They passed them from one generation to another. Thus, this noble heritage in our time is gaining more and more importance in the process of educating the generation" (Gabdullın 1974, 80).

If the main features of expression and emotions conveyed by language in the content of proverbs are the psychological state of a person in living conditions, then expression is its linguistic image. The functional-semantic system in proverbs is based on the principles of expressiveness, accuracy, brevity, and accuracy that characterize psychological processes in a person's thoughts. The linguistic means of expression and emotion are characterized by psycholinguistic structures that express the sensual state, such as love, admiration, delight, hatred, disgust, or gloom. For example, the proverb "good is at the top of the tree, and evil is under your feet" is a profound thought that gives a moral character to the modern generation. Such proverbs are widely found in the wisdom and spiritual treasure of the Kazakh people. Thus, the use of proverbs formulated by centuries of peoples' experiences in everyday life is becoming increasingly important.

The study of the origin and application of proverbs that have accumulated over the centuries and become the property of the people is recognized as a global trend. Many nations and nationalities that inhabit the globe treat their ancestral heritage with special respect and want them to become cognitive edifications for the future generation. Therefore, in our study, we took the work of researchers from foreign countries and the CIS as a basis, studying the history of the origin of proverbs. Russian scientists V.P. Zhukov, V.I. Dal, G.L. Permiakov, V. Kunin, Yu.M. Sokolov, V.P. Anikin, V.M. Mokienko, A.G. Nazaryan, A.A. Potebnya and foreign scientists R. Reidout, K. Whiting, W. Mieder, A. Taylor, A. Dundes, R. Norrick, F. Schindler, J. Spears, D. Bitnerova, and P. Durcho analyze paremiology as a branch of philological sciences depending on the structural and semantic features of proverbs. In particular, German linguist V. Fleischer considers proverbs as a macro text that summarizes the real-life experience of ordinary people and notes that they reflect the moral values of each era (Fleischer 1982, 80–82). The next German linguist, H. Burger, summarizes the proverbs as new units adding to the stock of phraseologists (Burger 2005, 17–43).

We can see that, in the studies of German scholars, proverbs were often considered phraseological; in particular, H. Lüger describes them as phraseological sentences (Lüger 1999), and A.F. Seiler argues they are phraseological phrases (Seiler 1922).

O.I. Natkho interprets proverbs as phraseologic material and paremiology as a branch of phraseological science (Natkho 2009, 433–9).

Bulgarian linguist V. Zangliger, analyzing the synonymous multiplicity of proverbs and the subject of changes, classifies them into lexical, grammatical, and structural and divides some reduced, compacted proverbs into separate groups (Zangliger 2010, 12–33).

Russian scientist V.P. Anikin argues that "the proverb is an opinion generalization of thousands of people, and from the statement 'the power of the proverb is the opinion of the masses of people' we can see the moral and educational power of proverbs. Every nation paid attention to the fact that the proverb spoken in their native language was built on thought and artistic imagery" (Anikin, 1957).

This classification is also found in the analysis of Kazakh linguists. These conclusions at the intersection of sciences reveal the importance of the proverbs and sayings research in the context of folklore and literary studies.

The methodological foundations of proverbs were previously formulated only by literary and theoretical analysis. However, under the new century's modern theoretical and cognitive methodology, historians have begun to pay attention to oral data, including proverbs that are inextricably linked with thought, culture, and human life, which have been created together with the people for centuries. The cognitive approach to proverbs and sayings study and draw conclusions compared to other data, allowing us to get acquainted with the era, period, society, economy, and culture of the population. In studying proverbs, the formation of works on generalization, systematization, grouping, textual analysis, and comparison into new searches requires analyzing Mashkhur-Zhusip Kópeiuly's proverbs. M. Kópeiuly is recognized as an outstanding Kazakh poet, thinker, scientist, philosopher, folklorist, historian, ethnographer, and orientalist who carried on the tradition of folk oral literature.

M. Kópeiuly is a well-known Kazakh poet who lived in the late nineteenth to early twentieth centuries. His work in the collection of oral folk art is vast, not to mention his ethnographic and journalistic works. He noted what he saw, felt, and heard for the benefit of the country. M. Auezov states,

we must not forget that, in addition to his works, Mashkhur was able to write down and convey intimate thoughts and judgments from the words of the great thinkers of the Kazakh people. Therefore, in the historiography section, as a scientific field of Kazakh oral and written literature, an adequate assessment of Mashkhur's merits should be valued adequately. (Auezov, 1961)

K. Zhusupov, studying the poet's work, notes that "with the acquisition of sovereignty by our country, it became possible to explore the rich heritage of Mashkhur-Zhusip Kópeiuly." Within the framework of the "Cultural Heritage" program, initiated with the support of the Head of State, the experts in Mashkhur studies intend to prepare and publish 20 volumes of Mashkhur Zhusip's works for the 150th anniversary of the poet's birth. Now the experts in Mashkhur studies are examining the poet's creative laboratory from different sites and note its relevance today (Júsipov 2008).

Mashkhur-Zhusip was born in 1859 in Kyzyltau, Naizatas region (the year of the ram, the month of the Arabian *erezhep* (*sawm*), on Friday, during Friday prayer). Kisyk, the wife of Boskynbai, cut off the baby's umbilical cord. He was the son of Kashkynbai and Karamys. According to the beliefs of the Kazakh people, the character of the child will be like the one who cut the omphalos at birth. His stubbornness of character passed from Kisyk. His parents called him Zhusip. The sage Izden said "this child was born on Friday, on Adam's birthday. May his name be Adam-Zhusip." In his memoirs, Mashkhur Zhusip shares the information about how he was given a name when was born: And completely unexpectedly, when I was thirty-nine years old, during a trip from Tashkent, the son of Kipchak-Ibrai Mukhammedzhan aksakal said: "Dear, people call you Mashkhur-Zhusip because they do not know your real name. Mashkhur has a twofold meaning: fame can be gained by kindness and evil. Your name is Mashkhur-Zhusip, and you are worthy of your name." And I was lucky to hear such words in the thirty-ninth year of my life from a wise man.

The poet writes about this in his work "Memoirs":

> I was called a man Zhusip in my infancy,
> The people called Mashkhur-Zhusip out of love for me.
> When I pick up a pen and a letter,
> My poems rush like the wind. (*Kazakh SSR Ġylym akademıasynyń Ortalyq Kitaphanasy. The Central Library of the Academy of Sciences of the Kazakh SSR.* Folder 1173, 20 p.)

Zhusip, intelligent from childhood, appeared before the general public at the age of nine and recited such lyric-epic poems as "Er Targyn" and "Kozy Korpesh-Bayan Sulu." The assembled people were pleased with the child's abilities and said the child should wear owl feathers from bad harvest and named him "Mashkhur" (*Kazakh SSR Ġylym akademıasynyń Ortalyq Kitaphanasy. The Central Library of the Academy of Sciences of the Kazakh SSR.* Folder 1173, 69 p.).

In 1886, Shorman's son, Musa, was nicknamed Adam Zhusip Mashkhur-Zhusip. It was written in the poet's memoirs:

> From the age of five
> I began to write with the name of God,
> And I saw the difficulties of life
> When I turned nine years old,
> Musa gave me the name "Mashkhur." (*Kazakh SSR Ǵylym akademıasynyń Ortalyq Kitaphanasy. The Central Library of the Academy of Sciences of the Kazakh SSR.* Folder 1173, 35 p.)

Based on this information, we can see that Mashkhur Zhusip had wisdom, genius, and foresight from childhood.

Literature Review

Proverbs and sayings of the Kazakh people have been collected and published in the country since the second half of the nineteenth century. Proverbs were first collected by Shokan Ualikhanov, Ibrai Altynsarin, Abubakir Divayev, and Mashkhur Zhusip Kópeiuly. Russians A.A. Vasiliev, F. Plotnikov, P.A. Melioransky, V.V. Katarinsky, and V. Radlov published one of the oldest branches of folk oral literature. In 1914, proverbs and sayings in the Kazakh language were first published in Kazan; 1923, *One Thousand and One Proverbs* in Moscow; 1927, *Kazakh Proverbs* (compiled by A. Divayev) in Tashkent; and 1935, *Kazakh Proverbs and Sayings* (U. Turmanzhanov) in Almaty. Studying the rich spiritual heritage of Mashhur Zhusip, we were guided by the works of scientists who substantiated the oral literature and folklore of the Kazakh people.

The works of A. Baitursynov, H. Dosmukhamedov, S. Seifullin, M. Auezov, S. Mukanov, B. Kenzhebayev, K. Zhumaliyev, A. Margulan, B. Shalabayev, M. Gabdullın, B. Akmukanova, A. Qaidarov, B. Adambeav, N. Torekulov, S. Omarbekov, R. Sarsembayev, and other scientists who analyzed the Kazakh proverbs are presented in this article as research sources. Russian scientists S. Dautuly, D. Abilev, S. Negimov, U. Abdimanuly, E. Zhusupov, A. Turyshev, D. Iskakuly, B. Sagyndykuly, S. Saurykova, A. Pazylov, S. Nurmuratov, B. Satershinov, A. Shagyrbayev, and B. Beisenov have also studied the works of Mashkhur Zhusip in the field of literature and language, pedagogy, ethno-pedagogy, and philosophy, and their ideas became the basis for substantiating the viability of the poet's rich heritage.

The study uses historical, comparative, generalizing, and descriptive analysis, theoretical and analytical analysis of scientific literature, and analysis, processing, and generalization of the study.

Analysis of Results

The collected proverbs of M.Zh. Kópeiuly are thematically diverse. His manuscripts contain 176 proverbs, numbered sequentially. The poet wrote where and from whom he took the proverbs, and he gave some explanatory information. He spoke about the circumstances, at what time, and why many proverbs appeared, and how important it was for them to be used and distributed among the population. The poet made his analyses, comparing many of the proverbs that he collected, while traveling around the country with versions of proverbs published in books. From this, we can conclude that Mashkhur-Zhusip was a collector of oral literature and engaged in research. Undoubtedly, the theoretical substantiation of the problem of revealing the genre nature of Kazakh proverbs among scientists studying folk oral literature and folklore is a significant contribution to the fund of literary studies. In the research of N. Kuandykuly, most proverbs and sayings collected by Mashkhur-Zhusip have not been introduced. Therefore, we can say that the revival and publication of proverbs and sayings preserved in Mashkhur-Zhusip's writings, archives, and systematization in the thematic and content structure can serve as the basis for research at present.

M. Kópeiuly's proverbs reflect the essence, everyday life, behavior, dreams, traditions, and customs of a person and reflect our people's national values and life principles. The breadth of the thematic content of proverbs in the poet's manuscripts is noted by the scale of their problems. Mashkhur-Zhusip's knowledge of the Russian language contributed to the fact that he wrote works aimed at such areas of science as oral literature, philosophy, history, ethnology, medicine, and cosmology inspired by Western civilization. Thus, depending on the nature of the implementation of Mashkhur Zhusip's proverbs, their specific features can be classified as follows:

- Proverbs reflect the truth of the world from an artistic point of view.
- The linguistic and cultural function of proverbs is reflected in language communication.
- The direct and indirect meanings of proverbs are intertwined with the worldview of the people.
- The thought given in proverbs is expressed and formulated using its own logical sequence.

According to these features, proverbs collected by Mashkhur-Zhusip can be grouped in the thematic system as follows:

1. Humanity, respect, solidarity, unity.
2. Human behavior, health, purity.
3. Skill, education, effort, science, training, education.
4. Country and native land, society, and family.
5. Justice, honesty, good deeds.
6. Infringement, silliness, evil, falsehood.
7. Prosperity, indigence, truth, belief, friendship.
8. Domestic animals.

This thematic classification tells us that Mashkhur-Zhusip paid attention to the axiological value, semantic significance, and lingua didactic depth of proverbs, which are expressed in connection with the life of the people, their way of life, and various human behaviors. According to researchers, the thematic variety of proverbs in the manuscripts of Mashkhur-Zhusip is divided in relation to the creation, religion, behavior, existence, lifestyle, and customs of a person. One of the features of the proverbs preserved in the writings of Mashkhur-Zhusip is that the poet makes an accent on the character of a person by referring to the behavior of domestic animals. For example, we see impressive hints in proverbs such as *Adam alasy—ishinde, mal alasy—syrtynd* (The secret and character of the person is not visible like animals), *Syryn bilmegen attyń syrtynan júrme* (It is better to stay away from someone you do not know well), or *Sengen qoıym sen bolsań, kúısegenińdi uraıyn* (You believe someone, but he or she does not live up to expectations).

In the proverbs collected by M. Kópeiuly about human behavior, moral qualities and spiritual ideals are interpreted as being derived from human nature. Behavior—which begins with a characteristic feature of the individual and expresses the entire national mentality, national consciousness, and worldview formed over the centuries—is a complex concept. The proverbs, which are expressed in the science of psychology, indicate that the national character is reflected in the personality of each people, expressed in the poet's phrases such as *Jorǵa júrisinen pul bolady, jaman júrisinen qul bolady* (A good horse becomes valuable by its ride, a bad person becomes a slave by his behavior) or *Aıdan—anyq, sútten-aq, kúnnen-jaryq, sýdan-tunyq* (Clearer than the moon, whiter than milk, brighter than the sun, clearer than water) that both good and bad character are expressed in actions, thoughts, and words. Using the proverb *Ulyń ósse, uly qylyqtymen, qyzyń ósse, qyzy qylyqtymen aýyldas bol* (*When your son grows up, live with a neighbor with a well-mannered son, when your daughter grows up, live with a neighbor who has a well-mannered daughter*) the poet describes the character of a good person in the sense of behavior. We are not mistaken if the poet's manuscript contains many proverbs and sayings from the "Koran" "Hadith-Sharif," which symbolize good deeds built on charity, friendship, and loyalty in everyday life along with communication between people.

Importance of Research

The article reveals the relevance of the work by studying the proverbs of M.Zh. Kópeiuly, written at the end of the nineteenth century, as a heritage of folk wisdom and everyday experience. Mashkhur-Zhusip defined the root of each proverb and told the people how it spread across the country. For example, the proverb *baılyq murat emes, joqtyq uıat emes* (wealth is not the purpose, poverty is not a shame) was said by Gaisa Bikei Ishan, who at that time lived in the vast steppes of Saryarka. The proverb has not lost its relevance even in modern times. Especially in the context of today's globalization, there is a weakening of virtue and charity among people that makes it possible to distinguish between the concepts of "wealth" and "poverty" as spiritual values and material needs. Mashkhur-Zhusip heard and wrote many proverbs from the famous people of that era. The poet proved that the proverb, *Qaradan han qoısa, qasıeti bolmaıdy, úlgisizden bı qoısa ósıeti bolmaıdy,* (If the Khan is not from an elite background, then do not expect nobility from him) was said by Shorman Musa and explained the meaning of it. In this article, we will talk about the importance of human nobility and intelligence.

Almost all the proverbs of Mashkhur-Zhusip are written in relation to culture, including the art of writing, music, and crafts and are aimed at a diversified generation. Among the thematically diverse proverbs, the meaning of science and education in human life is much touched upon. The author emphasizes that an educated person has undimmed intelligence. We can summarize this thought with the poet's proverb *Bilmegen aıyp emes, bilýdi izdenbegen aıyp*(This is not an accusation of ignorance, it is an accusation that he is not seeking knowledge.) If we analyze it from the semantic side, we can see how important it is to search and strive for knowledge. Among the proverbs collected by the poet we see that the proverb *Óziń bilme, bilgenniń tilin alma*! is related to the previous proverb. According to the poet, "there are people who know their illiteracy and listen to those who know and follow their advice, but there are some people who know nothing and do not want to accept and follow the advice." It follows that an educated person is simple minded, but an uneducated person is a selfish, arrogant person. Although some proverbs of Mashkhur-Zhusip Kópeiuly were used in that era, they were not used much later. However, such proverbs are considered valuable in their meaning, no matter how much time passes. One of such proverbs is *Er—egiz, enbekti zhalgyz* (A man is twin; work is lone). The point of this proverb is that if a man meets a worthy woman, he will have "double" success and happiness. If a man has bad relatives, wife, and children, then his business will never go uphill. If a husband and wife are together for better or worse, they will feel like "twins." If things are going well, success will accompany everywhere, even if there is only one person. Luck and happiness as twins will go side-by-side. If a person's business does not develop successfully, then he will climb, and even the dry land will seem like a swamp. The word "twin" here has a semantic structure that expresses similar meanings in accordance with the common features of a particular object or phenomenon (Hasenov, 1959).

In the history of human beings, the word "twin" has been used to describe the common birth of two children from the same mother. Then this word was used as "couple," and the two things became known as twins. In the Kazakh language, the definition of similar concepts is used depending on the similarity of twins. In defining the semantics of "not alone," the meaning of the word "twin" is used. The word "twin" is also included in the number of words that are used in the numerical value. It has the value of a particular exact number and the words which are formed through them. There are many proverbs and sayings in paremiology that include the word "twin." Therefore, Mashkhur-Zhusip Kópeiuly's proverb *Er—egiz, enbekti zhalgyz* means if a person's business is going up in the world, he gets a double benefit.

Mashkhur-Zhusip used ancient words in his proverbs. His word combination *Bergen asta bereke bar, bermegen asta pitá bar* (Be a friend, be an enemy, share a meal) became a proverb. For example, the word "pitá" means "grime." This proverb was exposed to linguistic ecology and is now out of use. The impact of some proverbs in M. Kópeiuly's manuscripts on linguistic ecology, which is not used today, leads to a decrease in social and public relations in the linguistic environment.

Modern cultural exchanges develop interaction with other languages in the speaker's mind and reveal the partly physiological and partly social nature of language ecology. According to lingua ecological principles, the keenness of the word in proverbs, the depth of expressed thought, the spiritual significance, and the power of the word are combined with the national character and personality that give our people the whole reality. The proverbs of Mashhur-Zhusip reflect the social realities of that time. At the same time, the task of today's linguistic ecology is to preserve the national heritage of the Kazakh people, including the use of proverbs and improve the vocabulary of informants and language culture. After all, lingua-ecology is a socio-cultural phenomenon that allows us to preserve and enrich the language.

From the point of view of the goals and objectives of language ecology, it is important to preserve the viability of proverbs, which are considered one of the root branches of the worldview, mentality, and language of the Kazakh people in the development of the linguistic sphere. According to the traditions of our ancestors, proverbs that are passed down from generation to generation are used correctly, and they are aimed at preserving the communication ecology. Such proverbs like *At jamany jorǵa bolady, adam jamany molda bolady* (the worst horse can be a pacer, and the worst person will become a leader) or *Qısyq arba jol buzar, dúmshe molda din buzar* (a bad cart can ruin the road, and a bad leader religion) are not used nowadays.

The proverb *Er ekenin bileiin, er óltirshi kóreiin* (If you are a man, kill the enemy) is outdated and has fallen out of use. In the distant years of hostilities, the meaning of this proverb was probably powerful. However, in today's calm, peaceful time, no one goes to kill someone to show courage. Among the proverbs subject to linguistic ecology, the proverb *Kózi soqyr soqyr emes, keýdesi soqyr* (Better blind than the blind in mind) is also not used. The meaning of the proverb is about the person; the inner world is narrow; the chest gives the image of a dark person. *Iesin syılaǵannyń itine súıek sal* (If you respect the owner, feed his dog) has different meaning. This proverb is also not widely used (Kópeıuly, 2010).

Thus, the educational, artistic power of M. Kópeiuly's proverbs will remain important and have not lost their value no matter how much time has passed.

Conclusion

Kazakh proverbs are a unique node of centuries old folk wisdom and rich experience as represented by a short and concise form that complements the meaning of what has been expressed. Since the second half of the nineteenth century, the collection and publication of Kazakh proverbs have been characterized by the continuation of the dialogue between generations. Since proverbs are connected with the life of the people, their subjects are different and have been studied in numerous scientific papers. They indicate that proverbs are a mirror of human life.

In the science of paremiology, various aspects of the study of proverbs and sayings combine linguistic, cultural, and semantic positions recognized as relics.

The truth is that the proverbs in the manuscripts of Mashkhur-Zhusip are of value that develops socio-historical changes in the life of the Kazakh people and complements their didactic content at each historical stage. Furthermore, the use of the poet's proverbs as one of the points of the *Rukhani Zhangyru* (Spiritual Revival) program in the context of today's globalization is associated with the national education of the younger generation.

In conclusion, the legacy of Mashkhur-Zhusip in the history of humankind has profound educational value and strength and is the beginning of wisdom.

Bibliography

Anikin, V. P. 1957. *Russkiye narodnyye poslovitsy, pogovorki, zagadki i detskiy fol'klor* [Russian folk proverbs, sayings, riddles, and children's folklore]. Moscow: Uchpedgiz.

Auezov, M. 1961. *Ádebı mura jáne ony zertteý.* (Literary heritage and its study). Almaty.

Burger, H. 2005. "30 Jahre germanistische Phraseologieforschung" [30 years of German phraseology research]. *HERMES – Journal of Language and Communication in Business* 35: 17–43.

Fleischer, W. 1982. *Phraseologie der deutschen Gegenwartssprache.* [Phraseology of contemporary German]. 80–82. Leipzig: VEB Bibliographisches Institut.

Gabdullın, M. 1974. *Qazaq halqynyń aýyz ádebıetı: Joǵary oqý oryndarynyń stýdentterine arn.* [Oral literature of the Kazakh people: Designed for university students]. Almaty: Mektep.

Hasenov, Á. 1959. *Qazirgi qazaq tilindegi san esimder.* [Numerals in the modern Kazakh language]. Almaty: Zhazushy.

Júsipov, Q. 2008. *Mashkhúr-Zhusip Kópeıuly.* Pavlodar: Kerekw.

Kazakh SSR Ǵylym akademıasynyń Ortalyq Kitaphanasynyń qoljazbalar qory. Manuscript collection of the Central Library of the Academy of Sciences of the Kazakh SSR. Folder 1173, 20p.

Kazakh SSR Ǵylym akademıasynyń Ortalyq Kitaphanasynyń qoljazbalar qory. Manuscript collection of the Central Library of the Academy of Sciences of the Kazakh SSR. Folder 1173, 69p.

Kazakh SSR Ǵylym akademıasynyń Ortalyq Kitaphanasynyń qoljazbalar qory. Manuscript collection of the Central Library of the Academy of Sciences of the Kazakh SSR. Folder 1173, 35p.

Kópeıuly, M. J. 2010. Collected works. *Eldi kórse, ıt ozady.* [When it sees the country, the dog overtakes]. Vol. 10. Almaty: El-shejire.

Lüger, H. H. 1999. *Satzwertige Phraseologismen: Eine pragmalinguistische Untersuchung.* [Sentential phrases: a pragmatic-linguistic investigation]. Vienna: Praesens.

Natkho, O. I. 2009. "English paremias in the linguistic picture of the world." In *Language. Text. Discourse: Scientific Almanac*. Stavropol: Stavropol State Pedagogical Institute. 7, 433–39.

Qaıdar Á. 2004. *Halyq danalyǵy* [People's wisdom]. Almaty. Tolǵanaı.

Seiler, F. 1922. *Deutsche Sprichwörterkunde*. (German proverbs). München: C. H. Beck'sche Verlagsbuchhandlungs Oskar Becker.

Zangliger, V. 2010. Variantnost' i sinonimiya poslovits [Variability and Synonymy of Proverbs]. *Bulgarian Russian Studies*, no. 3–4: 12–33.

Gender Linguistic Picture of the World in Kazakh Proverbs

GULZHAN SHOKYM
Doctor of Philological Sciences, Professor

ELMIRA BURANKULOVA
Ph.D. student

KARYLGA DUISENOVA
Master of Pedagogy, Confucius Institute, K. Zhubanov Aktobe Regional University

Introduction

The idea of a linguistic picture of the world goes back to the works of Von Humboldt, L. Weisberger, Sapir, and Whorf. Thus, the famous philosopher and linguist of the nineteenth century Von Humbolt argued that language is a necessary condition for the implementation of the thinking process; in addition, a person's perception of the surrounding reality directly depends on the native speaker of which language he is. The differences in languages are manifested in the way the world conceptualization (Uryson 2003, 224).

O.V. Orlova also believes that the linguistic picture of the world is a set of knowledge about the world captured in vocabulary, phraseology, and grammar. It is a "space of meanings," part of the internal organization of human knowledge about the world, which includes the national and cultural experience of the people (Orlova 2010, 110).

Based on this, the linguistic picture of the world includes the most important socio-psychological features that were developed by the nation during its historical development under the influence of environmental factors, living conditions, lifestyle, traditions, and culture. Therefore, the study of the linguistic picture of the world of a particular people gives us the opportunity to get the widest idea of the perception of the world, thinking, and mentality of these people.

V.A. Maslova says the term "linguistic picture of the world" is nothing more than a Metaphor, because in reality, the specific features of the national language, in which the unique socio-historical experience of a certain national community of people is recorded, create for native speakers not some other, unique picture of the world, different from the objectively existing one. Rather, it creates only a specific coloring of this world, due to the national significance of objects, phenomena, processes, and selective attitude to them, which are generated by the specifics of the activity, lifestyle, and national culture of these people (Maslova 2001, 65).

Modern studies of the linguistic picture of the world are conducted in two directions. First, based on the system semantic analysis of the vocabulary of a certain language, the general system of representations reflected in this language is reconstructed, regardless of whether it is specific to this language or universal. On the other hand, separate linguistic-specific concepts with two properties are studied: they are key for a given culture, and at the same time, the words representing them are difficult to translate or are not translated at all into other languages. Such studies can be found in the works of A. Vezhbitskaya, V.V. Kolesov, E.A. Pimenov, M.V. Pimenova, A.D. Shmelev, and E.S. Yakovleva (Pimenova 2014, 108). The linguistic picture of the world is expressed in stable phrases, phraseology, idioms, and proverbs. After all, this layer of the language contains such important information as folk wisdom, the system of spiritual values, public morality, and the attitude of representatives of the nation to the world, people, and other nations. The study of the linguistic picture of the world is possible through the analysis of linguistic material. Our research is based on the analysis of the gender linguistic picture of the world of proverbs of the Kazakh language. What is the gender linguistic picture of the world? The gender picture of the world encompasses all the diversity of representations of gender relations and ideas. The gender linguistic picture of the world is a verbalized form of the gender picture of the world, its deep layer, a set of knowledge and ideas about the world, a worldview which is based on the functioning of gender stereotypes captured in the language form (Vandysheva 2007, 93).

"Proverbs and sayings are the set of the minds of the people, the definition of which is summed up by the centuries-old events that they have seen, experienced, and are associated with events and phenomena that are constantly repeated in nature and life" (Adambayev 1996, 15).

The wisdom of proverbs has guided people in their social interactions for thousands of years throughout the world. Proverbs contain everyday experiences and common observations in succinct and formulaic language, making them easy to remember and ready to be used instantly as effective rhetoric in oral or written communication (Mieder 2004).

According to A. Qaidar, today's phraseology, proverbs, and sayings reflect everyday life in a language formed because of a phenomenon. They gradually stabilize and, because of semantic changes, rise to the rank of ethnophraseology and proverbs. If they before were originally related to animals, plants, the celestial world, and natural phenomena, then today everything is devoted to human life, behavior, good and bad qualities, or internal and external appearance (Qaidar 1998, 214). Proverbs address different aspects of life, including education, work, human aspirations, personal concerns, and relationships. Since proverbs are generally regarded as truths and serve as advice for people, they are important tools with which to instill values and transform the social order (Lee 2015, 559). Marlis Hellinger and Hadumod Bußmann note that another area of the implicit discursive negotiation of gender, irrespective of whether the language does or does not have grammatical gender, are frozen expressions such as idioms, metaphors, and proverbs (2001, 16).

The study of the gender aspect of phraseology as an anthropocentric phenomenon is currently considered one of the leading trends in linguistics of the twenty-first century. Research on this topic allows us to explain such problems as "a person in a language" and "the language and culture of the people". The most important culturally significant fragment is not just the image of a person but its male and female components, its gender attribute. The reflection of the gender aspect in phraseology is the main object of research in gender linguistics.

The purpose of the article is to describe the gender-linguistic representation of female and male images in Kazakh proverbs and substantiate their continuity with the worldview of the Kazakh people.

Literature Review

It is known that the problem of general phraseology is considered in linguistics in various aspects and attracts the attention of many researchers. In Kazakh linguistics, Y. Kengesbayev, A. Qaidar, U. Aitbayev, A. Iskakov, T. Sairambayev, N. Uali, G. Smagulova, S. Satenova, G. Kosymova, G. Sagidolda, R. Avakova, R.E. Zhaysakova, S.E. Isabekov, M. Sabitova, S. Zhetpisov, L.S. Voitik, Z.K. Konakbayeva, D. Mederbekov, S.N. Muratov, A.E. Tazhmuratova, M.T. Tezekbayev, F.R. Akhmetzhanova, B. Uizbayeva, K. Ryspayeva, G. Boranbayeva, H. Kozhakhmetova, S. Zhapakov, and many scientists have conducted research in various aspects related to the definition of types, composition and structure of phraseology, features of semantic division, grammatical nature, lexical and semantic division, their use in fiction and their function in oral speech, differences and similarities in other languages, and patterns of phraseological phenomena (Zhirenov 2016, 27).

The study of the linguistic picture of the world in the gender paradigm becomes particularly relevant. Meanwhile, many of its key (methodological) issues remain poorly studied.

Methodology and Methods

In this article, a number of methods were used, such as the philological method, the general scientific descriptive method, and the method of linguistic and cultural description. These methods were supplemented by linguistic and cultural commentary. The research material was collections of proverbs of the Kazakh language.

Discussion of the Results

Through the analysis of the linguistic picture of the world of various languages, national peculiarities are manifested and explained. It is precisely this picture that is the formative principle and determines the nature of thinking, which, as E.Y. Lukyanova notes, is reflected in different types of texts, such as in oral folk art like paremias (Lukyanova 2009, 39).

Proverbs emanate from people's experiences, mentality, and ways of thinking at a certain point in time. The rich linguistic data found in proverbs enables us to study the cultural beliefs and social values of a society, including its attitudes towards the two genders (Lee 2015). When considering the gender aspect of proverbs and sayings, it is important to reveal their national and cultural background and the sources of their spiritual culture because in each proverb we can see the national worldview, national philosophy, and certain cultural information.

The gender meaning of Kazakh proverbs and sayings is that a man is a defender of the country, a hero, a breadwinner, an educated, a talented person, a person of honor and authority. His wife is a loving wife, good housewife, mother; and his father and mother are advisers, respected people; and his sons and daughters are well mannered and polite teenagers (Shokym 125).

Authors who research proverbs divide them into groups. E. Khuzina and R. Mukhtarova divide phraseological units characterizing a person into following thematic groups: (1) appearance, physical qualities; (2) character;

(3) intellectual and other abilities; (4) marriage, marital status, relations between a man and a woman; (5) moral qualities; (6) social status, occupation; and (7) general characteristic (Khuzina et al, 2018, 214). For the analysis, we select Kazakh proverbs and sayings about a woman and a man, which were classified by these thematic groups:

1. Appearance. The appearance of man is associated with his country: *Erdiń kórki-elimen, Otan kórki-jerimen* (The beauty of the man is the country, the beauty of the Motherland is the land), *Kelisti kelbet erde bar, Qymbatty qazyna jerde* bar (Man has handsome appearance; the land has precious treasures).

In Kazakh culture, the beauty of woman is not important as these proverbs show *Sulý—sulý emes, súıgen sulý* (Beautiful is that woman you love), *Suqtanba qapyda "sulý" dep qur betke, Adamdyq—aqylda, sulýlyq—júrekte* (Humanity—in the mind; beauty-in the heart).

2. Characters and other qualities. One of the main characters of Kazakh men is honor: *Qoıandy qamys, erdi namys óltiredi* (A rabbit is killed by a reed; a guy is killed by pride), *Jigitke jar qymbat, namys pen ar qymbat* (To a guy a wife is dear; honor and conscience are dear).

Generosity: *Jomart bergenin aıtpas, Er aıtqanynan qaıtpas* (He will never say what he has given. Man said, man did).
Talks little: *Emen aǵashtyń uilgeni—synǵany, Er jigittiń eki sóılegeni—ólgeni* (The bending of an oak tree is broken, The man spoke twice; he is dead).
Good character of a young girl is also mentioned in proverbs such as *Qyz qylyǵymen súıkimdi* (A girl with good character is lovely), *Qyz minezdi, ul ónerli bolsyn* (Let the girl have a character, the boy has talent).
In Kazakh proverbs, intelligence is shown as the main qualities of man and woman: *Jerdiń sáni—egin, erdiń sáni—bilim* (The beauty of the earth is the harvest; the beauty of the man is knowledge), *Alǵyr jigit aqylyna qaraı is qylar, Olaq jigit ońaı jumysty kúsh qylar* (The able young man will act according to his wisdom, but the weak man will make trouble with even easy work), *Aqyldy qyz bilimge júgirer, Aqylsyz qyz sózge iliger* (A wise girl runs for knowledge, but a foolish girl lacks knowledge) (Malaysarin 2010, 61).

3. Marriage and families. The image of a wise, all-knowing woman, the keeper of the family who can shake the cradle with one hand and the world with the other is represented in Kazakh proverbs: *Ana bolǵan*

dana bolady (Being a mother is wise), *Ana jaqsylyǵyn aýyrsań bilersiń* (You know the goodness of a mother when you are sick), *Ananyń basqan jerinde peıish bar* (There is a paradise where the mother walks) (Malaysarin 2010, 76).

The attitude of the Kazakh people to the "woman" can be clearly seen in the following proverb: *Jaman áıel jaqsy erkektiń tórdegi basyn kórge súıreıdi, Jaqsy áıel jaman erkektiń kórdegi basyn tórge súıreıdi* (A bad woman drags a good man's head to the grave; a good woman drags a bad man's head to the higher respectful place). From the above proverb, it is clear that the Kazakh people divided women into good and bad. It is said that a good wife educates and disciplines her bad, uneducated husband.

In the Kazakh tradition, a woman is considered equal to a man in everything, including in the ability to work. Therefore, the Kazakh paremiological picture of the world is characterized by the image of an active woman. Many proverbs show the defining role of a woman: *Áıeli joq úı jetim* (A home without a wife is an orphan).

Kazakh proverbs define a man as an active person, endowed with this quality by nature, which determines his desire for dominance. *Batyr jigit jol bastar, aqyn jigit toı bastar* (The hero starts the path; the poet starts the wedding).

Kazakh proverbs show that the role of women in the Kazakh mentality is one step lower than that of men. For example, the following Kazakh proverbs can prove it: *Astyńdaǵy atyńa, qoınyńdaǵy qatynyńa senbe* (Trust neither horse nor wife).

Implications of the Study

The language of each nation can be called a folk encyclopedia, which contains all the knowledge about the world and the experience of previous generations. The language contains much of what the people have learned throughout their history; "we must understand what our ancestors once discovered for themselves, restore, at least in general terms, the picture of their knowledge of the world and explain these achievements to ourselves as the success of civilization and the human spirit in their national forms-because any culture is born and develops in national forms" (Kolesov 2000, 8).

Thus, in modern linguistics, the need for such studies is considerable. That is why the study of proverbs from a gender perspective makes it possible to better understand the history, culture, psychology, and worldview of people, thereby making communication between them more understandable.

Conclusion and Recommendations

Gender as a social construct finds a vivid embodiment in the language picture of the world. The proverbs reflect the history and worldview of the people who created them, their traditions, and customs. The study shows that proverbs and sayings clearly demonstrate the image of a man and a woman as part of their linguistic picture of the world. The analysis of proverbs and sayings allowed us to obtain the following results:

From proverbs and sayings that form the concepts of "man" and "woman," the national nature of the images of a man and a woman is comprehensively revealed. Proverbs and sayings that form the concept of "man" and "woman" in the Kazakh language provide a lot of information in creating an image, reflecting the specifics of the national worldview, and reflecting the realities of an ethnic group from different angles.

The indisputable advantages of a man are recognized as courage, loyalty to the word, strength, and intelligence.

B. Hassanuly notes that "the manifestation of the gender factor should be studied at all levels of the language," noting the ways of forming a gender orientation in Kazakh linguistics:

1. Comparative gender linguistics.
2. Gender paralinguistics. This direction should be formed based on non-verbal signs in the Kazakh language. The research conducted in Kazakh from the point of view of gender paralinguistics will contribute to the development of many areas of life (art, public speaking, etc.).
3. Gender lexicography. This direction should be implemented based on the Kazakh language and other languages.
4. Gender and language acquisition. Research in this direction is essential for language planning (Khasanuly 2003, 287). The task of studying the place of men and women in Kazakh culture through language in accordance with the national worldview of the Kazakh people has not been fully solved. In this regard, it is important to study the nature of men and women, their place in society, in the family in accordance with the worldview, and the spiritual and cultural values of the nation through proverbs.

On this basis, we recommend deeper research of the gender aspect of Kazakh proverbs and comparative research with Turkic languages as well as other languages. As one of the most important issues of modern linguistics, to study gender-linguistic, cognitive-linguistic, ethnolinguistic, and social-linguistic features of Kazakh proverbs is a demand of modern science.

Bibliography

Adambayev, B. 1996. *Halyq Danalygy* [Folk wisdom]. Almaty: Rauan.

Hellinger, M., and H. Bußmann. 2001. *Gender Across Languages the Linguistic Representation of Women and Men.* Netherlands: John Benjamins Publishing Company.

Khasanuly, B. 2003. "Qazaq til biliminde genderlik baǵytty qalyptastyrýdyń ózekti máseleleri" [Topical issues of gender orientation in Kazakh linguistics]. In *Psıholıngvıstıka jáne áleýmettik til bilimi: qazirgi kúıi jáne bolashaǵy; Halyqaralyq konferentsıa materıaldary* [Psycholinguistics and sociolinguistics: status and prospects; Proceedings of the International Conference]. Almaty: Sanat. 284–288.

Khuzina, E., and R. Mukhtarova. 2008. "The Lexico-Semantic Analysis of the Common and Various in the World of Gender Picture in the English and Tatar Linguistic Cultures." *Tarih Kültür ve Sanat Arastirmalari Dergisi* [Journal of History, Culture and Art Research]. 7 (4): 214–22.

Kirilina, A. V., and M. Tomskaya. 2005. "Lingvisticheskie gendernye issledovaniya" [Linguistic gender studies]. *Otechestvennye zapiski* [Domestic notes] 2 (22): 112–132.

Kolesov, V. V. 2000. *Drevnyaya Russia: nasledie v slove. Mir cheloveka* [Ancient Russia: heritage in the word. The world of man]. Series "Philology and Culture" St. Petersburg: SPbGU Publ.

Lee, J. 2015. "Chinese Proverbs: How Are Women and Men Represented?" *Multidisciplinary Journal of Gender Studies* 4 (1): 559–85.

Lukyanova, E. Yu. 2009. "Azykovaya kartina mira i ee vliyanie na strukturno-funkcional'nye i pragmaticheskie osobennosti reklamnogo teksta: Yazykovaya kartina mira v lingvistike" [The linguistic picture of the world and its influence on the structural, functional and pragmatic features of the advertising text: The linguistic picture of the world in linguistics]. In *Materials of the I International Scientific Conference on December 2–4, 2009*, edited by L. M. Ermakov, 39–43. Federal Agency for Education, Tambov. Tambov: Publishing House of Tambov State University named after G. R. Derzhvin.

Malaysarin, Zh. 2010. *Kazak makal-matelderi* [Kazakh proverbs and sayings]. Almaty: Ana Tili.

Maslova, V. A. 2001. *Lingvokulturologia* [Linguoculturology]. A textbook for students. Higher. Studies. Institutions / V. A. Maslova. Moscow: Publishing Center "Academy."

Mieder, Wolfgang. *Proverbs: A Handbook.* 2004. Greenwood Publishing Group.

Mieder, Wolfgang. 2004. *Proverbs : A Handbook.* Greenwood Folklore Handbooks. Westport, Conn.: Greenwood Press.

Mukhtarova, R., E. Tsyganova, and S. Radionova. 2020. "Analysis of English and Tatar Proverbs with a Gender Component." In *Proceedings of the International Conference Digital Age: Traditions, Modernity, and Innovations (ICDATMI 2020).* Vol. 489.

Orlova, O. V. 2010. *The Linguistic Picture of the World and National-Cultural Identity.* Moscow: GASK. 110.

Pimenova, M. V. 2014. *Yazykovaya kartina mira* [Language picture of the world]. [Electronic resource]: textbook. Manual / M. V. Pimenova. Moscow: FLINT. 108.

Qaidar, A. 1998. *Kazak tilinin ozekti masselerii* [Topical issues of Kazakh linguistics]. Almaty: Ana tili.

Shokym, G. 2012. *Genderlik linguistika negizderi* [The basis of gender linguistics]. Almaty: Ekonomika.

Uryson, E. V. 2003. *Problemy issledovaniya yazykovoj kartiny mira v semantike* [Problems of studying the linguistic picture of the world in semantics]. Russian Academy of Sciences. V. V. Vinogradov Institute of the Russian Language. Moscow: Languages of Slavic Culture.

Vandysheva, A. V. 2007. "Gendernaya yazykovaya kartina mira yazyk: diskurs; tekst" [Gender linguistic picture of the world language: Discourse; Text]. *Materials of the III International Scientific Conference*, 93–94. Rostov: Southern Federal University.

Weisberger, L. 2004. *Rodnoj Yazyk I Formirovanie Duha* [Native language and the formation of the spirit]. Moscow: Editorial URSS. 232.

Zhirenov, S. A. 2016. "Lingvisticheskie svojstva frazeologizmov kazahskogo yazyka" [Linguistic identity of phraseology of the Kazakh language]. *Bulletin of Abai KazNPU: Series "Philological Sciences"*, No. 1 (55): 27–29.

Linguistic Characteristics of the Images of "Kyz-Kelin-Ana" in the Concept of "Woman"

GULMIRA ABDIMAULEN
L.N. Gumilyov Eurasian National University, Nur-Sultan

Introduction

The words "*qyz, boıjetken, bıbi, jar, qalyńdyq, qurby, qaryndas, sińili, ápke, táte, kelin, jeńge, jesir, kelinshek, qatyn, toqal, ana, báıbishe, ene, áje, kempir, qudaǵı, qudasha, sheshe*" form the thesaurus entry for *áıel* (woman), with meanings varying by age, place, and social role of the girl in society. The word *áıel* embodied words as *kyz-bibi, kyz-kurby, kyz-apke, kyz-kelin, kyz-áıel, kyz-zhenge, kyz-ana* in the macro-frame structure of the paremiological world in the Kazakh language (Sagidolda 2011, 253–255). The greatest goal of every woman in life is to bring a generation and raise them as good people. Its meaning is revealed within the framework of the following proverb *Ul ósirgeniń—urpaq ósirgeniń, qyz ósirgeniń—ult ósirgeniń* (the family line grows by raising boys; the nation grows by raising girls). Realizing that today's generation is the nation of tomorrow, we understand that women are very responsible for their tasks. The article combines proverbs and sayings about a girl, daughter-in-law, and mother, which are absorbed into the Kazakh consciousness, and their meaning is revealed. Comparing the meaning of the proverbs and sayings used in the early twentieth century with the proverbs of the late twentieth and early twenty-first century, new moments of the image of *qyz-kelin-ana* are visible. Collections of proverbs and sayings published in the Kazakh language are used as a source. In a typical Kazakh family, which has not yet lost its language and traditions, a girl occupies a special place. From infancy to marriage, every Kazakh girl grows up freely, pampered by her parents, brothers, sisters, and relatives. The rules of use, value, and importance of ancient proverbs and phraseological phrases concerning girls in the country are described in the article. Several English proverbs that are similar in meaning to Kazakh proverbs are also given as examples.

Methods

The materials are studied and recorded in historical and diachronic directions in the context of synchronous description. Comparative, historical etymological, ethno-linguistic cognitive, and component and synthesis methods are used to achieve the result. In addition, descriptive, ethno-linguistic, and conceptual methods of analysis are used in some places. Information is obtained from the literary heritage of the Kazakh people, phraseological, linguo-cultural, and ritual collections, dictionaries, and proverbs.

The Results

The life trend changes over time, but proverbs and sayings do not lose their meaning. This proverb can serve as proof of this *Elý jylda el jaña, júz jylda qazan* (the country will be renewed in 50 years and destroyed in 100). The frequent use of proverbs and sayings in everyday colloquial speech is equivalent to the revival of the national heritage. Proverbs and sayings are used to refer to growing girls in a Kazakh family. The results of the research work will be to show the future generation a special picture of the girl's place in society.

Discussion

Only language can reveal the results of any science. Language is the most important, fundamental, and stable indicator of an ethnic group. N.I. Tolstoi, in his work *Iazik i narodnaya cultura* (Language and folk culture), says that "language is related to culture, ethnicity, and mentality." It is also a component and tool of the culture (Tolstoi 1995, 16). Tolstoi distinguishes three categories of language: literary, sacred, and folklore languages. He argues that language can also be considered separately from culture (Tolstoi 1995, 36). A. Qaidar reveals this relationship between language and nation: "language is the foundation of the national spirit," and "one language is one nation." Language Is the soul of a people. The people's way of life is manifest in their language. The specifics of the people are also known through language. The most important information about the population is provided by its language. Language is a mirror of the people (Qaidar 2004, 567). S. G. Ter-Minasova connects language with culture, focusing on spoken language. They preserve the values of the nation, their worldview, attitude towards other peoples, and their positions. Phraseology and proverbs provide information about the culture, history, and geographical location of the entire population. However, the utilization of phraseology and proverbs are not the same in all languages. They are like spices. If we use spices for food, phraseology and proverbs are also a word (Ter-Minasova 2018, 93). According to G. S. Sagidolda, "phraseology and proverbs perform an important linguistic function in depicting a traditional picture of the world. In other words, language reflects the attitude of the people to the world, spiritual and material culture, and life. They help to revive the ancient elements of Ethnos' understanding of the universe, the world. Phraseology and proverbs are involved in the creation of a single language image of the world" (Sagidolda 2011, 60). There is considerable consensus among scientists about language, culture, society, people, proverbs, sayings, and traditions.

In general, proverbs and sayings in the Kazakh consciousness are not the product of one era. The collection and publication of proverbs and sayings in the Kazakh language consisted of two stages. The first stage is the second half of the nineteenth century, where proverbs and sayings were collected, printed, and published. In the second stage, proverbs and sayings were addressed in research. Shokan Ualikhanov was the first scientist who recorded Kazakh proverbs and sayings on paper. He wrote more than 200 proverbs and sayings in the 1850s (Qasymova 2004, 10). A. Qaidar, in *Khalyq danalygy* (Folk wisdom), suggests the following definition:

> Proverbs and sayings are the 'Golden Bridge' which connects the past life of the people and the present with the future. They will be a guarantee for the preservation of spiritual and cultural traditions in the human mind, society, and language. This means that an ethnic community deprived of wealth loses its past, and such a community has no future. (Qaidar 2004, 7)

Áıel-Qyz (woman-girl). The lexeme *Áıel* is associated with many other concepts in the language, consciousness, faith, traditions, proverbs, and phraseology of the Kazakh people. It is not enough to use only the personal word *Áıel* and reveal its conceptual meaning. It consists of many branches, such as: *áıel-qyz, sulý-qyz, qyz-báısheshek, qyz-gúl, qyz-óris, kelin, qyz-kelin, jas-kelin, dana-kelin, dara-kelin, áıel-ana, áıel-urpaq*, etc. Girls, daughter-in-law, and mothers are women. It is clear that in one Kazakh family there will be *a daughter, a daughter-in-law*, and *a mother*. All of them are women, but their status is different. In that regard, the following word associations in proverbs are notable: girls—favorite, free, beautiful, and nice; daughter-in-law—noble, gentle, calm, shawl, greeting, cradle, and mothers—smart, kind, caring, etc. The lexical meaning of the word "woman" changes depending on the degree of developmental growth. The beginning of the word *áıel* (woman) begins with the word *qyz* (girl). It is interpreted by the concepts of being very gentle, carefree, charming, beautiful, transparent, and ideal. After all, there is only an interest in beauty and elegance in the mind and intuition of a young girl. She is so clean, so carefree. The dream of a girl is to wear beautiful jewelry, put on beautiful clothes, play with nice toys, dance like a flower, bend, sing songs, etc. This proverb reveals its meaning, *qyzdyń kózi qyzarǵandada* (girls quickly pay attention to shiny things) (Barzhaksyuly, Baitursynuly, and Bokeikhanuly 1993, 27). Similarly in English, "the brains of a woman are in her curls" (Schipper 2003, 60) and "a mother's wish is a daughter's duty" (Doyle, Mieder, and Shapiro 2012, 181). These each address this life stage which in general has been quite short. Our ancestors, who knew this quality of a girl, brought up girls with manners, likening them to flowers, stroking their forehead, saying beautiful words, and giving them all the sweets. However, it is true that the girl will go to the status of "daughter-in-law" and then "mother" in the future. Therefore, the girl's parents managed to bring her up depending on her age to a great life, prepared for the subsequent social statuses. In this regard, the great Kazakh batyr Bauyrzhan Momyshuly expressed the following opinion about girls. "Being a strong hero, I can't stand an hour in a foreign, unfamiliar country. And the girl goes to a new environment alone, which she does not know at all. She gets along with this country, raises her offspring. She respects the people of that country and also dominates her own honor. That is why the most heroic person on earth is a girl" (Akmeshit Weekly 2020). The girl was raised with great respect, protection, and sometimes the people of the village pay attention to it. This proverb reveals its meaning, *Qyzǵa qyryq úiden, qala berse qara kúńnen tyıý* (each girl had forty strong guards) (Barzhaksyuly, Baitursynuly, and Bokeikhanuly 1993, 27). The girl's parents always mention that such freedom at her home is short-lived, and when the girl reaches the marrying age, such actions will be forgotten. The transition of a "girl" to the status of a "daughter-in-law" was accompanied by the following proverbs: *qaıtyp shapqan jaý jaman, qaıtyp kelgen qyz jaman* (both the girl who returns, and the enemy who returns are evil), *tórkini jaqynnyń tósegi jınalmaıdy* (if a married girl is close to her own parents, her case will not finish), *tórkinge sengenniń tóbesi tesik* (if a married girl trusts her parents, there will be no prosperity in her family), *tórkin dese qyz tózbeıdi, kókpek dese túıe tózbeıdi* (a married girl constantly misses her relatives) (Barzhaksyuly, Baitursynuly, and Bokeikhanuly 1993, 27). That is, through these proverbs, it is said that a girl who has passed to the status of *kelin* does not have the opportunity to return to the status of *qyz*. As a result, in proverbs and sayings of the early twentieth century, we can see that in addition to raising girls freely, they were kept in strict order. One of the most widely used proverbs is *"qyzym saǵan aıtamyn, kelinim sen tyńda"* (daughter, I tell you, daughter-in-law, you listen) in the second half of the twentieth century and the beginning of the twenty-first century (Keikin 2002, 77). It is a subtle way to criticize a girl who has come to someone's strange house as a daughter-in-law. She was also a daughter-in-law who had previously grown up freely in another house. The mother-in-law remarks—to the daughter-in-law through her daughter so as not to offend the bride. This is the pinnacle of culture. Proverbs that have been used a lot lately: *Qyz qonaq"Qyz óris,"* *"Qyz jat jurttyq"* (the girl is a guest, the girl is a field, the girl is a stranger) (Shariphanuly 2011, 543); *"Qyz—aýyldyń kórki"* (the girl is the beauty of the village) (Shariphanuly 2011, 542), and in English, "Our girlhood determines our womanhood" (Kerschen 1998, 39). These proverbs inform that the girl's dignity has increased.*Qyzy bardyń kózi bar, uly bardyń ózi bar* (if you have a daughter, you have eyes, and if you have a son, you have yourself), *Bir jaqsy qyz eki jaman ulǵa tatıdy* (one good girl is valued for two bad boys), *Qyz ósse úıge jut, ul ósse úıge qut* (a girl is a symbol of poverty, a boy is a symbol of wealth) (Shariphanuly 2011, 544). In this proverb, we see an increase in the status of girls in the Kazakh family and sometimes equating girls with boys. It may also be the result of gender policy.

Áıel-kelin (woman—daughter-in-law). Combining the proverb *"jaqsy úıge kelgen kelin kelin bolady, jaman úıge kelgen kelin kelsap bolady"* (a bride who comes to a good house will be a bride, a bride who comes to a bad house will be a log) (Barzhaksyuly, Baitursynuly, and Bokeikhanuly 1993, 28) with the proverb *balany jasynan, kelindi basynan* (it is necessary to raise the child from the beginning, the daughter-in-law from the very beginning) (Barzhaksyuly, Baitursynuly, and Bokeikhanuly 1993, 27), we can see that there are many changes in the life, consciousness, and psychology of a girl who has entered the strange country and, house as a daughter-in-law. There is a long-standing habit of criticizing the new bride by the public in the Kazakh tradition. A girl is obliged to practice the upbringing and manners received from her parents when she receives the status of *"daughter-in-law."* The girl's mother prepares her daughter in advance so that she can quickly get used to her new home. The mother prepares her daughter from an early age, telling her that there are rules of living in each family that has been formed over the years. This proverb reveals its full meaning: *"Ata kórgen oq janar, ene kórgen ton pisher"* (the boy continues his father's, the girl continues her mother's profession) (Barzhaksyuly, Baitursynuly, and Bokeikhanuly 1993, 28). However, it is very difficult to get into a strange environment. We know that many people will help the daughter-in-law to adapt quickly to a new place. We understand its argument from the following proverb, *"Balanyń ózi týǵandaı, kelinniń ózi kelgenda"* (both the child and the daughter-in-law seem to have grown up on their own) (Barzhaksyuly, Baitursynuly, and Bokeikhanuly 1993, 28). The mother-in-law has a strong duty to adapt her daughter-in-law to the new environment. First her husband, then other family members help her. Whoever speaks to the daughter-in-law and loves her, she also tried to love and respect them in this way. The proverb *"Kelinniń betin kim ashsa, sol ystyq"* (the person who opens the bride's face will be close to her) refers to the Kazakh tradition of "betashar," where the new daughter-in-law is placed in the house, covering her face. The mother of her husband unveils the face of the bride in public after the singer's special song. (Barzhaksyuly, Baitursynuly, and Bokeikhanuly 1993, 28). However, in ancient times, the proverb *"ulyń ósse úlgimen aýyl bol, qyzyń ósse qylyqtymen aýyl bol"* (be close to with good people for the future of the son and daughter) (Barzhaksyuly, Baitursynuly, and Bokeikhanuly 1993, 28) was based on the principle. The English proverb is Marry your son when you will, your daughter when you can (Schipper 2003, 164). Parents of both sides call their sons and daughters future couples from the very beginning of their childhood. Such tradition is called "atastyrý." It is a serious relationship between the two families, and the future couple grew up knowing and seeing each other from childhood. This is a guarantee that the girl will feel free in the future, without crying in a strange place.

The word *"kelin"* is used in the same sense as the word *"qatyn"* in the Kazakh language. A woman becomes respected by other people thanks to her husband. Man and woman are a single pair that does not separate. The following proverb proves this *"Baqa jaryǵy sýmen, qatyn jaryǵy ermen"* (a frog is beautiful with water, a woman is beautiful with her husband) (Barzhaksyuly, Baitursynuly, and Bokeikhanuly 1993, 25). Therefore, where a woman is mentioned, her man is also mentioned. It is impossible to consider them separately. A woman is one step lower than a man and depends on him in the Kazakh consciousness. in this regard, I prefer to use the following proverb *Jaqsy qatyn jarym yrys* (if a woman is good, there will be a lot of welfare, harmony, kindness) (Barzhaksyuly, Baitursynuly, and Bokeikhanuly 1993, 25). E.V. Sevortyan explains in his etymological dictionary that *"kelin"* comes from the Turkish word *"gelin,"* that is, gives the concept of *"a newlywed girl"* or *"young bride."* In this case, V. V. Radlov explains that "kel" in the word "kelin" is the verb "kel" (to come), and "-n" is the formative (Sevortyan 1980, 17). It means the concept of a "visitor" who comes from one place to another. As a result, from proverbs and sayings of the beginning of the twentieth century, we understand that the daughter-in-law was a fragile person who did not have power in her head, depended on someone else, and also was the mainstay of the family.

And now, let us analyze the meaning of the proverbs of the second part of the twentieth century and the beginning of the twenty-first century. The following are examples from the proverbs of this period: *"Kelini jaqsy úıdiń, keregesi altyn"* (the wall of the house change for the gold if the daughter-in-law will be good) (Shariphanuly 2011, 294), and the English variant is *"Woman is the key of the life`s mystery"* (Kerschen 1998, 40), *Kelindi qaıynenenıń topyraǵynan jaratqan* (the daughter-in-law is very similar to her mother-in-law) (Shariphanuly 2011, 292), English cognate is *All brides are child brides in their mother's eyes* (Kerschen 1998, 30), *"Jaqsy kelin qyzyńdaı, jaqsy kúıeý ulyńdaı"* (a good daughter-in-law will be like a daughter, a good husband will be like a son), *"Jaqsy kelin qurdasyńdaı bolar, jaqsy ulyń syrlasyńdaı bolar"* (a good daughter-in-law and son will be like a friend), *"Kelinniń aıaǵynan, qoıshynyń taıaǵynan"* (from the feet of the daughter-in-law, from the stick of the shepherd. It is good that the daughter-in-law is good from the first day, and if the Shepherd has a good and strong tool, that is, a stick, the sheep will graze well) (Shariphanuly 2011, 293) and the English cognate is *"Who finds a wife finds a good thing"* (Kerschen 1998, 30). From these proverbs, we noticed that the status of the daughter-in-law in the family has increased for the better, the care and attitude to her has changed and enlarged. In some families, the phrase "we see my daughter-in-law as our daughter", has recently been widely spoken.

Áıel–Ana (woman–mother). The symbol of the prosperity of each family is the mother! The most beautiful, wonderful word in the Kazakh language is *ana*. This word is read as *ana* without any changes from right to left, from left to right. *Ana* is a wonderful priceless soul that from ancient times to the present day does not lose its value, dignity, quality, strength, and place in the family is a wonderful and priceless soul. This word is associated in the Kazakh consciousness with the word's kindness, patience, compassion, sincerity, inexhaustible love, and care. It is impossible to explore, understand, and discover the nature of the mother. God made it very wide in all respects. A woman reaches the status of *ana* only when she has a child. Therefore, mother and child are an integral being that fulfill each other. The mother gives all the best qualities to her child through her milk. Motherhood is an activity that transcends even good deeds around the world. Maternal love cannot be expressed in words. These words are for all mothers on earth.

Instead of the word *ana*, the words *sheshe, shesheı* or *ene* are often used in the Kazakh spoken language. Every person came into the world thanks to his or her mother. If you take any mother of Kazakh family, then their fate, life credo, love for the child, blessing, and desires are similar to each other. The concept of *Aiel-ana* does not lose its dignity, meaning until the respect for them ceases in the Kazakh consciousness. Most of the proverbs from the first half of the twentieth century are related to parents and children. Parents are dear to any child. *Ata kórgen oq jonar, ene kórgen ton pisher* (the boy repeats the action of the father, the girl repeats the action of the mother), *Áke turyp ul sóılegennen bez, sheshe turyp qyz sóılegennen bez* (the son has no right to speak in the place of the father, and the girl has no right to speak in the place of the mother) (Barzhaksyuly, Baitursynuly, and Bokeikhanuly 1993, 28), *"Aģaıynnyń qadirin jalaly bolsań bilesiń, ata-ananyń qadirin balaly bolģanda bilesiń"* (you know the dignity of a relative when you have a problem, the dignity of a parent when you have a child) (Barzhaksyuly, Baitursynuly, and Bokeikhanuly 1993, 29). Under these proverbs, all generations are described as substitutes of their parents, repeaters of the upbringing received from them. It is clear that a mother`s care for her child is very broad from the meaning of these proverbs: *Ákeli jetim—arsyz jetim, shesheli jetim—erke jetim* (orphanhood without a mother is much more difficult than orphanhood without a father), *"Sheshesi bar jetimniń basynda taraq pen qyl oınar, sheshesi joq jetimniń basynda bıt pen sirke oınar"* (an orphan with a mother will have little trouble, and an orphan without a mother will have a lot of trouble) (Barzhaksyuly, Baitursynuly, and Bokeikhanuly 1993, 28.). A mother never lets her child suffer. Mothers are ready to give their souls for their children. The love of the mother for the child is more powerful than the kindness of the father.

In the second half of the twentieth century and the beginning of the twenty-first century, the character of proverbs in the sense of "woman-mother" is described as follows. *Ananyń kóńili qyzynda, qyzynyń kóńili qyz-ylda* (mother always worries about her child but the child has nothing in his mind) (Keikin 2002, 77), *Ana balasyn arystannyń aýzynan alar* (a mother can take her child from the mouth of a lion (a mother is not afraid of anything when she needs to protect her child)), *Ana júregi teńizden tereń* (mother's heart is deeper than the sea), *Ana júregi—ómir tiregi* (mother's heart is the pillar of life), *Ana meıirimi aspannan da sheksiz* (mother's mercy is infinitely greater than heaven), *Ananyń mahabbaty, ajaldy da jeńedi* (mother's love conquers death), *Anasyz ómir—sóngen kómir* (there is no life without a mother) (Shariphanuly 2011, 144–148), and in English "A mother can take care of 10 children, but (sometimes) 10 children cannot take care of one mother" (Doyle, Mieder, and Shapiro 2012, 181). "A woman's place is any place she wants to be" (Doyle, Mieder, and Shapiro 2012, 289) It is quite clear that the child's act, the beauty of his soul, is transmitted through the mother's milk and the warmth of his heart in the meaning of all proverbs. The mother endowed her child with the best qualities. The gentle tone and hand of the mother are invaluable wealth for the child. The meaning of the word "mother" has not changed in comparison after a long time. This means that any mother will protect her child and grow up with mercy. The mother has a special place in every family. The status of motherhood has the same function for all nations and people.

When the topic of motherhood is touched on, another topic that should be mentioned is *ana til* (native language). It is used with the word *ana* only in the Kazakh language. We provide such valuable information through our language, don't we? And we should not forget that this language was given to us thanks to our mother!

Conclusion

The Kazakh people were eloquent and often used proverbs in everyday oral speech. The transmission of thoughts through proverbs is developed in the speech culture of our ancestors. This trend continues to this day.

At the beginning of the twentieth century, Kazakh girls grew up free and pampered, judging from the proverbs and sayings, yet the discipline for them was strict. Over time, at the end of the twentieth century and the beginning of the twenty-first century, there was an increase in the status of a girl in the Kazakh family. In addition, sometimes there are cases when they are equated with the level of boys. This is also the result of gender policy.

At the beginning of the twentieth century, we see the daughter-in-law as a woman who has no power in her head, depends on someone else, comes from a strange place to an unknown place, and is criticized a lot. In addition, she is a fragile person who is the mainstay of family well-being. At that time, "daughter-in-law" had only the status of "performer," who could not openly express her own opinion to anyone, everor, anywhere. It is known from the proverbs of the second half of the twentieth century and the beginning of the twenty-first century that the status of the "daughter-in-law" in the public sphere increased. This result is accompanied by an increase in the social situation and education of the country. The result of gender policy is that women receive education, work in the same field as men, and begin to openly express their thoughts in a public environment. This is the merit and result of the independence of our country.

When we speak about the status of *Ana*, we can say that all of them, regardless of nationality, language, and religion are equal. The function of mothers is the same everywhere. The love of mothers for the child is boundless. They are people who do not change, do not lose their value, and perform their functions. Although there were some changes in the linguistic characteristics of the status *qyz* and *kelin*, it was found that the status of *ana* remained unchanged.

Bibliography

Akmeshit Weekly. 2020 "Zher Betindegi Eŋ Batyr Adam Kim?" [Who is the most heroic person on earth?]. *Aqmeshit aptalyǵy*, January 31, 2020. https://old.aqmeshit-aptal ygy.kz/zanalyk/11239-zher-betndeg-e-batyr-adam-km.html

Barzhaksyuly, A., A. Baitursynuly, and A. Bokeikhanuly. (1923) 1993. *Myń bir maqal, jıyrma úsh joqtaý* [One thousand and one proverbs; twenty-three songs – poems (lamentations)]. Almaty: Kúnshyǵys.

Doyle, C. C., W. Mieder, and F. R.Shapiro. eds. 2012. *The Dictionary of Modern Proverbs*. New Haven: Yale University Press.

Keikin, Zh. 2002. *Qazaqtyń 7777 maqal mátelderi*. [7777 Kazakh proverbs and sayings]. Almaty: Ölke.

Kerschen, L. 1998. *American Proverbs about Women: A Reference Guide*. Westport, CT: Greenwood Press.

Qaidar, A. 2004. *Khalyq danalyǵy*. [Folk wisdom]. Almaty: Toganay T.

Qaidar, A. 2009. *Kazaktar ana tili aleminde: etnolingvistikalyk sozdik*. [Kazakhs in the world of the native tongue: Ethnolinguistic dictionary]. Vol. 1. Almaty: Daik-Press.

Qasymova, S. K. 2004. *San komponetti maqal-mátelderdiń ulttyq-mádeni negizi. [National and cultural basis of numerical proverbs and sayings]*. Astana: Nurlı älem.

Sagidolda, G. S. 2011. *Turki-mongol dunie beinesining tildik fragmentteri* [Linguistic fragments of the turkmongol world image]. Astana: B.O.Zh.

Schipper, M. 2003. *Never Marry a Woman with Big Feet: Women in Proverbs from Around the World*. New Haven: Yale University Press.

Sevortyan, E. V. 1980. *Etımologıcheskıı slovar túrkskıh ıazykov. Na býkvy "B, G, D".* [Etymological dictionary of the Turkic languages. On the letters "B, G, D"] Moscow: Nauka.

Shariphanuly, M. 2011. *Kazakhtyn makal-matelderi* [Kazakh Proverbs and sayings]. 2 vol. Astana: Master.

Ter-Minasova, S. G. 2018. *Til jane madenietaraliq comunikasia* [Language and intercultural communication]. Almaty: National Translation Bureau.

Tolstoi, N. 1995. *Iazik i narodnaya cultura: Otcherki po clobiyanskoi mifologii I etnolinguistike* [Language and folk culture: Essays on Slavic mythology and ethnolinguistics] Moscow: Indrik.

Chapter 4 The Role of Proverbs in Pedagogy

Cognitive and Linguo-cultural Aspects of Transference of English Proverbs and Sayings into the Kazakh Language

GULNAR BEKKOZHANOVA
Al-Farabi Kazakh National University, Almaty

ROZALINDA SHAKHANOVA
Abay Kazakh National Pedagogical University, Almaty

GULMARIYA OSPANOVA
Al-Farabi Kazakh National University, Almaty

Introduction

Since the Republic of Kazakhstan is a sovereign country, a subject of international relations and receives the status of state, the possibility of using the Kazakh language has broadened. As the language of the Republic and the State, participation of the Kazakh cannot be ruled out at the level of international relations. Linguistic units, like phraseology and proverbs, create certain difficulties in learning a foreign language and working on translations. Literary texts are rich in meaningful parts of the verbal composition that characterize periods in the life of the people, relations, and social phenomena. This means that people inherit a rich source of linguistic units. Thanks to these linguistic units, the younger generation learn to love their country, gain education, inherit cultural norms and human values such as honesty and modesty, and avoid such qualities as slander, falsehood, and pride.

Literary texts in the Kazakh language were generated from an ancient genre of folk art. Many of them appeared before writing. Therefore, the question of their primary sources is open for discussion. The main sources of the emergence of English texts were also of folk, literary, and biblical origins, borrowing from other languages and Shakespeare's quotes.

Before talking about the study of literary texts in English and Kazakh, we should mention the findings that provoked a discussion among linguists about the scope to which proverbs belong. For example, the formation and development of phraseology in post-soviet linguistics was contributed by V.V. Vinogradov, N.M. Shansky, V.N. Telia, M. Chernysheva, M.M. Kopylenko, A.V. Kunin, Y.V. Arnold, Y. Kengesbayev, S. Yergaliev, R. Zhusipova, A.T. Qaidar, B. Manasbaev, and others. Their works provide justification for the fact that literary texts belong to the foundations of the field of phraseology. G.L. Permiakov warns that the field of phraseology should be studied by corresponding the works of scientists and literary specialists, especially the field of proverbs and sayings.

Based on these statements and the results of their own research, the characteristics of literary texts and the transference of proverbs and sayings have certain characteristics. The characteristics are revealed through the uniqueness of ethnocultural values such as stability, consistency, and utility that allow them to be fully studied in this field, including them among phraseological units.

In the twenty-first century, in accordance with new theoretical and cognitive methodology, it became necessary to consider language alongside the thinking, culture, and everyday practical activities of a person. It required the development of a new direction in linguistics and the anthropocentric paradigm that could be established on its basis. At the same time, in modern linguistics and the study of literary texts, new approaches appeared in its formation. These approaches form theoretical principles and scientific methods, raising a variety of issues that require comprehensive study of the national language.

Proverbs and sayings reflect the thoughts of each nation, its worldview, and philosophy. Literary texts are distinguished by accuracy of thinking, depth of content, and compactness. They assess the various sectoral phenomena of life, summarize thoughts, and express opinions based on the experience of the people throughout centuries. In cognitive and linguistic units, linguistics is insufficient to analyze the linguistic nature of literary texts when they were formed in a specific area. Texts reveal national features and the ethnolinguistic nature. Therefore, the definition and consideration of ways to transfer Kazakh proverbs and sayings into English and the comparison of them on a cognitive and linguistic basis are the relevance of this research.

Literature Review

These universal cognitive patterns (models) are the product of language's complex cognitive activity that is characteristic of the human in general. It is born in the deep structures of language. Cognitive models, meanwhile, show an intermediate image between human thought and consciousness. The information received is encoded in cognitive models. The unity of language and knowledge is studied within linguistics.

In the mid-twentieth century, cognitive linguistics was considered at the level of basic teaching in the modern anthropocentric paradigm. A lot of research was being done in this direction. As a result, by the end of the twentieth century, the theoretical directions of cognitive science in Europe had matured.

In this connection, there were published research papers related to the field of cognitology by foreign scientists J.R.R. Tolkien, G. Lakoff, R. Langaker, T. Van Dyck, H.Y. Schmidt, M. Johnson, and M. Wittenstein. Researchers pay special attention to the function of language in describing the "linguistic picture of the world" within the framework of cognitive sciences.

We consider that these studies have made a significant contribution to the definition of theoretical bases and units of cognitive linguistics. The study of the peculiarities of the functioning and implementation of cognitive elements in human consciousness was not mentioned.

Methodology

The main research methods used in this work are cognitive, comparative, and contrastive analysis. Cognitive and linguo-cultural comparative analysis of English and Kazakh proverbs and sayings through their components and transference of equivalents was used to reveal the main ways of transference of proverbs and sayings. The ways of transference of English proverbs into the Kazakh language have been analyzed according to ethnolinguistic, linguo-cultural, and cognitive bases with their equivalents in the dictionaries of English-Kazakh-Russian dictionaries of proverbs and sayings.

In this connection, we used dictionaries of proverbs and sayings in English and Kazakh languages and made statistical analyses. More than 100 proverbs and sayings have been analyzed, revealing the ways of transference in studied languages. We tried to distinguish cultural realia and understandings of different objects through cognitive and linguo-cultural peculiarities of proverbs and sayings in Kazakh and English languages. Cognitive modeling was used to distinguish the cognitive and linguo-cultural peculiarities of English and Kazakh proverbs and sayings.

Theoretical Basis of Transference of Proverbs and Sayings

The main ways to transfer English language proverbs and sayings into other languages dominate general linguistics, as well as in many studies in a separate linguistics anthropocentric paradigm. The main reason for this is that the anthropocentric principle in linguistics puts primarily the ethno-cultural values of the nation as the consumer of the language. The anthropocentric paradigm opens new directions within its framework, such as ethnolinguistics, linguistics, cognitive linguistics, and lingua-psychology. According to S. Japaqov:

> The surrounding reality is connected with the language of conscious knowledge of life and categorization of human experience, since meaningful information obtained during human cognitive activity. It is expressed in linguistic ideas and linguistic forms and expressed through speech. Cognitive processes in dialectical forms are closely related to language, since language consolidates people's social experience and knowledge of the world. And what we know about the structure of consciousness depends only on language. Only language allows us to report these structures and depict them in any natural language. (Japaqov 2003, 21)

In particular, cognitive linguistics avoids the restriction of traditional linguistics and sees deep and comprehensive laws recognized through linguistic "external" manifestations. The cognitive method for the study of proverbs and sayings in language signs should take into account the processes of conceptualization and categorization. According to E.S. Kubryakova and others, "the linguist should reveal objective reality at the end of the idea, assume it in separate system, linguistic forms, but also know how the linguistic units, natural integrity is formed within linguistic transmissions, categories associated with the perception of the world and how they reflect human cognition" (Kubryakova et al. 1996, 37).

In Russian linguistics, the importance of cognitive linguistics is determined by V.A. Maslova states: "cognitive linguistics is an analysis of language by speech analysis, different contexts, matching lexemes, written in terms of concepts. Its definitions in different words and definitions, analysis of phraseology, postulates, speeches, aphorisms, in which concepts are represented" (Maslova 2001, 25).

For cognitive linguistics to be recognized as a separate branch of science, it must have basic concepts, characteristic basic categories, and units.

Researchers of anthropological linguistics consider linguistic knowledge, conceptuality, conceptual system, cognition, cognitive models, verbality, mentality, and concepts in this field. World image, conceptual field, and national cultural units are also the main concepts of cognitive linguistics. Further research shows that the question of the actions of these concepts in human consciousness, their manifestation in language, and thus the ability to recognize the "linguistic picture of the world" are currently in the category of the main and most pressing problems for linguists. Conceptuality is reflected in the result of knowledge in the process of cognition. As L.A. Morozova points out that "conceptualization is interpreted as different forms of knowledge of the process of structuring knowledge from some minimal conceptual units" (Morozova 1973, 93). G. Smagulova defines "cognitive linguistics as a branch of linguistics that considers the human language as a system of symbols, a mechanism and means of cognition that allows us to present a common message, transfer it from one state to another" (Smagulova 2007, 53).

Today, having its own concepts, principles, and theoretical foundations, this linguistic field has been developed. At first, the term "cognitive" itself was perceived as an unclear problem. The conceptual units were not systematized, therefore opinions and views on cognitive linguistics were also not formed.

However, some scientists, putting structural linguistics against cognitive linguistics, interpreted the cognitive approach as an "uprising," a "turning point" born at the end of the twentieth century. As a result, the correspondents evaluated cognitive linguistics as an indicator of interdisciplinary communication, a stream of language teachings. Y. Kengesbayev, considering cognitive science or cognitive psychology, names the prerequisites for the development of linguistics as linguistic typology, ethnolinguistics, neurolinguistics, psycholinguistics, and comparative-historical linguistics (Kengesbayev, 2006). The principles and categories of semasiology form the results of human knowledge and the laws of language typology allow us to explain the universal structure of language (Kopylenko et al, 1989, 17).

G.L. Permiakov expresses the following idea about the units that form the basis of the final idea of cognitive science: "the mouse represents its manipulations with external (mental) representations of types of frames, plans, scenarios, models and other structures of knowledge" (Permiakov 1979, 95). Therefore, cognitive linguistics, being a linguistic approach in the cognitive system, allows us to consider the cognitive nature of language from a deep point of view. The cognitive image of a language can be seen under any lexical units in the language. For example, proverbs and sayings, phraseology, set expressions in the national language as lexical units that were formed based on the worldview of the people throughout centuries.

Findings and Discussion

The Main Approaches to the Study of the Transference of English Proverbs and Sayings into the Kazakh Language

Proverbs and sayings in any language are concise statements, and they are the basis of spoken language, "the pearl of thought." The first examples of them were born with the birth of a people. They have been combined for many centuries in the process of their formation, development, and growth. They are changed and updated in accordance with various social and class desires in different times. It can be said that there is no sphere of life that is not mentioned in proverbs and sayings.

The most productive writers who have contributed to English proverbs were poets and writers, such as Browning, Byron, Cowper, Dickens, Johnson, and Austin. The contribution of other cultural communities to the fund of English proverbs is also significant. There are also scientists who have considered proverbs and sayings of the English language and have written special research papers. For example, L.Y. Selyanina's dissertation, "Variants of Postulates of the English Language," the features of English proverbs are considered. R.B. Jusipova likewise analyzes the structure of English proverbs in her work, "Synonymous Meaning of Proverbs in English and Kazakh Languages" (Jusipova 2003, 55).

There are also special, comprehensive research papers on English proverbs and sayings. In the work of L.Y. Shvydkoy, proverbs and aphorisms are combined into one group under the name "cliche," and their synonymous series is given. The analysis of S.Y. Vyaltseva's English proverbs are stylistic, and E. Akhundova's research is devoted to syntactic features. Works on the study of set expressions of the English language are closely related to the name of A.V. Kunin. Through his extensive scientific work, "The Course of English Language," "The Course of Phraseology of Modern English Language," and the "Anglo-Russian Phraseological Dictionary," he made a significant contribution to the science of the language and guided research on a comparative basis (Kunin 1986, 55).

The main difference between the roots of Kazakh and English paremiology is that a large group of Kazakh mentality is formed depending on the individual (poets, bies, chechens, akylgeys, wise old people, etc.). Kazakh proverbs are transmitted orally from generation to generation. The main source of the English proverbs is religion, especially the Bible, and a special place is occupied by expressive, meaningful examples of words of such great personalities as Shakespeare.

A.V. Kunin, known for his comprehensive research and views on the phraseology of the English language, also adheres to the views of the above scholars. Based on the structural and semantic features of non-motivated individuals, he proposes to consider them as "communicative phraseological units." The author also includes a group of proverbs, the synonyms of which are literal and not considered as "traditional" set expressions (Kunin 1986, 30). For example: "All's well that ends well" (*satti ayaqtalgan istin bari jaqsi*), or "Appearances are deceitful" (*kelbet—aldamshi*), or "Better late than never" (*eshten kesh jaqsi*).

There are many monographs devoted to the study of Kazakh proverbs and sayings. Among them, B. Shalabayev was one of the first to specifically consider this group of set expressions and identify their main semantic groups and genre features. In his work, "Oral Literature of the Kazakh People" M. Gabdullın defines the vital meaning and function of proverbs and sayings, describing the economy, profession, and life of the Kazakh people (Gabdullın [1958] 1996). S. Nuryshev considers them from the point of view of the history of development (Nuryshev 1959, 112).

In the English language, *Manners make the man* (Adamdi adam etetin onin adeptiligi) is often used among the population. The expression is compact but significant, and it depends on the principles, traditions, and requirements of the time of the Middle Ages. Especially in the fourteenth century, in England, the main conditions of culture and rules of behavior were emphasized, and strict compliance was required. Special collections containing the rules of decency began to be published. Over time, some of these positions have become popular proverbs.

Proverbs and sayings also correspond to the realities of real life in different eras, to the early concepts of the people. Proverbs and sayings are used with the same composition as phraseology, and their words cannot be replaced. They are used in any context, either morphologically or sintactically, unchanged, ready-made.

The more educated a person is, the greater the influence on other people. In addition, the rational words of famous poets and writers such as A. Kunanbayev, Zh. Zhabayev, and W. Shakespeare were skillfully used among the population (Sarsenbaev 1998, 124).

In proverbs and sayings, the problem of labor is touched upon a lot. The Kazakh thinker Abay, based on the popular proverbs A good dog deserves a good bone (*Jaqsi itke jaqsi suyek tiisti*), What we do willingly is easy (*Qalap jasagan is jenil boladi*), Must rise at five (*Jumis jasaytin beste turw kerek*) says that success is achieved through work (Abay ensiklopediyasy 1995, 156).

In the proverbs and sayings, a variety of human dignity takes its place. In the course of the study, there are a large number of proverbs in both languages, which are considered within the framework of this topic. If we consider the communicative motivation of proverbs, the group of proverbs included in this group is divided into two parts. The first alternative is the corresponding proverbs:

> Calamity is man's true touchstones (*Erdi kebenek ishinde tani*)
>   Every man has a fool in his sleeve (*Uydin jili swigin qis tuskende bilersin*)
>   A bird may be known by its song (in Kazakh it is: *Kisi qatesiz bolmas, qol baqasiz bolmas, Isine qarap adamin tani*)

And in the second group, there are proverbs that have no analogues, which are related to the peculiarities of the worldview, everyday life, and history of the people. For example, *Qizga qiriq uyden tiyim, ayel joli jinishke* (Every dog has his day), *Ozinnen twmay ul bolmas, satip almay qul bolmas* (Every Jack has his Jill).

The son had a special place in the Kazakh family and society. He is the owner of the house and family. He did not extinguish the hearth; he understood that he was the leader of the dynasty. A son imitates his father, teaches the upbringing of his father, and a daughter receives education from her mother. In Kazakh, *Uyada ne korsen, ushqanda soni ilersin* means that the upbringing of a child and the place where he grew up is of great importance (Argingazina 2004, 92). For example: "As the tree, so the fruit" (*Agashi qanday bola, jemi de sonday*), "Charity begins at home" (*Qayirimdiliq uyden bastaladi*), or "As the twig is bent, so is the tree inclined" (*Shibiq qalay enkeyse, tal da solay bagittaladi*).

Thematic grouping is distinguished by the fact that semantic proverbs can be easily found in one group. First of all, since many proverbs and sayings have a variable meaning, there are so many topics that it is difficult to include them in the same group. Secondly, it is quite difficult to define the subject group of some proverbs and sayings. The ideographic classification "according to language characteristics" proposed by A.T. Qaydar is quite suitable for revealing the communicative features of proverbs and sayings in English and Kazakh.

A number of English and Kazakh proverbs and sayings have mutual correspondence in terms of composition, structure and meaning, and there are also absolute equivalents, i.e. types of equivalents (Qaidar 1998, 31). Such transference can be seen in the examples provided in Table 11.1 of English proverbs and Kazakh cognates.

Table 11.1. Examples of proverbs.

English proverbs	*Transference into Kazakh*
If you haven't achieved anything by the age of 36, no one will believe in your feats at the age of 40.	*Otizinda orda buzbasan, qirqindi qirip keldim degenine eshkim senbeydi (qirga shiga almaysin).*
Depression is the sea; submerge in it and you will sink. Risk is about a boat; trust it and you will float.	*Wayim tubi tungiiq, batarsin da ketersin.*
The boat of a daring man never sinks even during a storm.	*Tawekeldin kemesi swga batpaydi. Tawekel tubi jelqayiq, minesin de otesin.*

The linguistic picture of the world that exists in a particular linguo-cultural community is determined by the study of the totality of human language and culture. English proverbs often consist of only one sentence, while the vast majority of Kazakh proverbs are two- or several-point. In Kazakh proverbs, the comparison of thought with another situation or phenomenon can be attributed to the category of linguistic features.

The linguist criticizes those who do not know the value of the word and says, "*Oner aldi—qizil til*" (Talent begins with eloquent speech). This proverb underestimates the art of the word. "*Maqal—soz atasi*" ("The proverb is the father of the word"). Proverbs are distinguished by the accuracy of the word, its compactness. Proverbs and sayings serve as proverbs of wisdom. In any of them there is a rhythm, harmony, music, and intonation that is characteristic of poetry (Adambayev 1996, 57).

Proverbs are a wonderful success of logical and imaginative thought, philosophical words born from experience. First of all, you need to look for the meaning of the word in the proverb. It contains ethical, philosophical, and collective content. The results of the proverb can never be refuted by the people. For example, B. Adambayev in "Folk Wisdom" says "the proverbs and sayings of each person are a logical formula, a rule created by the people themselves. It is remembered in the context of any event, problem, and returns to the language. Thus, it is possible to formulate the basic requirements of proverbs and sayings for behavioral culture, art, and literature, saying that it is easy to eat what is difficult, which requires a lot of thinking, a long story" (Adambayev 1996, 81).

Folk pedagogy is a science that has been formed and enriched over the centuries. Our people called it "*Maqal—sozdin munarasi*," transferred as

"The tower of speech is proverb," and gave such an assessment to one of the noble genres of folk oral literature. The tower is located at the height of the mind. The advantage of proverbs and sayings is that they compress thoughts, are expressive and touching in a few words, sharp and meaningful. The common people are the owner of proverbs and sayings that arise in a new way in accordance with the requirements of the new era, as well as the keeper of ancient, sorted, and beautiful gems (Aldasheva 1998, 97).

The proverb is said as *Maqal—sozdin atasi* ("The father of the word is a proverb") in Kazakh. It is in our hands to preserve the national heritage, which contributes to the growth of our consciousness, realizing the need for proverbs and sayings in life. If we grow up drinking in the proverbs and sayings of our native people, which are included in the principles of folk pedagogy, our fruits will be abundant and full.

Peculiarities of Proverbs and Sayings from the Point of Cognitive Linguistics

It is known that cognitive science has its origins in ancient times because cognition and reason, which are the object of cognitive science, are concepts whose relationship has been debated since ancient times. This means that the most important and fundamental problem of cognitive science is the classical problem—language and thinking.

According to L.S. Barkhudarov and Y.Y. Retsker, cognition of the environment with the help of names is only the lower stage of the cognitive structure, and the highest stage of this process is the ability to notice and understand the meaning. We can conclude that Plato's restriction of the cognitive function of language within such a framework is due to the formation of an approach to consider language from the point of view of a natural sign, rather than considering it as a symbolic sign in that era (Barkhudarov and Retsker 1968). According to Y.Y. Retsker, the relationship between thinking and language (the relationship between the origin of thought and the expression of words) have not lost their value even today (Retsker 1974, 32). Kazakh writer S. Muqanov (1980), in "The Field of Reasoning," explains that if we consider the Confucian teaching of China, to understand the meaning of a thing, only a return to its original ideological reality, to its "ideal" meaning, to its "correct" name, opens the way to the knowledge of this thing.

Q. Beysenov, in his "Trends in the Development of Thought on the Kazakh Soil in the 10th Century," which was the period of the Muslim renaissance, quotes Abu Hayan, who noted the importance of any element of the language and the close relationship between language and thinking. It can be seen in the works of scientists studying medieval works (Beysenov 1994).

We can say that the scientist's research has become a landmark for many researchers in this direction. The mental space of A.D. Shveitser (2003, 86) is caused by the connection of the cognitive approach with the problems of traditional logic-pragmatic.

E.S. Kubryakova, V.Z. Demyankov, Yu.G. Pankrats, L.G. Luzina concluded, "We know about structures and knowledge only thanks to the language, which allows us to relate to these structures and describe their love for the original language" (Kubryakova et al. 2006, 21).

In the history of the development of linguistics, three different paradigms have been identified. These are: comparative-historical, systematic-structural, and anthropocentric.

Y. Kengesbayev considers "a special method of studying the language is a comparative-historical method," characterized as the first paradigm of linguistics of the entire nineteenth century, in the twentieth century special attention was paid to the systematic-structural paradigm as a system of words. He names them as symbols. On the basis of his basic research, textbooks and academic grammars were written that determine the paradigm and syntagmatic relations, functions of the language at various levels and became the main ideas of many researchers (Kengesbayev 2006, 29). Also, as K.A. Jamanbaeva notes, deep inner needs are awakened by proverbs. This process is known to consciousness through emotion. Now, in order to satisfy his inner need, he again turns to the world of symbols. Thus, the nature of needs with a deep foundation is determined by symbols. That is, consciousness resolves its dependence on external factors or the need for internal growth and improvement by accumulating a certain model, form (Jamanbaeva 1998, 8).

In general, cognitive linguistics aims to explain the mechanism of assimilation and use of natural language and to create a corresponding model of it. For this purpose, cognitive categories are used. It combines language, psychological, and physiological information related to speech, such as intention, memory, memory, understanding, planning, and management.

The Importance of the Research

Interlinks between Language and Culture: Linguo-cultural and Ethnolinguistic Approach

In this chapter, we focus on cognitive and linguo-cultural studies to describe the national language. The power of the native language, both the speaker and the bearer of the ancient, intimate, and long-standing history of culture, is shown in the fact that each nation expresses its own way of life through language, the recognition of culture in another country through language; there is an inextricable link between language and culture.

It is important to note the history of the Kazakh people. The numbers associated with the numbers seven, twelve, nine (seven blue, seven universe, seven lovers, twelve members, nine parcels) are names born from the experience of everyday cultural life of the Kazakh people. They are intertwined with the meaning of folk names of time dimensions (twelve moments, days, two, birth of March, etc.). The study of the sources of the national language mentioned in the works of these authors can be attributed to the field of study of the subject of linguistic and cultural studies.

When studying the nature of the word, they were guided by the most important conclusions of the philosophy of language in explaining its nominative function. The number of patterns and images, meanings, and typical forms that are included in the cognitive image of a person increases. Therefore, the cognitive sphere of human activity depends on two categories:

- "intellectual higher categories" or a special combination of such concepts as knowledge, consciousness, thinking, intelligence, creativity, imagination, dreams, and symbols;
- referring to the categories of "everyday life," i.e. a chain of actions guided by the principles of practical action, memory, attention, recognition, and perception the main conclusions of cognitive linguistics are as follows:
    1. cognitive linguistics is the most important branch of linguistics.
    2. the relationship between language and cognition is a form of cognitive linguistics.
    3. language laws and cognitive principles manifest in human consciousness and memory.
    4. cognitive linguistics relates to other sciences.

Language reflects and colors the global picture of the world in the process of conceptualization and categorization of knowledge about the world through the mental manifestation of cognitive structures. The concept system or conceptual system is the main part of the conceptual, linguistic picture of the world, the rubricator. The relationship between language symbols and the phenomena of cultural and social reality depicted in them forms the content of cognitive semantics and methods of verbalization.

Thus, from the study of language and lexical units, cognitive linguistics goes beyond the territory of the language circle and connects with the problems of science on the general principles of individual cognitivism that govern mental processes in the human mind, as well as the subjects of lingua-cultural study, ethnolinguistics, psychology, and philosophy.

Conclusion

Proverbs and sayings are lexical units that reflect the history of the people, their social life, intelligence, and wisdom, and are characterized by accuracy and compactness of thought:

- ways of transfering English proverbs and sayings to the Kazakh language are studied on a cognitive, linguistic, and cultural basis.
- through proverbs and sayings, you can see the culture, consciousness, and traditions of the past life of the English people, which is one of the most important pieces of information for the translator.
- in the way of transfering proverbs and sayings in English, there are appropriate alternatives, explanations related to the thinking and consciousness of the Kazakh people.
- in the theory of translation, it is not enough to analyze the linguistic nature of proverbs and sayings on a cognitive and linguo-cultural basis, for their national features are revealed.
- a number of Kazakh and English proverbs and sayings have a mutual correspondence in terms of composition, structure, and meaning.

Today, the transference of proverbs and sayings in English into other languages is increasingly dominated by the anthropocentric paradigm in linguistics, as well as in many studies of individual linguistics. The main reason for this is that the anthropocentric principle in linguistics first puts the values of the nation that uses the language at the forefront. The anthropocentric paradigm opens up new areas within its framework, such as ethnolinguistics, linguocultural studies, cognitive linguistics, and lingua psychology.

While analyzing proverbs and sayings from the point of cognitive linguistics, our research aims at explaining the mechanism of assimilation and use of natural language and to create a corresponding model of it. Cognitive linguistics expands the understanding of ways and structures of information transmission and storage through language, and it allows us to solve a number of applied tasks related to machine translation, information and search, computer systems, and similar.

Bibliography

Abay ensiklopediyasy [Abai encyclopedia]. 1985. Almaty: Atamura.

Adambayev, B. 1996. *Agylshin jane Qazaq Maqal-matelderining Qurylymdyq jane Maginalyq Uqsastyqtary* [Structural and semantic similarities of English and Kazakh proverbs]. Almaty: Ana Tili.

Adambayev, B. 1999. *Halyq Danalygy* [Folk wisdom]. Almaty: Atamura.

Akkozin, M.1990. *Qazaq maqaldary* [Kazakh proverbs]. Almaty: Ana tili.

Aldasheva, A. 1998. *Awdarmatanw: Lingvistikalyq jane Lingvomadeni Maseleler* [Translation Studies: Linguistic and linguo-cultural issues]. Almaty: Arys.

Argingazina, Sh. B. 2004. *Agylshin jane qazaq tilderindegi etistikti frazeologizmderding leksika – semantikalyq sipaty* [Lexical and semantic nature of verb phraseology in English and Kazakh languages] Almaty.

Barkhudarov, L. S., and YA. Y. Retsker. 1968. *Kurs lektsiy po teorii perevoda* [Course of lectures on translation theory]. Moscow: Progress.

Beysenov, Q. 1994. *Qazaq topyragingda qalyptasqan gaqliyatty oy keshw urdisteri.* [Processes of rational thinking formed on Kazakh soil]. Almaty: Gylym.

Catford, J. A. 1965. *Linguistic Theory of Translation.* London: Oxford University Press. 103.

Draxe, T. 1612. *Bibliotheca Scholastica Instructissima or, a Treasure of Ancient Adagies, and Sententious Proverbes.* London.

Gabdullın, M. (1958) 1996. *Qazaq Halqınıŋ Ayız Ädebıyeti.* [Oral literature of the Kazakh people]. Reprint, Almaty: Sanat.

Gumbold, V. 1984. Fon. *Yzbrannyye trudy po yazykoznaniyu.* [Background. Selected works on linguistics]. Moscow: Progress.

Jamanbaeva, K. A. 1998. *Til qoldanysining lingvomadenitanymdyq negizderi: émociya, simvol lingvistikalyq sana.* [Linguocultural bases of language use: emotion, symbol, linguistic consciousness]. Almaty: Gylym.

Japaqov, S. 2003. *Epikalyq frazeologizmderding lingvomadenitanymdyq negizderi.* [Cognitive bases of epic phraseology]. Almaty: Ana tili.

Jusipova, R. B. 2003. *Agylshin jane qazaq tilderindegi maqal–matelderding sinonimdik maginasy.* [Synonymous meaning of proverbs in English and Kazakh languages]. Almaty: Ana Tili.

Kengesbayev, Y. 1946. *Qazaq tilining idiomdary men frazalary* [Idioms and phrases of the Kazakh language]. Almaty: Xalıq muğalimi.

Kengesbayev, Y. 2006. *Qazaq lingvistitka gylym joninde zerttewler.* [Origin of phraseology in English]. Almaty: Gylym.

Kopylenko, M. M., and Z. D. Popova. 1989. *Ocherki po obshchey frazeologii* [Essays on general phraseology]. Voronezh: Voronezh University.

Koller, W. A. 1990. "Linguistic Approach to Translation, Its Range and Limitations." In *Translation Theory in Scandinavia. Proceedings from the Scandinavian Symposium on Translation Theory (SSOTT) III: Oslo, 11–13 August 1988, Oslo.*

Kubryakova, E. S., V. Z. Demyankov, Yu. G. Pankrats, and L. G. Luzina. 1996. *Kratkiy slovar' kognitivnykh terminov* [A short dictionary of cognitive terms]. Moscow: Faculty of Philology, M.V. Lomonosov Moscow State University.

Kubryakova, E. S., V. Z. Demyankov, Yu. G. Pankrats, and L. G. Luzina. 2006. *Kratkiy slovar' kognitivnykh terminov* [A short dictionary of cognitive terms]. Moscow: Vysshaya shkola.

Kunin, A. V. 1970. *Angliyskaya frazeologiya* [English phraseology]. Moskva: Vysshaya Shkola.

Kunin, A. V. 1986. *Kurs frazeologii sovremennogo angliyskogo yazyka* [Course of phraseology of modern English]. Moscow: Vysshaya Shkola.

Levitskaya, T. R., and A. M. Fiterman. 1963. *Teoriya i praktika perevoda s angliyskogo yazyka na russkiy* [Theory and practice of translation from English into Russian]. Moscow: Progress.

Maslova, V. A. 2001. *Lingvokulturologiya* [Linguoculturology]. Moscow: Prosveshenie.

Maslova, V. A. 2004. *Lingvokulturologiya* [Linguoculturology]. Moscow: Academia.

Morozova L. A. 1973. *Khudozhestvennyye formy poslovits* [Literary forms of proverbs]. Moscow: Moscow University.

Muqanov, M. 1980. *Aqyl-oy oresi* [The field of the mind]. Almaty: Qazaqstan.

Nuryshev, S. 1959. *Qazaqting xalyq maqaldarining qalyptasw tarixy.* [History of the development of Kazakh folk proverbs]. Almaty: Atamura.

Permiakov, G. L. 1979. *Poslovitsy i pogovorki narodov Vostoka* [Proverbs and sayings of the peoples of the East]. Moscow: Nauka.

Qaidar, A. 1998. *Kazak tilinin ozekti masselerii* [Topical issues of Kazakh linguistics]. Almaty: Ana Tili. 304.

Retsker, YA. Y. 1974. *Teoriya perevoda i perevodcheskaya praktika* [Theory of translation and translation practice]. Moscow: Academia.

Sarsenbaev, R. 1998. *Maqal – matelderding awdarylwy* [Translation of proverbs]. Almaty: Atamura.

Satenova, S. K. 1997. *Kazakh tilindegi kos tagandy phraseologizmderdin tildik zhune poeticalyk tabigaty* [Linguistic and poetic nature of phraseological units in the Kazakh language]. Almaty: Gylym.

Shveitser, A. D. 2003. *Perevod i lngvistika* [Translation and Linguistics]. Moscow: Academia.

Smagulova, G. 2007. *Körkem mätin lingvistikası* [Linguistics of literary texts] Almaty: Gylym. 201.

Smith, L. P. 1990. *English Idioms.* London: Constable. 207.

Ysina, G. Y. 2008. *Stereotipy i natsionalnaya yazykovaya kartina mira* [Stereotypes and the national language picture of the worl]. Almaty: Gylym.

Yslam, A. 2004. *Ulttyq-madeni madeniet kontekstindegi duniening lingvistikalyq swreti* [Linguistic picture of the world in the context of national culture]. Almaty: Gylym.

Case Study of Teaching Paremiological Units in Digital Education

ROZA ZHUSSUPOVA
L.N. Gumilyov Eurasian National University, Nur-Sultan

AIZHULDYZ TOLEGEN
L.N. Gumilyov Eurasian National University, Nur-Sultan

Introduction

Since ancient times, parameliological unit have been commonly used in society. In ancient times, people did not have the opportunity to put their thoughts in written form, so they had to remember catchy sayings. Subsequently, PU as the lingua-culturological national standard was spread orally from generation to generation, and along these lines renamed as "paremia." PU (paremiological units) is the scientific term, whereas it is more commonly known as "proverbs and sayings."

Scientists in their own ways determine the circle of concepts that fall under the definition of paremia, and they put forward various grounds for their classification. Generally, the word paremia has two main meanings and two reading options: *paremia* or *parimiya*—an element of worship in the theological liturgy, an excerpt from the Holy Scriptures; paremias are read during the service. In philology, paremia is defined as a stable utterance, which is a holistic sentence of didactic content.

Paremiology studies the origin, development, and existence of paremies, such as proverbs, folk and weather sayings, and riddles. Attempts to establish a paremiological minimum have still been oriented by the concept of a set of proverbs that all members of society know, or an average adult is expected to know. Therefore, the concept of paremiological minimum has been in fact reduced to proverbs that an average adult is expected to be familiar with. Thus, the proper term used should be the proverbial minimum.

Regarding the origins of proverbs, Mieder (2004) states that proverbs, like riddles, jokes, or fairy tales, do not fall out of the sky, and neither are they products of a mythical soul of the folk. Instead, they are always coined by an individual either intentionally or unintentionally, as expressed in Lord John Russell's well-known one -line proverb definition that has taken on a proverbial status of sorts: "A proverb is the wit of one and the wisdom of many."

The origin and sources of English proverbs are diverse and are determined by the peculiarities of the historical dynamics of the English language, national specificity of British culture, and the results of contacts with other cultures in the world. According to their origin, English proverbs are traditionally divided into native and borrowed (mainly from Latin and French).

The first English PU were found in old chronicles and early English records. In fact, every nation has its collections of proverbs. Scholars stated that the process of collecting proverbs has significant practice. According to Mieder, "all over Europe, the sixteenth and seventeenth centuries are considered the Golden Age of the proverbs."

PU is like a code because it is a regulation that cannot be changed. The ideas and policies laid down in society are consolidated as truth. No one dares to violate these strong social norms. It is impossible to disagree with the value of paremias, the same as, it is impossible to ignore the law. PU controls reverence for centuries-old concepts of life. Such values are passed continuously from the older to the younger generation. PU are discussed in folklore studies as one of the divisions of oral folk literature, and in linguistics as a permanent syntax. English, Russian, and Kazakh linguists provided an infinite number of paremiological definitions in their languages.

In 1988, Baymahanova et al. published the first proverbial dictionary, entitled "English Proverbs and Sayings and Their Equivalents in Russian and Kazakh." PU are divided into 10 themes in this proverbial dictionary, along with their counterparts in the English, Russian, and Kazakh languages.

General proverbs in the Kazakh language are transmitted from generation to generation orally, so it is difficult to identify the exact date of origin. For example, for the fifteenth to nineteenth centuries, K. Omiraliev in his poetry showed that Kazakh songs occupied an important place in national oratory. In addition, he said that the genre of these oratory poems was close to the proverbial genre. From the second half of the nineteenth century, he began to collect oral proverbs and write them in newspapers, the first-person being Shokan Ualikhanov. In fact, the Kazakh PU entered the treasury of world culture because they reflected not only the identity and cultural heritage of the Kazakh people, but they had also absorbed the wisdom of centuries-old enrichment of cultural experience with other nations. In one of the Kazakh sayings, it was said that speech without proverbs was like food without salt. All Kazakh ancient manuscripts were characterized by richness in proverbs and sayings, the people always respecting the value and power of words. The legends described how the *biys* (speakers and connoisseurs of the word) solved conflicts between people by proclaiming just one phrase.

Paremias have been studied by different scientists—folklorists, ethnographers, and linguists. As Valerij M. Mokienko noted while in the twentieth century the main purpose of studying proverbs was to get to know "the spirit of nation," today there was more attention to purely linguistic characteristics of these units—their usage in spoken and written language, interaction with the folkloric fund of other nations, and problems of translation into other languages.

The cultural aspect of PU has important implications for developing learners' cultural and intercultural competence in SLA. Moreover, Intercultural Communicative Competence (ICC) was to be added as a distinct component to the kinds of competences involved in communicative competence (CC) and, hence, to the aims of language teaching. Furthermore, the ICC goals as stated by Byram et al. described acquiring ICC as well as linguistic competence, prepare learners for interaction with people of other cultures, enable them understand and accept people from other cultures as individuals with other distinctive perspectives, values, and behaviors and help them see that such interaction is an enriching experience. Therefore, the aim on the part of language learners was not to become native speakers but adequate intercultural speakers, who acted as mediators between two cultures, interpreting and understanding other perspectives. CC was related to cultural awareness as well as to metaphorical comprehension. A foreign language learner is culturally aware to communicate effectively. Mieder highlighted the importance of including proverbs that belonged to the paremiological minimum in SLA because they were "clearly a part of the cultural literacy of native speakers". Inclusion of proverbs also helped immigrants and tourists to interact with native English speakers more easily in America. Mieder argued, "Proverbs continue to be effective verbal devices and culturally literate persons, both native and foreign, must have a certain paremiological minimum at their disposal in order to participate in meaningful oral and written communication."

Thus, we asserted in this literature review that the speech of a speaker who used PU in multilingual intercultural communication becomes acute. It was considered that both PU structure and the content were useful in SLA, especially when it came to teaching and understanding culture, as proverbs conveyed the values and metaphors shared by a culture. Work with proverbs and sayings in the lessons helped to diversify the educational process and to make it brighter and more interesting.

Methodology

PU in Digital Teaching of English to Multilingual Students

Mobile Applications as an Effective Tool in Teaching Proverbs. In recent years, reference to mobile assisted language learning (MALL) was made to digital processing systems that promote active learning, information creation, research, and discovery on the part of learners, and enabled remote communication and data sharing to take place between teachers and learners via mobile phones. It was an extended notion of technology that acknowledges their advancement from pure knowledge processing mechanisms and clarified their function in classrooms as opposed to their broader application of schools and learning centers. MALL has become a foreground teaching and learning methodology that uses mobile phones/devices with some form of wireless connectivity.

In this part, the research on organization of learning with using mobile devices as a new educational technology was considered, the model for constructing such a learning method was analyzed, and the pros and cons of mobile learning were presented. Mobile applications were studied, and the degree of students' readiness for the introduction of this kind of training was analyzed. MALL was implemented in the following options:

1. Support for the traditional learning process
2. Full-volume mobile learning
3. Blended learning

Mobile devices were lighter in weight and smaller in size. Digital tools supported the educational process. In our study, we considered the possibilities of using mobile applications in teaching English, namely in PU teaching through digital tools as an effective technique. Some free apps were presented for learning proverbs digitally that were implemented during the English lessons with the students of third year. The Proverb digital applications were:

1. English Proverbs Pro
2. Russian English Proverbs Dictionary
3. English Proverbs and Meanings
4. English Idioms, Phrases and Proverbs
5. English Proverbs

6. Proverbs and Meanings English
7. English Proverbs—A fun Game
8. Proverbs Fun Quiz

These free apps helped learning of English proverbs because they have a vast collection of proverbs with descriptions/meanings. Some apps practice English in an entertaining and simple way that are designed as games/quizzes and completely developed by educators to help students solve obstacles while learning English. They are challenging for all, with more than 1,000 sayings/proverbs for various language proficiency.

As a result of researching applications, we applied some of them practically in different modes, we used the dictionary of proverbs as a translation to find the equivalents, and we used the game form to practice the proverbs.

Over the past years, we have not only heard about MALL but also actively understood it and worked on it. Therefore, we decided to additionally conduct a SWOT analysis of the use of mobile applications. It is shown in Table 12.1 below:

Teachers used them in the classroom for developing students' vocabulary skills, listening comprehension, linguo-cultural and speaking abilities. Mobile applications were very effective in incorporating effective critical thinking

Table 12.1. Mobile learning apps SWOT analysis.

Strengths	Enhances student motivation	Weaknesses	Implementation is still incomplete
	Flexibility of learning		Needs internet connectivity
	Makes learning fun		Addictiveness of mobile apps
	Easy access to accurate educational tools		Limited access due to technical restrictions
Opportunities	Supports the educational process	Threats	It is not clear if the usage of apps will consistently be a productive part of the education process
	Enhances student digital literacy		Chaotic environment—a lot of new applications of various quality
	No time and location restrictions		
	Improve teaching/ learning skills		Lack of live communication

skills of learners. Therefore, we strongly recommended using smartphones as frequently as possible.

Procedure

The Practical Implementation of Using Applications in PU Teaching. This review intends to examine whether and how PU were used in Kazakhstani education as part of English teaching. In addition, views of students and teachers were sought, and teaching aids examined in order to reveal the situation regarding proverb teaching in English language classrooms.

Due to the limited number of proverb studies in the classroom in our country, we developed a questionnaire in accordance with the studies of Turkish scholars for future English teachers, with some questions being adapted from Hanzén. The questionnaire was structured to assess students' attitudes about learning/teaching English proverbs, their opinions regarding their understanding of proverbs and perceptions of the degree to which they had English teachers and used course books.

The participants of the experimental teaching were university students studying English as a foreign language and English teachers. We designed a questionnaire for both students and teachers. The Questionnaire for students consisted of two sections. The first section covered the general student point of view on proverbs and their usage thereafter to both observe certain activities on proverbs and obtain questionnaires to figure out what had been changed. The next part was aimed at testing how their teachers used and learned proverbs during lessons. Survey's purpose was to find out whether teachers used proverbs in their teaching, which ones they perceived useful for teaching, and how they used them. To find out what attitudes there were toward using proverbs, a written questionnaire was chosen.

Questionnaire to English Teachers. In the survey took part 15 English teachers, 12 of which were upper secondary schools and three were university teachers. The questionnaire contained three questions aimed to check how they dealt with proverbs and also included questions such as:

1. ***Do you agree that learning English proverbs is an important part of the English language learning experience?***
   A. Strongly Agree
   B. Agree
   C. Neutral
   D. Disagree
   E. Strongly Disagree

Table 12.2. Importance of PU learning.

ITEM	Strongly Agree		Agree		Neutral		Disagree		Strongly disagree	
	N	%	N	%	N	%	N	%	N	%
1	3	20	10	67	2	13	0	0	0	0

The first question referred to the significance of studying English proverbs for learning in the English language and for good communication in general.

Table 12.2 shows that most of the respondents of the survey agree (67%), and (20%) strongly agree, but 13% of teachers were neutral. The results indicate that educators say that PU learning was an essential part of their learning experience and was required for successful communication in the target language. Usually, teachers tried to use various teaching aids during their classes, except for textbooks.

2. What kinds of teaching materials do you use to teach PU?
- Dictionary
- Proverb Lists
- Worksheet on Proverbs
- Texts
- Mobile applications
- Materials from everyday life

You can see these different types of teaching materials represented in the piec chart in Figure 12.1.

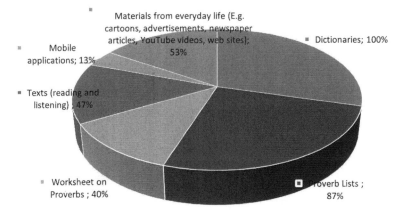

Figure 12.1. Teaching materials.

3. How do you deal with PU that you find in the textbook?
- Explain it
- Compare with Kazakh equivalent
- Discuss the meaning
- Discuss metaphorical use
- Discuss cultural issues concerning the proverb
- Discuss the communicative use of the proverb
- Work with a theme around the proverb
- I do not deal with it I have not noticed any and therefore I do not deal with it
- Anything else (clarify):_____

The most chosen alternatives about how to interact with PU contained in the textbook, seen in Figure 12.2, were the first three: compare it to the Kazakh or Russian equivalent, focus on the topic of the proverb, and analyze the meaning. No respondent chose "I have not found all of them, but I don't bother with them." Ten teachers examined the usage of culture, then analyzed the meaning and clarified it. Eight teachers chose the communicative application of proverbs, and another eight said that they discussed the metaphorical use.

In the following survey 39 students participated. The questionnaire contained three questions aimed to identify students' perceptions as they taught several proverbs. Students' survey consisted of two parts: the first designed to test knowledge of proverbs and the use of mobile applications; the second

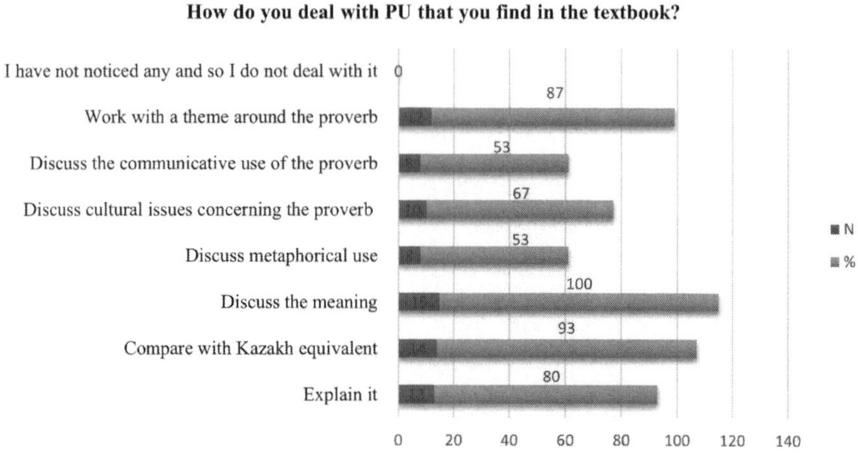

How do you deal with PU that you find in the textbook?

Figure 12.2. Ways of dealing with proverbs in teaching.

part, how their teachers' taught sayings and in what situations they used proverbs, whether they included activities to teach proverbs and strengthen knowledge about them.

Students' Survey

1. *My English teachers at high school taught sufficient English proverbs.*
   A. Strongly Agree
   B. Agree
   C. Neutral
   D. Disagree
   E. Strongly Disagree

As you can see in Table 12.3, the answers to the first question in the item showed that many respondents (44%) did not believe that their English teachers taught enough English proverbs.

2. *My English teachers at high school used to employ English proverbs in the teaching of* _____
   A. Grammar
   B. Vocabulary
   C. Pronunciation
   D. Writing
   E. Culture

According to Table 12.4, outcomes of the survey demonstrate that almost all the participants answered that teachers use proverbs to teach vocabulary (23%), and (18%) of them believe that they used sayings to write essays. However, most of the respondents (26%) found it acceptable to stay outside the poll. As we saw, the usage of proverbs in grammar and pronunciation training was at a low level. Therefore, this study required further empirical

Table 12.3. Sufficiency of teaching English proverbs by teachers at high school.

	Strongly Agree			Agree		Neutral		Disagree		Strongly disagree	
ITEM	N	%		N	%	N	%	N	%	N	%
1	4	10		6	15,4	12	30,8	10	26	7	18

Table 12.4. The use of proverbs in teaching different language skills.

	Grammar		Vocabulary		Pronunciation		Writing skills		Culture teaching		Abstained	
ITEM	N	%	N	%	N	%	N	%	N	%	N	%
1	3	8	9	23	2	5	7	18	8	21	10	26

experiments to test the role of PU training in the development of language skills and components.

3. What teaching materials other than coursebooks did your English teachers employ to teach English proverbs?
   - Dictionary
   - Proverb Lists
   - Worksheet on Proverbs
   - Texts
   - Mobile applications
   - Materials from everyday life
   - Others (clarify)_____

The findings of the survey are presented in pie chart in Figure 12.3. Teachers used supplementary resources other than textbooks to teach proverbs in their classes. Among the additional materials used, materials from real life

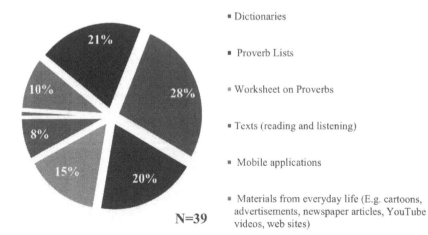

Figure 12.3. Teaching materials used in the study of proverbs.

(26%), worksheets (39%), texts (21%), and dictionaries (72%) were indicated by the students to have been the mostly used ones. However, (54%) of the participants responded that their instructors did not deal with proverbs, that they are usually overlooked. Only one of the students (3%) reported that his or her English teacher used mobile applications. The result of the third question confirmed that teaching proverbs digitally was not popular among our teachers. Therefore, we investigated different apps, discussed their advantages and disadvantages, and created a SWOT analysis of the smartphone applications.

Taking online polls was a simple way to ask respondents for instant feedback on just about anything. This survey was conducted through the application Survey Monkey poll in real time. Once the data had been collected, Survey Monkey used its several reporting features to process the data to provide an in-depth analysis.

To determine the use of educational digital applications in PU teaching by students we conducted another brief questionnaire.

Results of the questionnaire regarding proverbs with 39 university students are seen below in Figures 12.4 and 12.5.

The results of a survey on the impact of using a mobile app on learning showed that students prefer to use mobile apps. As we see, 87 (8%) of the

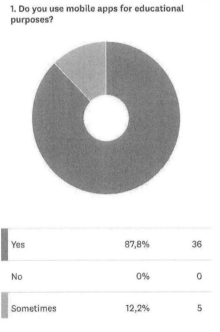

1. Do you use mobile apps for educational purposes?

Yes	87,8%	36
No	0%	0
Sometimes	12,2%	5

Figure 12.4. Usage of mobile applications.

**2. Do you find it convenient to use mobile
applications? (Are there any disadvantages?)**

Yes	95,12%	39
No	0%	0
Other (clarify)	4,88%	2

Figure 12.5. Impact of the app on students.

**4. What categories of educational
applications are you interested in?**

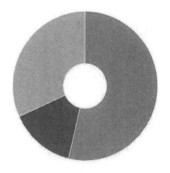

For learning vocabulary	53,66%	22
To study grammar	14,63%	6
For learning proverbs, idioms and phrases	31,71%	13

Figure 12.6. Student preference of educational applications.

students always used applications for educational purposes, and only 12 (2%) of them used it sometimes. Almost 95% of the participants described it as convenient, but approximately (5%) two students thought that they had some cons. The cons were that it took up a lot of memory in the phone and that some apps were paid, while the student had no financial support or opportunity to pay in order to use the whole content offline.

Figure 12.6 displays the students' choice for educational applications.

The majority of the learners, 53 (7%) used apps for learning vocabulary, 14 (6%) studied grammar rules, and 32% chose them for learning proverbs, idioms, and phrases.

Through various surveys and experiments, we concluded that students preferred to study and use PU in their speech. Also, teachers tried to use different materials. The study of proverbs in digital format was not developed yet.

The Results of Experimental PU Digitally Teaching

In this part, the methods for data collection are presented which describe the pilot experiments carried out in the construction of the instruments. The methods for collecting and processing data are provided.

The target audience for this study was forty-one pre-service English teachers. They all were full-time third-year students at university. Experiment lasted from September till December 2019, and classes were held regularly. All students used smartphones with a special mobile app tailored to their needs as a supporting tool during the whole semester. Twenty-three students served as a control group.

The findings of the need analysis showed that the biggest weakness of the students was studying English PU and identifying their correct parallels in both Russian and Kazakh. Therefore, the lesson material included physically completed proverbs and sayings, and the learners were required to identify the meaning of the proverbs and find their equivalents in native language. Each lesson was given as a test, and on average it consisted of ten new proverbs on each subject.

After the following tasks were given for conducting the pre- and post-tests.

Task 1. Complete the following proverbs

1. Екі ..... бір оқпен атып өлтіру.
   To kill two birds with one stone
2. Туған жердей жер болмас, ...
   There is no place like home.

3. Көзден кетсе, ...
Out of sight out of mind.

4. Ерте тұрған жігіттің ырысы артық, ...
The early bird catches the worm.

5. Өзге елде сұлтан болғанша, ...
It is better to be the sole of the shoe to your own birthplace, rather than the sultan of another place.

6. Еңбек етсең ерінбей, ...
No song, no supper.

7. Жел тұрмаса, ...
There is no smoke without fire.

8. Басы қатты болса, ...
All is well that ends well.

9. Бір қарын майды ... ...
One drop of poison spoils the whole tun of wine.

10. Досына қарап, ...
A man is known by the company he keeps.

Task 2. Give the equivalents of the proverbs in Russian or Kazakh

1. Every country has its customs.
   Answer: Әр елдің салты басқа, иттері қара қасқа.
   Answer: Сколько стран, столько обычаев.

2. Appearances are deceptive—never judge from appearance.
   Сырты жалтырауықтың іші қалтырауық.
   Наружность обманчива.

3. Every cook praises his own broth.
   Сиыр баласын торпағым дер, қарға баласын аппағым дер.
   Всяк кулик своё болото хвалит

4. A friend in court is better than a penny in a purse.
   Жүз сомың болғанша, жүз досың болсын.
   Не имей сто рублей, а имей сто друзей.

5. Walls have ears.
   Үй артында кісі бар
   У стен есть уши

6. Many hands make light work.
   Жұмыла көтерген жүк жеңіл
   В коллективе работа спорится

7. No sweet without (some) sweat.
   Әрекет болмай — берекет жоқ.
   Без труда не выловишь и рыбку из пруда.

8. Measure thrice and cut once.
   Жеті рет өлшеп, бір рет кес
   Семь раз отмерь, один раз отрежь.
9. Better late than never.
   Ештен кеш жақсы
   Лучше поздно чем никогда
10. Never put off till tomorrow what you can do today.
    Бүгін бітер істі ертеңге қалдырма
    Не откладывай на завтра то, что можно сделать сегодня

In this study, three instruments were used. They included pre-test, diagnosis, and post-test materials. Pre-test was one of the methods used in the experimental study. In preliminary testing, selected PU were tested before completing the study to make sure students were familiar with such vocabulary points. Equivalents of PU that were intended for use in the study were given to students in previous classes. Fifteen proverbs with their equivalents were chosen from the book by Ahmetova. A sample of the tasks were presented above in Tasks 1, 2. In addition, the results of two groups were examined to see how much application-based learning was successful in learning PU. The results are presented in Tables 12.5 and 12.6.

As can be seen from Table 12.5, the experimental (EG) and control group (CG) had almost similar results in preliminary testing since there was a difference in the number of respondents. The same result was almost found between two groups when they tried to continue the PU. The number of participants who could not find PU equal continuation too, but CG students suggested more options.

As Table 12.6 shows, according to the post-test analysis, the EG = 88% got a higher percentage than the CG = 76, 5%. Compared with the pretest results, most of the respondents could show a good result. The number of students who did not answer at all significantly decreased in EG = 5%, but CG =11%. The same result was found among the respondents in both groups who could not find the proverbial parallels. The variations between EG and CG were meaningful, based on the descriptive statistics in the Table 12.6. This can be explained by the fact that, during practical experiments, the research group practiced proverbs using proverbial smartphone apps.

The average percentage of pre- and post- tests for each of the groups are illustrated graphically in Figure 12.7.

The post-test findings show that most students who did not use the software to practice during normal classes had performed poorly, even though they had the ability to review such points discussed and written down during

Table 12.5. Analysis of the pre-test.

Group	Test Pre-test	Questions	Respondent continued proverbs N	%	The respondent could not find the continuation of the proverbs N	%	Suggested another option N	%
Experimental group N=19								
1	17	89,5	2	10,5	0	0	2	16
84	2	10,5	1	5,3	3	15	78,9	3
15,8	1	5,3	4	17	89,5	2	10,5	0
0	5	16	84	2	10,5	1	5,3	6
18	94,7	0	0	1	5,3	7	17	89,5
2	10,5	0	0	8	16	84	3	15,8
2	10,5	9	13	68	5	26	1	5,3
10	14	73,7	3	15,8	2	10,5	Results	
	159	83%	24	12%	9	5%	Control group N=23	Pre-test
1	18	78	3	13	2	8,7		
2	18	78	2	8,7	3	13		
3	16	69,6	3	13	4	17,4		
4	19	82,6	2	8,7	2	8,7		
5	20	87	1	4	2	8,7		
6	17	74	4	17,4	2	8,7		
7	13	56,5	5	21,7	5	21,7		
8	15	65	5	21,7	3	13		
9	16	69,6	3	13	4	17,4		
10	19	82,6	0	0	4	17,4	Results	
	171	74%	28	12,5%	31	13,5%		

Table 12.6. Analysis of the post-test.

Group	Test		The respondent was able to find the equivalent of proverbs		The respondent could not find the equivalent of the proverbs		Did not answer at all	
	Post-test	Questions	N	%	N	%	N	%
Experimental group N=19								
1	18	94,7	1	5,3	0	0	2	17
89,5	2	10,5	0	0	3	16	84	2
10,5	1	5,3	4	16	84	2	10,5	1
5,3	5	17	89,5	2	10,5	0	0	6
18	94,7	0	0	1	5,3	7	15	78,9
3	15,8	1	5,3	8	16	84	3	15,8
0	0	9	16	84	2	10,5	1	5,3
10	18	94,7	1	5,3	0	0		
Results	**167**	**88%**	**18**	**9,5%**	**5**	**2,5%**		
Control group N=23	Post-test							
1	18	78	3	13	2	8,7		
2	18	78	2	8,7	3	13		
3	17	74	4	17,4	2	8,7		
4	19	83	2	8,7	2	8,7		
5	20	87	1	4	2	8,7		
6	17	74	4	17,4	2	8,7		
7	16	69,6	4	17,4	3	13		
8	15	65	5	21,7	3	13		
9	16	69,6	3	13	4	17,4		
10	18	78	1	4	3	13		
Results	**174**	**76,5%**	**29**	**12,5%**	**26**	**11%**		

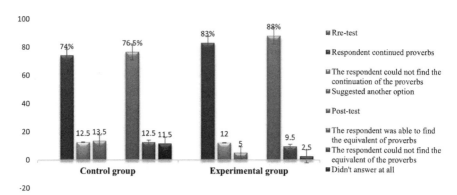

Figure 12.7. The average percentage of pre- and post-tests.

classes in face-to-face lectures of their own. Nevertheless, the notifications were not provided to encourage them to review them, and so they had less chances to introduce themselves to the target language. Statistical analysis, as well, confirmed the results. On average, the students who used *English Proverbs Pro, Russian English Proverbs Dictionary,* or *Proverbs and Sayings Master (Pro)* hit 88%, and the students in CG reached 76%. This indicates that using a mobile application as an aid to teach PU was more effective than a traditional teaching method.

To sum up, the results demonstrated that studying foreign languages with the application was successful in growing university students' academic success. In general, students believed that a mobile application better influenced their knowledge.

Conclusion

To summarize the work done, the case study was devoted to the linguistic and cultural studies of English/Kazakh/Russian paremias and their use in digital format. Using digital technology in proverbs study was the best way to save the teacher's time and encourage students. The purpose of the study was depicted in conducting experimental teaching. The following objectives of the work were done:

- PU examples were gathered in electronic format.
- The PU role in language and culture has been analyzed.

- Peculiarities of using applications in PU teaching and learning were revealed.
- A PU comparative analysis in three genetically unrelated and culturally diverse languages—Kazakh/Russian/English—were conducted.
- The implementation of English/Kazakh/Russian PU in digital learning were examined and experimentally tested.

Different methods were used during the research. First, descriptive theoretical literature analysis was employed to review numerous issues concerning features of PU. Second, comparative analysis was used to compare English proverbs with their equivalents in Kazakh/Russian. Further, a contrastive method was applied to demonstrate semantic contradictions of paremiological types. Statistical method was used to analyze the attitudes towards learning and teaching PU through applications. The questionnaires were evaluated using descriptive statistics for the evaluation of the results. More than ever, the role of educational technologies in learning is of great importance. Recommendations were given for further detailed research focusing on proverbs in English teaching.

To conclude, in this study, we attempted to provide a summary of MALL value and usage in PU teaching in a multilingual classroom. This work discussed how teachers used PU to keep students engaged in English learning. First, teachers were motivated to use digital resources because the use of educational technology in PU teaching provided better interaction with students and information reception because the students received knowledge visually, audibly, and kinesthetically.

In further perspective of this research, it is important to review PU in ELT from various digital technologies, as well as expanding creating websites, mobile apps to the Apple platform, iOS, with activities for PU teaching.

Bibliography

Aasland, E. 2018. "Contrasting Two Kazakh Proverbial Calls to Action: Using Discourse Ecologies to Understand Proverb Meaning–making." *Proverbium: Yearbook of International Proverb Scholarship* 35: 1–14.

Adnan, Zaid. 2016. "Using Proverbs as a Lead-in Activity in Teaching English as a Foreign Language." *International Journal on Studies in English Language and Literature (IJSELL)* 4(10): 1–5.

Ahmetova, S. G. 2017. *Paremiological Dictionary. English Proverbs and Their Equivalents in Russian and Kazakh.* Almaty: Lingua.

Byram, M., B. Gribkova, and H. Starkey. 2002. *Developing the Intercultural Dimension in Language Teaching: A Practical Introduction for Teachers*. Strasbourg: Council of Europe.

Hanzén, M. 2007. Thesis. "When in Rome, do as the Romans do": Proverbs as a part of EFL teaching. *Högskolan För Larande Och Kommunikation (HLK)* 36: 1–24.

Hrisztova-Gotthardt, H., and M. A. Varga. 2015. *Introduction to Paremiology: A Comprehensive Guide to Proverb Studies*. Berlin: De Gruyter.

Ivanov, E. E., and Yu. A. Petrushevskaya. 2015. *English Proverbs: From Literary Texts, in Literary Texts; Etymology, Usage, Variability; Teaching Materials*. Mogilev: Moscow State University named after A. A. Kuleshova.

Jabu, M. 2016. "Exploring the Role of Teaching Using Folklore in Developing Grade R Learners' Mother Tongue." *Stud Tribes Tribals. Kamla-Raj* 14(2): 129–37.

Klimova, B. 2019. "Impact of Mobile Learning on Students' Achievement Results." *Education Sciences* 9(2): 2–12.

Kulkenov, M. 2012. *Kazakh Anthology of Proverbs*. Almaty: Ölke.

Lazar, Stošić. 2015. "The Importance of Educational Technology in Teaching." *International Journal of Cognitive Research in Science, Engineering and Education* 31(1): 111–113.

Mieder, W. 1993. *Proverbs Are Never out of Season: Popular Wisdom in the Modern Age*. New York: Oxford University Press.

Mieder, W. 1996. "Proverbs." In *American Folklore: An Encyclopedia*, edited by J. H. Brunvand, 597–600. New York: Garland.

Mieder, W. 2004. *Proverbs: A Handbook*. Westport, CT: Greenwood.

Mohammad, J. R., and B. Elham. 2014. "The Effect of Proverbs on Learning Vocabulary through Visual Organizers." *International Journal of English Language Teaching* 2(4): 11–20.

Mokienko, V. M., T. G. Nikitina, and E. K. Nikolaeva. 2010. *Bolshoy slovar' russkikh poslovits* [Big dictionary of Russian sayings]. Moscow: Olma.

Stæhr, L. S. 2008. "Vocabulary Size and the Skills of Listening, Reading, and Writing." *Language Learning Journal* 36: 139–52.

Syzdykov, K. 2014. "Contrastive Studies on Proverbs." *Procedia-Social and Behavioral Sciences* 136: 318–21.

Zhulduz, R., D. Zhankara, and N. L. B. H. Ali. 2019. "Various Aspects of Paremiological Units." *PEOPLE: International Journal of Social Sciences* 4(3): 985–96.

Part II The Anti-proverbs of the Kazakh Language

In recent years, the study of the modification and transformation of proverbs has become one of the most important issues in world linguistics. Since it is the result of a living process arising from the usual and accidental use of a proverb, change is therefore in the very nature of the proverb.

Qaidar argues that in paremiology, variability is inherent in the nature of proverbs, and states: "Variability is not a strictly notorious phenomenon, but a living phenomenon suitable for use in any area of language, if necessary, adaptable to change and flexible formulations. "(2004, 107–108).

In the press and the world of the Internet, due to the skill of the addresser, there are often cases in the Kazakh language when proverbs are changed. For example, a proverb may be based on a traditional proverb while retaining its structural characteristics, such as *"ül ösirme, qyz ösir, qalyŋmaly onyŋ köl-kösir"* (Do not bring up a boy, bring up a girl; you will get the money for the bride); this new creation adopts the structure of the famous proverb, *"mal ösirseŋ—qoi ösir, önimi önyŋ köl-kəsir"* (If you raise livestock, raise sheep; it is profitable). The form of the new proverb is grammatically and lexically modified through the replacement of two words, and its meaning revives traditions in modern Kazakhstani society, which shows the importance of the tradition of daughter's farewell, welcoming the bride, and "money given for bride." Hence, we understand the pragmatic function of modern proverbs as an irreplaceable literary tool in describing the life of a nation.

Thus, the anti-proverb is a new creation that arises from the surrounding social context, is based on a well-known proverb that already exists in the language, gives new meaning to the linguistic structure of the sentence, and makes it completely understandable and practical for the reader (Reznikov, 2009). In general, though the phenomenon of a change in the Kazakh proverb took place in the language, they were not called anti-proverbs based on the experience of world proverbs . In this work, we use the term for the first time in

Kazakh scholarship and include examples from Kazakh journalism and online. Our collection includes about 100 anti-proverbs and pseudo-anti proverbs that served as a starting point for modern variations of the Kazakh language.

New paremiological units (anti-proverbs) of the Kazakh language are created in different ways; some are created in accordance with traditional paremiological models and are very interesting material for cognitive-discourse analysis. They are free units with their own meaning regardless of context. Despite the fact that it consists of elements of the usual proverb, anti-proverbs explain a different idea with new content from traditional proverbs (62;65;67;72;78;90). Some new formations are created by changing the composition of the proverbs. This type of modification helps to attract the attention of the addressee, since the author, modifying the composition of the paremia, explicates a more significant component and focuses on the information contained in this component (9;16;25;51;61). The next group of anti-proverbs are created by contamination, the formation of a new word or stable phrase because of the crossing of two different proverbs or expressions, and this phenomenon of contamination is often used by authors to create a comic effect or a pun (3;38; 45;49; 80; 86), replacing proverb components with variant words, mainly with synonyms. There are two types of synonyms: stylistic (1;2;52;55;56) and contextual (42–2;46;48;60). The anti-proverb is coined by means of polysemy (32). Reception of "phonetic mimicry" is a sound assimilation of a word or its transformed version to other words. This technique is based on a partial morpho-phonetic transformation of the component, leading to a complete change in the semantics of the component and the entire proverb (24;33;37;62;65). Another type of stylistic device, based on wordplay in a metaphorical and literal sense, that is used in this corpus is called wellerisms. They make fun of established cliches and proverbs, showing that they are wrong in certain situations, often if taken literally. In this sense, a wellerism that includes proverbs is a type of anti-proverb. Wellerism usually consists of three parts: a proverb or saying, a speaker, and often a literal explanation with humor (96;100).

The following list of Kazakh anti-proverbs is organized according to the order of the Cyrillic alphabet. Here is the structure of each entry:

Traditional Proverb
- English translation
- Meaning, literal and/or figurative
- English equivalent if there is one

Anti-proverb #1
   English translation:
   Brief description of the context that will explain to readers its usage

* Language mechanism(s) used in creating this anti-proverb
* URL address of the publication from where the quote is taken

Anti-proverb #2, etc.

Bibliography

Qaidar, A. 2004. *Khalyq danalygy.* [Folk wisdom]. Almaty: Toganay T. 560 p.
Reznikov, A. 2009. *Old Wine in New Bottles: Modern Russian Anti-Proverbs.* Burlington: University of Vermont.

1. *Traditional proverb: Адам аласы ішінде, мал аласы сыртында.*
   · English translation: quality in a person inside and in an animal outside.
   · Meaning, literal and/or figurative: This proverb explains that you cannot be deceived by appearance without being sure of inner essence (i.e., the nature of a person cannot be determined by appearance).
   · English equivalent if there is one: Appearances are deceptive.
   Anti-proverb: Адам аласы ішінде, мал аласы тысында.
   · English translation: A person's bad intention is inside, and an animal's color is outside.
   · Brief description of the context that will explain to readers its usage: The evil of man is invisible to the eye, and the color of the beast is visible from the outside.
   · Language mechanisms used in creating anti proverbs: Replacing proverb components with stylistic synonyms.
   · URL: https://tengrinews.kz/kazakhstan_news/nege-makal-mateldn-jartyisyin-gana-aytyip-jurmz-386191/
2. *Traditional proverb: Ағаға қарап іні өсер.*
   · English translation: Observing the older brother the younger grows.
   · Meaning, literal and/or figurative: (1) Usually, a child is inclined to repeat the actions and words of an older adult. This is because he is trying to imitate the actions of the people around him; (2) if we want the next generation to be polite, moral, and cultured, this means that the previous generation of brothers, parents.

Anti-proverb: Ағаны көріп іні өсер.

- English translation: The little brother grows looking at the eldest brother.
- Brief description of the context that will explain to readers its usage: I think we grew up emulating Abeken's passion for art, writing, his polite demeanor, his humility in his pursuit of the well-being of adults and children, and even his politeness in choosing and wearing fashionable clothes.
- Language mechanisms used in creating anti proverbs: Replacing proverb components with stylistic synonyms.
- URL: https://aqjolgazet.kz/27716/tostikbajdyn-tyyagy-esse/aleu met/

3. *Traditional proverb: Ағайын тату болса, ат көп, абысын тату болса, ас көп, төртеу түгел болса төбедегі келер.*
   - English translation: If brothers get along—there is large livestock if daughters-in-law get along—there is much food.
   - Meaning, literal and/or figurative: Means peace and respect among relatives.

Anti-proverb: Ел мен ел тату болса, төбедегіні келтірер.

- English translation: If people live in peace, everything will be possible.
- Brief description of the context that will explain to readers its usage: If there is peace among people, then there would be unity and there would not be the border.
- Language Mechanisms Used in Creating anti-proverbs: The proverb is based on the phenomenon of contamination. It expands the content of the context by combining two different proverbs and adapting them to an ellipse.
- URL: The newspaper "Altyn Orda," 16.07.2000.

4. *Traditional proverb: Ағаш көркі—жапырақ, адам көркі—шүберек.*
   - English translation: Leaves decorate a tree; clothes decorate the person.
   - Meaning, literal and/or figurative: A person looks good in outerwear, attractive clothes attract attention.
   - English equivalent if there is one: —Clothing makes the man.

Anti-proverb: Ағаш көркі—жеміс, адам көркі—жақсы іс.

- English translation: The beauty of a tree is a fruit, the beauty of a man is a good deed
- Brief description of the context that will explain to readers its usage: The proverb explains that a person is beautiful when relatives,

friends, and good people surround him. Unity and peace are considered good deeds.

- Language mechanisms used in creating anti-proverbs: New lexical content of the same syntactic structure.
- URL: https://tengrinews.kz/kazakhstan_news/nege-makal-mateldn-jartyisyin-gana-aytyip-jurmz-386191/

5. *Traditional proverb: Ажалы жеткен тышқан мысықтың ернін тартып жатады.*
   - English translation: The dying mouse tugs at the cat's lips.
   - Meaning, literal and/or figurative: A proverb is used to say that a person should try to the last, even if this is already the end.

Anti-proverb: Ажалы жеткен тышқан мысықтың үстіне секіреді.
   - English translation: The dying mouse jumps on the cat.
   - Brief description of the context that will explain to readers its usage: When danger threatens, then a person can start an attack, aggression first.
   - Language mechanisms used in creating anti-proverbs: Replacing proverb components with contextual synonyms.
   - URL: https://tengrinews.kz/kazakhstan_news/nege-makal-mateldn-jartyisyin-gana-aytyip-jurmz-386191/

6. *Traditional proverb: Айдағаны бес ешкі, ысқырығы жер жарады.*
   - English translation: Only five goats are chasing, and whistle so that the earth cracks.
   - A proverb that has arisen among pastoralists is used when it is necessary to show people's actions the disproportion and inconsistency with their result. For a Kazakh cattle breeder, it seems absurd for a small number of goats to make a big noise; therefore, the shepherd's action in a figurative sense is interpreted as any absurd bragging. Despite its narrow professional origin, the proverb does not limit the lexicon of pastoralists but is widely used and has structural stability. It has a tinge of sarcasm and is used to express the irony created by the enhanced contrast of external meaning and subtext.
   - English equivalent, if there is one: Great boast, small roast.

Anti-proverb: Айдағаны бес ешкі, желілерде ысқырығы жер жарады.
   - English translation: Only five goats are chasing, and one whistle so that the network cracks.
   - Brief description of the context that will explain to readers its usage: He brags about his little things as if he is doing great things on a global scale. One makes such a noise over his affairs and prevents people from living calmly and measuredly.

- Language Mechanisms Used in Creating anti-proverbs: The syntactic structure of the traditional proverb is extended.
- URL: https://vk.com/wall348809512_603

7. *Traditional proverb: Айран ішкен құталар, аяқ жалаған тұтылар.*
   - English translation: Those who secretly drink sour milk will escape, those who drink remaining will be accountable for that.
   - Meaning, literal and/or figurative: This proverb means that innocent people are usually punished.
   - English equivalent, if there is one: The little thieves are hanged, but great one's escape.

Anti-proverb: Айран ішкен құтылып, шелек жалаған тұтылады.
   - English translation: Those who secretly drank sour milk escaped, those who liked the bucket with remaining were caught.
   - Brief description of the context that will explain to readers its usage: In life there are situations when people who secretly drank sour milk could escape, those who licked the bucket were caught, mostly it happens in corrupt countries. Sad to say that is also happening in our country.
   - Language mechanisms used in creating anti-proverbs: Replacing proverb components with stylistic synonyms.
   - URL: https://martebe.kz/anatty-s-z-azyna/

8. *Traditional proverb: Ақ иілін бүгілмес*
   - English translation: White does not bend.
   - Meaning, literal and/or figurative: A pure person does not bow his head, bend, or bow down in front of anyone.
   - English cognate, if there is one: *Better bend than break.*

Anti-proverb: Ақ иілін сынбайды.
   - English translation: White does not break.
   - Brief description of the context that will explain to readers its usage: This anti-proverb posits that the innocent person does not give up - no evil can break an honest person. Therefore, he does not lose face in front of anyone.
   - Language mechanisms used in creating anti-proverbs: Replacing proverb components with stylistic synonyms.
   - URL: https://bilim-all.kz/quote/13615

9. *Аққуды атпа, досыңды сатпа.*
   - English translation: Don't shoot the swan, and don't betray a friend.
   - Meaning, literal and/or figurative: In Kazakh upbringing, a swan cannot be killed, it teaches to be faithful to friendship.

Anti-proverb: Аққуды атпа, сотталасың.

- English translation: Don't shoot a swan, you'll be convicted.
- Brief description of the context that will explain to readers its usage: a swan as a bird listed in the Red Book of Kazakhstan has been taken under protection, and therefore hunting this bird is prohibited.
- Language mechanisms used in creating anti-proverbs: Syntactic restructuring.
- URL: https://vk.com/wall-101941802_449

10. *Traditional proverb: Ақылсыз достан ақылды дұшпан артық (Шалкиіз жырау).*
    - English translation: Smart enemy is better than a silly friend.
    - Meaning, literal and/or figurative: Having a silly friend can lead to problems while an intelligent enemy will not harm a person.

Anti-proverb: Біліксіз досыңнан білекті дұшпан артық.
    - English translation: Powerful enemy is better than a silly friend.
    - Brief description of the context that will explain to readers its usage: Having a friend who is not intelligent won't be helpful when you need help; instead of him, an enemy with power will be more helpful.
    - Language mechanisms used in creating anti-proverbs: Replacing proverb components with stylistic synonyms.
    - URL: https://www.zharar.com/index.php?do=shorttexts&action=item&id=10543

11. *Traditional proverb: Алып анадан, ат—биеден.*
    - English translation: Strongman is born from a mother, horse—from a mare.
    - Meaning, literal and/or figurative: Mother is the flower of life, the blessing of the family, the educator of all mankind and mother is the beginning of all life.

Anti-proverb: Алып анадан
    - English translation: Strongman is born from woman
    - Brief description of the context that will explain to readers its usage: A brilliant writer, a wise scientist, a leader of a country, an orator who grew up with satiety, a mother was born and raised.
    - Language mechanisms used in creating anti-proverbs: Reduction of the component composition of the proverb—ellipsis.
    - URL: https://tengrinews.kz/kazakhstan_news/nege-makal-mateldn-jartyisyin-gana-aytyip-jurmz-386191/

12. *Traditional proverb: Алыстан арбалағанша, жақыннан дорбала.*
    - English translation: Rather than carrying carts from a far, carrying them at close range in bags is better.

- Meaning, literal and/or figurative: It gives an idea that it is better and more effective to get things by working, creating and producing them yourself than to get things from afar, from someone, from abroad.
- English equivalent, if there is one: *A bird in the hand is worth two in the bush.*

Anti-proverb: Алыстан арбалағанша, Камазбен бір рейс жаса.

- English translation: Rather than carrying carts from a far, make one trip with the truck
- Brief description of the context that will explain to readers its usage: It is used as advice to make the work more effective.
- The syntactic structure of the traditional proverb is extended: The syntactic structure of the traditional proverb is extended.
- URL: https://vk.com/wall-101941802_449

13. *Traditional proverb:* Ананың көңілі балада, баланың көңілі далада.
   - English translation: All the thoughts of the mother are about the child; all the thoughts of the child are about the game.
   - Meaning, literal and/or figurative: From the moment we are born, our mother takes care of us, feeds us and lives for us. She wants us to grow up to be good people, no matter what she does. The child thinks about the game, and sometimes the child may not understand the concerns and situation of the parents.

Anti-proverb: Ананың көзі балада, баланың көзі далада.

- English translation: The mother's eyes are directed to the child, the eyes of the child to the outside.
- Brief description of the context that will explain to readers its usage: Mothers worry about their children and try to control by keeping them on observation. But children are careless and they think about playing.
- Language mechanisms used in creating anti-proverbs: A parallel structure is a syntactic sequence of sentence structures. Stylistic synonym.
- URL: https://www.wikiwand.com/kk

14. *Traditional proverb:* Аңдамай сөйлеген, ауырмай өледі.
   - English translation: Who talks recklessly will die without becoming ill.
   - Meaning, literal and/or figurative: This means that you should think before speaking, saying your word, and not hurting people by saying something wrong.
   - English equivalent: *A fool's tongue runs before his wit.*

Anti-proverb: Аңдамай сөйлеген, косякқа кіреді.
- English translation: Speaking without caution will get one into trouble.
- Brief description of the context that will explain to readers its usage: Any action without thinking can lead to problems.
- Language mechanisms used in creating anti-proverbs: The meaning is very much the same, but stylistically the wording is completely different. The association with the original proverb is achieved by preserving the structure and the first part, the second part is replaced by the borrowed Russian word, the AP belongs to the low colloquial register.
- URL: https://kaz.zakon.kz/4983086-ma-al-s-zd-mayonez-zaman-a-say-zha-a-ma.html

15. *Traditional proverb: Аспандағы сұңқардан қолдағы тұрымтай артық.*
- English translation: A fawn in the hands is better than a falcon in the sky.
- Meaning, literal and/or figurative: This proverb teaches a person to rejoice and be grateful already for what he has instead of chasing the unknown to find larger prey.
- English equivalent, if there is one: *A bird in the hand is worth two in the bush.*

Anti-proverb: Мат болған кәрөлден, шах қойған пешкі артық.
- English translation: Winning pawn is better than losing king.
- Brief description of the context that will explain to readers its usage: The ordinary worker is better than the authority with the problem.
- Language mechanisms used in creating anti-proverbs: Although the new formation is created in accordance with traditional paremiological models, the anti-proverb explains a different idea, a new content than the traditional proverb.
- URL: https://kaz.zakon.kz/4983086-ma-al-s-zd-mayonez-zaman-a-say-zha-a-ma.html

16. *Traditional proverb: Асықпаған арбамен қоян алады.*
- English translation: Even moving slowly, one can catch a hare.
- Meaning, literal and/or figurative: You can achieve a lot without slowing down.
- English equivalent if there is one: *Slow and steady wins the race.*

Anti-proverb: Асықпаған арбамен, асыққандар таксимен бара берсін.
- English translation: He who is not in a hurry, let him go by cart, and who is in a hurry—by taxi.

- Brief description of the context that will explain to readers its usage: Concerned with the modern way of life addressed to commuters who are not satisfied with public transport.
- Language mechanisms used in creating anti-proverbs: Extension of syntactic structure.
- URL: https://www.zharar.com/index.php?do=shorttexts&action=item&id=32791

17. *Traditional proverb: Ат аунаған жерде түк қалады.*
- English translation: Where the horse was lying, a tuft of wool remained.
- Meaning, literal and/or figurative: any work cannot be done without results, mistakes, etc.
- English equivalent if there is one: *You can't make an omelet without breaking eggs.*

Anti-proverb: Әйел жүрген жерде шу қалады.
- English translation: The noise remains where the woman was.
- Brief description of the context that will explain to readers its usage: Woman from nature is emotional and when she is not satisfied, she may quarrel.
- Language mechanisms used in creating anti-proverbs: Although the new formation is created in accordance with traditional paremiological models, the anti-proverb explains a different idea, a new content than the traditional proverb.
- URL: http://www.halyk-gazeti.kz/index.php?option=com_content&view=article&id=5797:2016-06-30-04-58-40&catid=5:2011-11-18-09-02-24&Itemid

18. *Traditional proverb: Ата-ананың қадірін балалы болғанда, білерсің.*
- English translation: You will honor (appreciate) your parents when you yourself become a parent.
- Meaning, literal and/or figurative: The meaning of this proverb is that when you'll have children and become parents. Then you'll understand your parents, how much they cared about you and how happy they were for you.

Anti-proverb: Ғаламтордың қадірін тариф біткенде білерсің.
- English translation: You will value the internet when the tariff expires.
- Brief description of the context that will explain to readers its usage: Modern life is connected to the internet and most mobile phones are connected to the internet via special tariffs.

- Language mechanisms used in creating anti-proverbs: Although the new formation is created in accordance with traditional paremiological models, the anti-proverb explains a different idea, a new content than the traditional proverb.
- URL: https://interesnoe.me/view/content/1

19. *Traditional proverb: Ат айналып қазығын табар, Ер айналып елін табар.*
   - English translation: The horse will return to its leash; the man will return to his country.
   - Meaning, literal and/or figurative: For a person who, for some reason, has left his native country, where he grew up, it is natural that one day he will return to his homeland

Anti-proverb: Админ айналып сайтын табар.
   - English translation: Admin will find his site.
   - Brief description of the context that will explain to readers its usage: People who created the website will find their accounts on the site.
   - Language mechanisms used in creating anti-proverbs: Reduction of the component composition of the proverb—ellipsis.
   - URL: https://surak.baribar.kz/618367/

20. *Traditional proverb: Аузы қисық болса да, байдың ұлы сөйлесін.*
   - English translation: Although his face is crooked, let the son of the rich speak.
   - Meaning, literal and/or figurative: Although he has nothing to say, in the past feudal era, the son of the rich (as a representative of the ruling class) had the right to speak first.
   - English equivalent if there is one: born with a silver spoon in one's mouth.

Anti-proverb: Аузы қисық болса да, байдың баласы сөйлесін.
   - English translation: Although his mouth is crooked, let the rich man's child speak.
   - Brief description of the context that will explain to readers its usage: This means the recognition of an official or an older adult who is not pleasant to hear, even if he is not very different from other people.
   - Language mechanism(s) used in creating this anti-proverb: Replacing proverb components with stylistic synonyms.
   - URL: https://abai.kz/post/73804

21. *Traditional proverb: Аш бала тоқ баламен ойнамайды.*
   - English translation: A hungry child does not want to play with a well-fed child.

- Meaning, literal and/or figurative: He who has everything cannot understand the needs and desires of a poor person.
- English equivalent if there is one: *The full man does not understand the hungry.*

Anti-proverb: Маскасы жоқ бала, маскасы бар баламен ойнамайды.

- English translation: A child with a face mask will not play with the child without a face mask.
- Brief description of the context that will explain to readers its usage: Appeared on the wave of Covid-19, when everyone was obliged to wear a face mask, as a caution even children were obeying the rule and stayed far from children without mask.
- Language mechanisms used in creating anti-proverbs: Replacing proverb components with contextual synonyms.
- URL: https://www.facebook.com/173266319881757/posts/7080 67626401621/

22. *Traditional proverb: Ашу—дұшпан, ақыл—дос, ақылыңа ақыл қос.*
   - English translation: Anger is enemy, intelligence is friend, add wisdom to your mind.
   - Meaning, literal and/or figurative: Usually, people look for an enemy in the outside world, but in fact we do not realize that the most dangerous enemy is in our inner world. One of the most dangerous enemies is anger.

Anti-proverb: Ашу—тапанша, ақыл—доллар.

   - English translation: Anger is a pistol; intelligence is a dollar.
   - Brief description of the context that will explain to readers its usage: Where there is anger, there is no mind. Anger darkens the mind and leads to insanity. An angry person becomes insane. Such a person does not know what to do.
   - Language mechanisms used in creating anti-proverbs: A stylistic mechanism, a metaphor is used to create modern Kazakh anti-proverb.
   - URL: https://kaz.zakon.kz/4983086-ma-al-s-zd-mayonez-zaman-a-say-zha-a-ma.html

23. *Traditional proverb: Аяқ киімің тар болса, дүниенің кеңдігінен не пайда.*
   - English translation: What good is the breadth of the world if you have tight shoes?
   - Meaning, literal and/or figurative: When a person has minor problems, he might not see his opportunities.

Anti-proverb: Өз етігің тар болса, дүниенің кеңдігінен не пайда.
- · English translation: What is good about the breadth of the world if your shoes are tight?
- · Brief description of the context that will explain to readers its usage: When a person has problems connected to him, he will not see any other opportunities.
- · Language mechanism(s) used in creating this anti-proverb: Replacing proverb components with stylistic synonyms.
- · URL: the newspaper "Leninshil zhas" 1983, 2 February.

24. *Traditional proverb: Балалы үй—базар, баласыз үй—қу мазар*
- · English translation: A house with children is like a bazaar, a house without children is like a grave.
- · Meaning, literal and/or figurative: In a family with many children, the market is full of fun, joy, and noise day and night, and in a childless family, on the other hand, the image is a grave-like cold and a faint sound of silence.

Anti-proverb #1: Балалы үй—базар, баласыз үй—азар.
- · English translation: A house with children is like a bazaar, a house without children will dwindle.
- · Brief description of the context that will explain to readers its usage: A child is both a blessing and a family holiday, and without a child there is no prosperity and happiness in the house. The family will fall apart sooner or later.
- · Language mechanism(s) used in creating this anti-proverb: The method of "graphic mimicry" is used, where there will be truncated one grapheme; "m" in "mazar."
- · URL: https://ridero.ru/books/anatty_s_z_azyna/freeText

Anti-proverb #2: WiFi бар үй — клуб, WiFi-i жоқ үй — тұлып.
- · English translation: House with WiFi is a club, a house without WiFi is hollow.
- · Brief description of the context that will explain to readers its usage: Nowadays, people can't imagine life without the internet because everything is connected to the internet, so people consider a place without internet useless.
- · Language mechanism(s) used in creating this anti-proverb: The association with the original proverb is achieved by preserving the structure, and both predicates of the proverbs, as in the original proverb, are formed from nouns, and the subjects are replaced by borrowed Internet words, AP belongs to the low colloquial register.
- · URL: https://interesnoe.me/view/content/1

25. *Traditional proverb: Балық басынан шіриді.*
   - English translation: Fish begins to stink at the head.
   - Meaning, literal and/or figurative: Some people may disturb public order such as the country's leadership, officials, by showing inappropriate behavior instead of setting an example for the people or simply irresponsible people.
   - English equivalent if there is one: *The fish rots from the head down.*

Anti-proverb: Банк басынан шіриді.
   - English translation: [the] Bank is destroyed from the top.
   - Brief description of the context that will explain to readers its usage: The problems that appear in the bank begin from the way it was organized and managed.
   - Language mechanism(s) used in creating this anti-proverb: Reception of "phonetic mimicry," sound assimilation of a word or its transformed version to other words. The words "balyq" and "bank" are alliterative, repetition of the consonant sound "b." The technique is based on a partial morpho-phonetic transformation of the component, leading to a complete change in the semantics of the component and the entire proverb.
   - URL: https://vk.com/wall-119897064_180

26. *Traditional proverb: Бас жарылса—бөрік ішінде, қол сынса—жең ішінде.*
   - English translation: If the head is injured—inside the hat, the arm is broken—inside the sleeve.
   - Meaning, literal and/or figurative: Not "divulge family, internal strife, quarrels, squabbles." In other words, everything that was said or done in a narrow circle should not be taken out of its framework.
   - English equivalent if there is one: to wash one's dirty linen at home. (French: *Il faut laver son linge sale en famille.*)

Anti-proverb: Бас жарылса бөркім бар ... кім көреді?
   - English translation: If the head is injured, I have the hat, who will see?
   - Brief description of the context that will explain to readers its usage: If the head injured, I have a hat ... who sees? The writer of the text has changed the original proverb to make it more expressive.
   - Language mechanism(s) used in creating this anti-proverb: Proverbs are stylistic constructions that are very expressive and play an important role in terms of imagery. Thanks to the functional style of this genre, it provides ample scope for skillfully describing

social, political, and social issues in an emotionally compelling way. Syntactic extension.

· URL: (The newspaper "Zhas Alash" 05.05.2010).

27. *Traditional proverb:* Бәлен жерде бақыр бар, іздеп барсаң, мыс шелек те жоқ.

· English translation: Somewhere, there is a bucket; even if you look for it, there is no copper bucket.

· Meaning, literal and/or figurative: This means that if you leave your homeland (a warm place), for the place which, as you think, someone will praise you, in search of good from afar, and what you find in your search is not even worth the nails of your homeland.

· Language mechanism(s) used in creating this anti-proverb: Replacing proverb components with stylistic synonyms.

· English equivalent if there is one: *The grass is always greener on the other side.*

Anti-proverb #1: Бәлен жерде алтын бар, барсаң бақыр да жоқ.

· English translation: Somewhere, there is gold, if you look for it, there is not even a copper bucket.

· Brief description of the context that will explain to readers its usage: Gold is everywhere, and if you go, there is not even copper, today more and more people are looking for jobs in online marketing and they were deceived.

· URL: http://qazaqjoly.kz/?p=11165

Anti-proverb #2: Бәлен жерде бақыр бар, барсаң бақыр тұрмақ қол жаулық жоқ.

· English translation: Somewhere there is a bucket, if you go to look for it, there is not even a handkerchief.

· Brief description of the context that will explain to readers its usage: The expression is used in relation to those who always think that everything is better in other lands than in their homeland, and who treat their country with disdain. Once they leave it, they do not find anything new in another country, since it is not about the location, but rather the consciousness of the person.

· URL: https://almaty.tv/kz/news/obschestvo/1908-tainstvenno-ischez-v-rossii-dgitel-almatinskoy-oblasti

Anti-proverb #3: Бәлен жерде бақыр бар, барсаң, тақыр да жоқ.

· English translation: Somewhere there is a bucket, if you go to look for it, there is nothing.

- Brief description of the context that will explain to readers its usage: Somewhere out there, in another place there is wealth. You go, finding neither money nor bare land.
  URL address of the publication from where the quote is taken: https://yvision.kz/post/199201

28. *Traditional proverb: Битке өкпелеп, тоныңды отқа жақпа.*
    - English translation: Do not burn your fur coat because of the fleas.
    - Meaning, literal and/or figurative: The proverb is based on the motto: "You cannot sacrifice big things for small things! If you do not lose, you will not win."

Anti-proverb: Биттің қаупінің күштілігі сонша, тонды отқа салуға тура келеді.
    - English translation: The danger of fleas is so great that you must burn your fur coat.
    - Brief description of the context that will explain to readers its usage: The need for the Latin alphabet in our country is expressed only when the President talks about the transition to the Latin alphabet. But what's stopping you? This also requires a presidential order. Otherwise, if we discuss every three years and leave it the same, we won't be switching to the Latin alphabet anytime soon.
    - Language mechanism(s) used in creating this anti-proverb: Proverbs are stylistic constructions that are very expressive and play an important role in terms of imagery. Thanks to the functional style of this genre, it provides ample scope for skillfully describing issues in an emotionally compelling way. Syntactic extension.
    - URL: https://inbusiness.kz/kz/news/%C2%ABbittin-kaupinin-kushtiligi-sonsha-tondy-otka-saluga-tura-

29. *Traditional proverb: Білімдіге дүние жарық, білімсіздің күні ғәріп.*
    - English translation: The world is bright for the educated, the day is strange for the silly.
    - Meaning, literal and/or figurative: A bright and good future awaits an educated person.

Anti-proverb: Білімдінің ойы ұзын, қалталының қолы ұзын.
    - English translation: An educated person has thoughts; the rich man has opportunities.
    - Brief description of the context that will explain to readers its usage: Comparing education and having money, they say that money provides many opportunities.
    - Language mechanism(s) used in creating this anti-proverb: Proverbs are stylistic constructions that are very expressive and play

an important role in terms of imagery. Thanks to the functional style of this genre, it provides ample scope for skillfully describing social, political, and social issues in an emotionally compelling way. Syntactic extension.

· URL: https://www.facebook.com.BD-211242482560306/

30. *Traditional proverb:* Бір елі ауызға екі елі қақпақ.
   · English translation: Cover your mouth with two fingers.
   · Meaning, literal and/or figurative: At any time, Kazakh people prefer to talk less and listen more. "A word is like a bullet," "One word, destroys one country"—these are the words of Kazakhs, which means that future descendants must be careful not to speak casually and not leave others in an awkward position.
   · English equivalent if there is one: *A shut mouth catches no flies.*

Anti-proverb: Екі елі ауызға төрт елі қақпақ.
   · English translation: Cover your mouth with your hand.
   · Brief description of the context that will explain to readers its usage: (Literally, аудармасы). If everyone was careful with their language, there would never be a fight. All problems are from the tongue. Good and bad, quarrels, gossip, everything goes on the tongue.
   · Language mechanism(s) used in creating this anti-proverb: Replacing proverb components with contextual synonyms.
   URL:https://www.elana.kz/eki-eli-auyzgha-tort-eli-qaqpaq/

31. *Traditional proverb:* Болар бала бесігінде бұлқынар, Болар құлын желісінде жұлқынар.
   · English translation: A child, or a good horse, exhibits their behavior from an early age.
   · Meaning, literal and/or figurative: The more stupid one is, the closer one is to reality. The more stupid one is, the clearer one is. Stupidity is brief and artless, while intelligence squirms and hides. Intelligence is unprincipled, but stupidity is honest and straightforward.

Anti-proverb: Болатын баланың бетін қақпа, өнерін әлеуметтік желіге сал.
   · English translation: Don't hide a child's talent, show it on the internet.
   · Brief description of the context that will explain to readers its usage: Nowadays people try to introduce their talent from the internet, so the advice for the parents is also to use the internet to get the opportunities to show children's talent.
   · Language mechanism(s) used in creating this anti-proverb: Proverbs are stylistic constructions that are very expressive and play

an important role in terms of imagery. Thanks to the functional style of this genre, it provides ample scope for skillfully describing social, political, and social issues in an emotionally compelling way. Syntactic extension.

· URL: https://vk.com/wall348809512_603

32. *Traditional proverb: Бірлік болмай, тірлік болмас.*
  · English translation: There is no life without unity.
  · Meaning, literal and/or figurative: People should refrain from such negative traits that have the destructive force of decay, jealousy, envy, hostility. Unity is the main guarantee of the unity of the country and the nation.

Anti-proverb: Бірлік (единица) болмай, тірлік болмас.
  · English translation: There is no life without money on the phone.
  · Brief description of the context that will explain to readers its usage: There is no life without charging a phone.
  · Language mechanism(s) used in creating this anti-proverb: the anti-proverb is coined by means of polysemy: the word "birlik" has two meanings: "unity," and "credit."
  · URL address of the publication from where the quote is taken: https://massaget.kz/layfstayl/bilim/gumanitarly-ylymdar/61688/

33. *Traditional proverb: Білегі күшті бірді жығады, білімі күшті мыңды жығады.*
  · English translation: Whoever has a strong hand will win one who has great knowledge, he can win thousands.
  · Meaning, literal and/or figurative: knowledge is an invincible weapon. A man armed with knowledge will never be defeated.
  · English equivalent if there is one: *Knowledge is power.*

Anti-proverb: Білегі күшті бірді жығады, блогы күшті мыңды жығады.
  · English translation: Someone with a strong hand will beat one, someone with a great blog will conquer thousands.
  · Brief description of the context that will explain to readers its usage: Someone with a strong hand will beat one, someone with a great blog will conquer thousands.
  · Language mechanism(s) used in creating this anti-proverb: Reception of "phonetic mimicry," sound assimilation of a word or its transformed version to other words. The words "bilim" and "blog" are alliterative, repetition of the consonant sound "b." The technique is based on a partial morpho-phonetic transformation of the component, leading to a complete change in the semantics of the component and the entire proverb.

- URL: https://surak.baribar.kz/618367/
34. *Traditional proverb: Біреу тойып секіреді, біреу тоңып секіреді.*
  - English translation: (literally) One jumps because of satiety, the other—of scarcity.
  - Meaning, literal and/or figurative: someone is faced with the inequality of social society, someone has a lot of wealth, someone does not even have enough money for food.
  - English equivalent if there is one: The lack of money is the root of all evil. George Bernard Shaw

Anti-proverb: Біреу көрiп күледi, біреу ерiп күледi.
  - English translation: (literally) One laughs at what he saw, another together with others.
  - Brief description of the context that will explain to readers its usage: Literally: someone laughs by himself; someone laughs without knowing about what he is laughing. It means a person should have his own opinion.
  - Language mechanism(s) used in creating this anti-proverb: Replacing proverb components with stylictic synonym.
  - URL: https://massaget.kz/mangilik_el/tup_tamyir/asyil_soz/36638/

35. *Traditional proverb: Біреуге мал қайғы, біреуге жан қайғы.*
  - English translation: One thinks about wealth, another about life.
  - Meaning, literal and/or figurative: If someone dreams of living and surviving on earth and someone dreams of making a living, raising livestock, and becoming rich.

Anti-proverb: Covid-19: Біреуге жан қайғы болса, біреу мал табуға кіріскен.
  - English translation: One thinks about health, another thinks about wealth.
  - Brief description of the context that will explain to readers its usage: If someone dreams of surviving during Covid-19, and someone dreams of making money and becoming rich. While the whole of Europe is fighting the disease, the Belarusian clubs are taking all sorts of other approaches.
  - Language mechanism(s) used in creating this anti-proverb: Change in the component composition of proverbs, as a rule, affects both the lexical and grammatical levels of the utterance. Expansion of the component composition.

- URL: https://www.ktk.kz/kz/news/video/2020/04/10/144 790/

36. *Traditional proverb: Біреудің әйелі біреуге қыздай болып көрінеді.*
  - English translation: Someone's wife looks to someone like a girl.
  - Meaning, literal and/or figurative: It always seems that things are better somewhere other than where you are.
  - Language mechanism(s) used in creating this anti-proverb: Replacing proverb components with contextual synonyms.
  - English equivalent, if there is one: *The apples on the other side of the wall are the sweetest.*

Anti-proverb #1: Біреудің байы біреуге, тауар артқан КамАЗ-дай көрінеді. Біреудің әйелі біреуге, Мерседестей сылаңдайды.
  - English translation: Someone's husband looks like a loaded truck with goods. Someone's wife looks like a beautiful car.
  - Brief description of the context that will explain to readers its usage: It is used to say about the modern evaluation of people by comparing them to cars.
  - URL: https://kaz.zakon.kz/4983086-ma-al-s-zd-mayonez-zaman-a-say-zha-a-ma.html

Anti-proverb #2: Көршілестің тауығы біреуге қаз боп көрінеді.
  - English translation: A neighbor's chicken looks like a goose to someone.
  - Brief description of the context that will explain to readers its usage: It is used to show that people are not satisfied with what they have.
  - URL: https://bilim-all.kz/tag/proverb

37. *Traditional proverb: Боранды күні қасқыр мен бала құтырады.*
  - English translation: On a stormy day, wolves and children are raging.
  - Meaning, literal and/or figurative: The proverb is used to show the reality; when it snows, children usually get gaiety and play, so do the dogs and wolves.

Anti-proverb: Боранды күні қасқыр мен блоггер құтырады.
  - English translation: On a stormy day, wolves and bloggers are raging.
  - Brief description of the context that will explain to readers its usage: It is used to say that when something extraordinary happens, the bloggers start announcing it.
  - Language mechanism(s) used in creating this anti-proverb: Reception of "phonetic mimicry," sound assimilation of a word or its transformed version to other words. The words "bala" and "blogger" are

alliterative, repetition of the consonant sound "b." The technique is based on a partial morpho-phonetic transformation of the component, leading to a complete change in the semantics of the component and the entire proverb.

· URL: https://vk.com/wall-98021698_1710

38. *Anti-proverb: Бүгін бар дүние ертең жоқ, "өзімдікі" дегенің өзгеге кетеді.*
   · English translation: Today you have tomorrow not, what is yours will be another's.
   · Meaning, literal and/or figurative: Nothing in this worl is eternal, the material world is changing, what you have may not be yours tomorrow.
   · Language Mechanisms Used in Creating anti-proverbs: Anti-proverb is created by contamination, the formation of a new phrase because of the crossing of two different proverbs.
   · Brief description of the context that will explain to readers its usage: Means the world is unstable
   · URL: https://bilim-all.kz/quote/14649

39. *Traditional proverb: Былай тартсаң арба сынады, былай тартсаң өгіз өледі.*
   · English translation: If you turn one way, the bull dies, if you turn the other—the cart will break.
   · Meaning, literal and/or figurative: Proverb is used to say about a hopeless situation.
   · English equivalent if there is one: *Damned if you do, damned if you don't.*

Anti-proverb: Былай тартсаң арба сынады, былай тартсаң өгіз өледі—жүк алға жылжыған жоқ. Өгіз өлсе тірілмейді, арба сынса жөндеуге болмайды.
   · English translation: If you pull like this, the cart breaks, if you pull like that, the bull dies—the load does not move forward. When a bull dies, it cannot be resurrected; if the cart breaks, it cannot be repaired.
   · Brief description of the context that will explain to readers its usage: It is used to say about the desperation of the situation.
   · Language mechanisms used in creating anti-proverbs: Change in the component composition of proverbs, as a rule, affects both the lexical and grammatical levels of the utterance. Expansion of the component composition.

- URL: https://pps.kaznu.kz/ru/Main/FileShow2/110014/111/2/21/0//

40. *Traditional proverb: Даяр асқа—тік қасық.*
   - English translation: Ready meal—a vertical spoon.
   - Meaning, literal and/or figurative: A person who does not work, who shares someone else's income, who is not directly involved in doing that, but who sits at the table when the food is ready.

English equivalent, if there is one: *Saepe alter alterius fruitur labribus* (from the labors of others it is often another who profits)

Anti-proverb #1: Піскен асқа—тік қасық.
   - English translation: For cooked meals, a spoon is ready.
   - Brief description of the context that will explain to readers its usage: A person is described who is willing to own ready-made food and everything ready without working.
   - Language mechanism(s) used in creating this anti-proverb: Replacing proverb components with stylistic synonyms.
   - URL: https://bilim-all.kz/quote/5332

Anti-proverb #2: Піскен асқа жеуші көп.
   - English translation: There are many people who eat cooked food.
   - Brief description of the context that will explain to readers its usage: There are always eaters for ready-made food.
   - Language mechanism(s) used in creating this anti-proverb: New lexical content of the same syntactic structure (partial).
   - URL: https://nurshashu.wordpress.com/2011/03/30

41. *Traditional proverb: Дерт көп, денсаулық біреу.*
   - English translation: There are lots of diseases, but there is only one health.
   - Meaning, literal and/or figurative: Health is the most important thing in a person's life. Maintaining health is very difficult because there are many diseases. A person must take care of himself to stay healthy.

Anti-proverb: Дерт көп, денсаулық қымбат.
   - English translation: There are lots of diseases, staying healthy is expensive.
   - Brief description of the context that will explain to readers its usage: Today there are many types of diseases and all of them have their own way of treatment and medicine, which cost much money.

- Language mechanism(s) used in creating this anti-proverb: New lexical content of the same syntactic structure.
- URL: https://egemen.kz/article/210572-dert-kop-densaulyq-qym bat

42. *Traditional proverb: Досы көпті жау алмайды, ақылы көпті дау алмайды.*
   - English translation: With many friends, the enemy will not defeat, with good intelligence, the argument will not prevail.
   - Meaning, literal and/or figurative: Those who have many friends will not be touched by the enemy; those who have a lot of intelligence will not be caught by litigation.

Anti-proverb #1: Досы көпті жау алмайды, жігіті көпті бай алмайды
   - English translation: With many friends, the enemy will not defeat, with boyfriends, a girl will not get married.
   - Brief description of the context that will explain to readers its usage: (literally) Whoever has many friends will not be touched by the enemy; whoever has many boyfriends, no one calls her to marry. It is better to have many friends in life, the girl should have a good upbringing.
   - Language mechanism(s) used in creating this anti-proverb: Replacing proverb components with contextual synonyms.
   - URL: https://alashainasy.kz/fromsocial/dosyi-kopt-jau-almaydyi-jgt-kopt-bay-almaydyi-104937/

Anti-proverb #2: Досы көпті жау алмайды, танысы бар сотталмайды.
   - English translation: With many friends the enemy will not defeat, someone with patron will not be sentenced.
   - Brief description of the context that will explain to readers its usage: Those who have many friends will not be touched by the enemy; those who have an acquaintance will not be caught up in litigation.
   - Language mechanism(s) used in creating this anti-proverb: New lexical content of the same syntactic structure (partial).
   - URL: https://vk.com/wall-101941802_449

43. *Екі қошқардың басы қазанға сыймайды.*
   - English translation: The heads of two rams do not fit in one cauldron.
   - Meaning, literal and/or figurative: This proverb refers mainly to people who compete with each other. Now there is a lot of talk about the ministry. It is also used in politics and interstate conflicts.

- English equivalent, if there is one: Two cunning men will not try to make a dupe of each other.

Anti-proverb: Екі бастықтың құйрығы, бір креслоға сыймайды.

- English translation: The backs of the two bosses do not fit in one chair.
- Brief description of the context that will explain to readers its usage: It is used to say about the situation when two authorities have to rule together and can not go along together.
- Language mechanisms used in creating anti-proverbs: Substitution of the lexical structure of proverbs.
- URL: https://kaz.zakon.kz/4983086-ma-al-s-zd-mayo nez-zaman-a-say-zha-a-ma.html

44. *Traditional proverb: Екі кеменің құйрығын ұстаған суға кетеді.*
  - English translation: If you run after two hares, you will catch neither.
  - Meaning, literal and/or figurative: The meaning of this proverb is that you cannot take on several things at once. In this case, you will not be successful in any of these cases.
  - Language Mechanisms Used in Creating anti-proverbs:
  - English equivalent if there is one: *A Jack of all trades is master of none.*

Anti-proverb: Екі кеменің басын ұстаған суға кетеді.

- English translation: Holding on to two ships, goes underwater.
- Brief description of the context that will explain to readers its usage: literally: the one who holds onto two boats will drown.
- Language mechanism(s) used in creating this anti-proverb: Replacing proverb components with stylistic synonyms.
- URL: https://azh.kz/index.php/kz/news/view/8869

45. *Ел мен ел тату болса, төбедегіні келтірер.*
  - Meaning, literal and/or figurative: If there is peace between the countries, they will achieve a lot.
  - Language mechanisms used in creating anti-proverbs: This proverb is created from two proverbs: "Ağayyn tatu bolsa, as köp" / If the relatives are friendly, then there are a lot of food /, Törteu tүgel bolsa, töbedegi keler / where there is understanding, much will be achieved/.

- Language mechanism(s) used in creating this anti-proverb: This is a contaminated version of two proverbs.
- URL: (The newspaper "Altyn Orda",16.07.2000).

46. *Traditional proverb: Ел болам десең, бесігіңді түзе.*

- English translation: If you want to be in one country, start from the cradle!
- Meaning, literal and/or figurative: It is necessary to pay special attention to the upbringing of a girl who will bring up a new generation in the future.
- Language mechanism(s) used in creating this anti-proverb: Replacing proverb components with stylistic synonyms.

Anti-proverb #1: Ел болам десең, ғылымыңды түзе.

- English translation: If you want to be in one country, develop science.
- Brief description of the context that will explain to readers its usage: The future of a country with undeveloped science is bleak. So far, the country has various programs for the development of science and the support of scientists, but their potential and impact do not deserve praise.
- URL: https://www.astana-akshamy.kz/el-bolam-deseng-ghylymyn gdy-tuze/

Anti-proverb #2: Ел боламын десең, маскаңды түзе.

- English translation: If you want to be in one country, wear the mask
- Brief description of the context that will explain to readers its usage: Wearing a mask in the event of COVID-19 protects the health of the country. If you want to be a healthy country, put on a mask.
- URL: https://www.facebook.com/173266319881757/posts/7080 67626401621/

Anti-proverb #3: Ел болам десең, экраныңды түзе.

- English translation: If you want to be in one country, control the TV.
- Brief description of the context that will explain to readers its usage: Today, issues in the field of domestic shows or social programs are often discussed. Showbiz and other lighthearted TV programs that avoid censorship and go beyond not only censorship of journalistic information but also ethics will soon overflow like mushrooms after rain. If the migration of Kazakhstani journalism goes in this direction, the situation will undoubtedly be dangerous.
- URL: https://ult.kz/post/-el-bolam-desen-efirindi-tuze

47. Traditional proverb: Ер жігіт елі үшін туады, елі үшін өледі.
- English translation: Man is born for his country; he dies for his country.
- Meaning, literal and/or figurative: A man must defend his country.

Anti-proverb: Шенеунік атақ үшін туады, билік үшін өледі.
- English translation: An official is born for glory, and he dies for power.
- Brief description of the context that will explain to readers its usage: The negative side of modern society is described.
- Language mechanisms used in creating anti-proverbs: New lexical content of the same syntactic structure (complete).
- URL: https://kaz.zakon.kz/4983086-ma-al-s-zd-mayo nez-zaman-a-say-zha-a-ma.html

48. Traditional proverb: Ерте тұрған еркектің ырысы артық, ерте тұрған әйелдің бір ісі артық.
- English translation: If a woman gets up early, she will have time for more than one thing, a horseman, if he gets up early, he will find one more happiness.
- Meaning, literal and/or figurative: Kazakh proverb calling for a cautious approach to getting up early. There are many benefits to getting up early.
- English equivalent if there is one: Early to bed and early to rise makes one healthy, wealthy, and wise. The early bird gets the worm.

Anti-proverb: Ерте тұрған әйелдің түстен кейін ұйқысы келеді.
- English translation: A woman who gets up early wants to sleep during the day
- Brief description of the context that will explain to readers its usage: A woman who gets up early wants to sleep in the afternoon.
- Language mechanisms used in creating anti-proverb: Substitution of the lexical structure of proverbs.
- URL: https://interesnoe.me/view/content/1

49. Traditional proverb: Еңбек етсең ерінбей, тояды қарның тіленбей (Абай)
- English translation: If you work without being lazy, you will be satisfied without asking.
- Meaning, literal and/or figurative: Everyone can see the fruits of their labor only if they work honestly and work hard.

- English equivalent if there is one: "A dream doesn't become reality through magic; it takes sweat, determination and hard work". Colin Powell

Anti-proverb #1: Еңбек етсең ерінбей, жетерсің мұратқа.
- Brief description of the context that will explain to readers its usage: If you work hard, you will achieve your goals.
- Language mechanism(s) used in creating this anti-proverb: Anti-proverb is created by contamination, the formation of a new stable phrase because of the crossing of two different proverbs.
- URL: https://goo.edu.kz/blogs/view/22/91800

Anti-proverb #2: Блоггер болсаң ерінбей, тояды қарның тіленбей.
- English translation: If you are a blogger, then you are full.
- Brief description of the context that will explain to readers its usage: if you work as a blogger, you will be satisfied without asking ...
- Language mechanism(s) used in creating this anti-proverb: New lexical content of the same syntactic structure (partial).
- URL: https://khabar.kz/kk/uzdik-azilder/item/113767-kyzyk-times-zhurgizushileri-zam

Anti-proverb #3: Сайт жасасаң ерінбей, тояды қарның тіленбей.
- English translation: If you create the site, then you are full.
- Brief description of the context that will explain to readers its usage: if you create a blog without laziness, you will be satisfied without begging.
- Language mechanism(s) used in creating this anti-proverb: New lexical content of the same syntactic structure.
- URL: https://khabar.kz/kk/uzdik-azilder/item/113767-kyzyk-times-zhurgizushileri-zam

50. *Traditional proverb: Жалғыз жүріп жол тапқанша, көппен бірге адас.*
- English translation: Wander with many until you find a way to walk alone
- Meaning, literal and/or figurative: The proverb shows the value of community and collectivity. To be a united and whole family, where everyone will be glad for each other.
- English equivalent if there is one: Two are better than one because they have a good return on their labor.

Anti-proverb: Жалғыз жүріп жол тапқанша, адастырмас көппен кеңес.
- English translation: Advise many people not to be lost then find a way to walk alone.

- Brief description of the context that will explain to readers its usage: It is used to say that it is better to get advice from people than do everything alone.
- Language mechanism(s) used in creating this anti-proverb: Substitution of the lexical structure of proverbs.
  URL: https://egemen.kz/article/108041-uly-dala-ulaghattary-5-bolim

51. *Traditional proverb: Жаман жолдастан, жақсы дұшпан артық.*
  - Translation: Better a good enemy than a bad friend.
  - Meaning, literal and/or figurative: The proverb says that it is better to have an evil, unpleasant, and open enemy than a hypocritical friend who speaks bad things about someone.
  - English equivalent if there is one: Better an open enemy than a false friend.

Anti-proverb: Жақсы жаудан жаман дос артық.
  - Brief description of the context that will explain to readers its usage: (literally) A bad friend is better than a good enemy. This is also a kind of game with the West. Putin knows that too. But now, the two superpowers have more "a bad friend than a good enemy."
  - Language mechanism(s) used in creating this anti-proverb: this anti-proverb is coined by means of lexical mechanisms, in this case, by antonymy.
  - URL: www.zhasalash.kz. 02.08.2016

52. *Traditional proverb: Жақсы сөз—жарым ырыс.*
  - English translation: A kind word is half the happiness.
  - Meaning, literal and/or figurative: A kind word can quickly reach the speaker. The speaker sees the good deeds first.
  - English equivalent, if there is one: Pleasant words are a honeycomb, sweet to the soul and healing to the bones.

Anti-proverb #1. Жақсы лебіз — жарым ырыс.
  - English translation: A good word is half wealth.
  - Brief description of the context that will explain to readers its usage: A kind word is half the happiness.
  - Language mechanisms used in creating anti-proverbs: the proverb component is replaced with a stylistic synonym.
  - URL: https://bilim-all.kz/quote/8247

Anti-proverb #2: Жақсы қаулы—жарым іс.
  - English translation: A good solution is half the battle.

- Brief description of the context that will explain to readers its usage: The good will and wish will help people to win more and have good results.
- Language mechanisms used in creating anti-proverbs: Substitution of the lexical structure of proverbs with the stylistic synonyms.
- URL: https://emle.kz/uploads/files/51b105703156b768745b2653bd121476.pdf p. 90

53. *Traditional proverb: Жақсының жақсылығын айт, нұры тасысын, жаманның жамандығын айт, құты қашсын.*
   - English translation: literally: Talk about the kindness of a good person to his face, let him shine with rays of joy, about what is bad in a bad person, speak to his face, let it tremble.
   - Meaning, literal and/or figurative: Properly spoken words inspire a person, increase one's enthusiasm for life, revive the soul.
   - English equivalent if there is one: Praise youth and they will prosper (Irish: *Mol an óige agus tiocfaidh sí*)

Anti-proverb: Жақсының жақсылығын айт...
   - English translation: Talk about the kindness of a good person.
   - Brief description of the context that will explain to readers its usage: The meaning of the proverb is we should talk about good people and be thankful for them.
   - Language mechanisms used in creating anti-proverbs: The final elements of a multicomponent unit are reduced. The reduction of the component composition is called ellipsis.
   - URL: https://philart.kaznu.kz/index.php/1-FIL/article/view/1122/1083

54. *Traditional proverb: Жаңбырмен жер көгерер, батамен ел көгерер.*
   - English translation: The earth will be green with rain, and the nation will be green with blessings.
   - Meaning, literal and/or figurative: Blessing is one of the ancient Kazakh traditions. Blessings are said at the parties, at various weddings and good deeds.
   - English equivalent if there is one: *Blessings start forth forever.*

Anti-proverb: Жаңбырмен жер көгерер, трафикпен сайт көгерер.
   - Brief description of the context that will explain to readers its usage: The earth will be green with rain, and the site will be green with traffic.
   - Language Mechanisms Used in Creating anti-proverb: Replacing proverb components with contextual synonyms.

- URL: https://surak.baribar.kz/618367/

55. *Traditional proverb: Жатқан жыланның құйрығын баспа.*
- English translation: Don't wake up a snake while it's quiet.
- Meaning, literal and/or figurative: This means that no one teases you or gets into trouble when you are not around.
- English equivalent if there is one: *Let sleeping dogs lie.*

Anti-proverb: Тыныш жатқан жыланның құйрығын баспа.
- Brief description of the context that will explain to readers its usage: (Literally) Don't step on the tail of a quiet snake—Don't step on the tail of a quiet snake, Russian neighbor, if you don't want trouble!
- Language mechanism(s) used in creating this anti-proverb: Replacing proverb components with stylistic synonyms.
- URL: https://m.tengrinews.kz

56. *Traditional proverb: Жел тұрмаса, шөптің басы қимылдамайды.*
- English translation: Everything happens for a reason; thus, if people are talking about something, there must be some truth behind this talk and rumors.
- Meaning, literal and/or figurative: According to the proverb, people do not speak in vain, nothing happens without a reason. It is often said when they believe a rumor is true.
- English equivalent: *There is no smoke without fire.*

Anti-proverb #1. Жел тұрмаса, жапырақ қимылдамайды.
- Brief description of the context that will explain to readers its usage: If there is no wind, the grass will not shake by itself.
- Language mechanism(s) used in creating this anti-proverb: Replacing proverb components with stylistic synonyms.
- URL: file:///C:/Users/W2/Downloads/514-37-924-1-10-20210628.pdf

Anti-proverb #2. Интернет жоқ болса желінің басы қимылдамайды.
- Brief description of the context that will explain to readers its usage: Without the Internet, the network will not work.
- Language mechanism(s) used in creating this anti-proverb: Substitution of the lexical structure of proverbs. Even though it consists of elements of a common proverb, an anti-proverb explains a different idea, new content, than traditional proverbs.
- URL: https://vk.com/wall348809512_603

57. *Traditional proverb: Жомарт адам жоқтығын білдірмес, жүйрік ат тоқтығын білдірмес.*

- English translation: Literally, the generous person does not show his poverty, the well-fed horse does not show his satiety.
- Meaning, literal and/or figurative: Generosity is a human virtue. It is still revered in modern Kazakhstani society. The proverb teaches us to be generous in any situation.
- Equivalent: *No one is as generous as he who has nothing to give.* (French proverb)

Anti-proverb: Жомарт жоқтығын, жүйрік тоқтығын білдірмес.
- Brief description of the context that will explain to readers its usage: the generous one does not show his poverty, the well-fed horse does not show his satiety.
- Language mechanism(s) used in creating this anti-proverb: The elements of a multicomponent unit are reduced. The reduction of the component composition is called ellipsis.
- URL: https://massaget.kz/qaarc/qa/11473

58. *Жылы, жылы сөйлесең—жылан інінен шығады, қатты, қатты сөйлесең—мұсылман дінінен шығады.*
- English translation: If you speak warmly, the snake will come out of its snake nest, if you speak harshly, then the person will leave the Muslim religion.
- Meaning, literal and/or figurative: The Kazakh people have always valued the power of words. They emphasize the importance of a kind word that creates a good mood and shapes the world. Proverbs are used to emphasize important qualities of a person. It also reminds us that any other use of the power of words is harmful in all respects to those who turn them into a destructive channel. Also, the snake in the proverb was not chosen at random as an antagonist. Among Kazakhs, the snake is an evil person.
- English equivalent, if there is one: *Good words are worth much, and cost little.*

Anti-proverb #1: Жылы-жылы сөйлесең, жылан інінен шығады.
- Brief description of the context that will explain to readers its usage: Half of the proverb has been shortened due to the norms of language. It means this proverb is long and has negative meaning from a stylistic point of view.
- Language mechanism(s) used in creating this anti-proverb: The final elements of a multicomponent unit are reduced. The reduction of the component composition is called ellipsis.

- URL: https://tengrinews.kz/kazakhstan_news/nege-makal-mate ldn-jartyisyin-gana-aytyip-jurmz-386191/

Anti-proverb #2: Жылы-жылы сөйлесең, жылан інінен шығады, қатты сөйлесең қайтып кіріп кетеді.

- Brief description of the context that will explain to readers its usage: If you talk warmly, the snake will come out of the den, and if you talk loudly, it will come back.
- Language mechanism(s) used in creating this anti-proverb: New lexical content of the same syntactic structure, blending.
- URL: https://anatili.kazgazeta.kz/news/56710

59. *Traditional proverb: Жүз теңгең болғанша, жүз досың болсын.*
    - English translation: Don't have 100 tenge but have 100 friends.
    - Meaning, literal and/or figurative: It is our task to find a friend in life, to find a companion. Everyone wants to have a loyal friend who will be there for him when he is in trouble.
    - English equivalent, if there is one: *A friend in need is a friend indeed.*

Anti-proverb #1: Жүз теңгең болғанша, бір досың болсын.
    - Brief description of the context that will explain to readers its usage: Don't have 100 tenge but have one friend.
    - Language mechanism(s) used in creating these anti-proverbs: replacing a single word, the proverb component with a stylistic synonym.
    - URL: https://www.zharar.com/index.php?do=shorttexts&action=item&id=37020
    o https://massaget.kz/jigitterge/psihologiya/42447/

Anti-proverb #2: Жүз теңгең болғанша, жүз мемің болсын.
    - Brief description of the context that will explain to readers its usage: Don't have 100 tenge but have 100 memos.
    - Language mechanism(s) used in creating these anti-proverbs: replacing a single word, the proverb component with a contextual synonym.
    - URL: https://uibdc.kz

Anti-proverb #3: Жүз теңгең болғанша, жүз гигабайтың болсын.
    - Brief description of the context that will explain to readers its usage: Don't have 100 tenge but have 100 gigabytes.
    - Language mechanism(s) used in creating these anti-proverbs: replacing a single word, the proverb component with a contextual synonym.

- URL: https://www.youtube.com/watch?v=VS4YbMrXY-o&list= RDCMUCOBmXp_2O09zqNR5qv2Qr-A3з,

60. *Traditional proverb: Заманың түлкі болса тазы болып шал.*
   - English translation: Keep up with your time.
   - Meaning, literal and/or figurative: (literally). If time is a fox, be a hound and grab it. Many people today live by the principle that if you pay for something, you can do it, if you don't pay, you are not able to get anything. The cunning people find ways to live easily and reach things without effort.
   - English equivalent if there is one: *A stitch in time saves nine.*

Anti-proverb: Заманың түлкі болса, бүркіт боп шал.
   - Brief description of the context that will explain to readers its usage: If your age is a fox, then be an eagle (like a hunter).
   - Language mechanism(s) used in creating this anti-proverb: substituting one or more words, the proverb component with a contextual synonym.
   - URL: https://vk.com/wall-26449296_29707

61. *Traditional proverb: Заттың жаңасы жақсы, достың ескісі жақсы.*
   - English translation: Make new friends, but keep the old, one is silver, the other is gold. Friends get better with age/time.
   - Meaning, literal and/or figurative: Of course, when a friend is old, you know that he or she is your real friend. Therefore, no one can replace him. Friends who come later don't even know what he knows.
   - English equivalent, if there is one: Friendship is like money, easier made than kept.

Anti-proverb: Жаңа дос келгенде, ескі достың көзінен жас шығады.
   - Brief description of the context that will explain to readers its usage: (literally) When a new friend comes, tears flow from the eyes of an old friend. The secret of the new friend is unknown. It is possible that from now on a new friend will replace your friend. In this sense, it is said that the tear of an old friend starts when a new friend appears.
   - Language mechanism(s) used in creating this anti-proverb: Some new formations are created by changing the component composition of the proverbs. This type of modification helps to attract the attention of the addressee, since the author, modifying the component composition of the paremia, explicates a more significant component and focuses on the information contained in this component
   - URL: https://kozhalar.kz/20208291-mani-ozgergen-maqaldar-3-

62. *Traditional proverb:* Интернатта оқып жүр, талай қазақ баласы (Абай).
- English translation: Many Kazakh children study in boarding schools.
- Meaning, literal and/or figurative: It is obligatory to teach a child, children study where their parents teach them (This taken from a poem by Abai).
- English equivalent if there is one: The aim of education is knowledge. Live and learn.

Anti-proverb: Интернеттен оқып жүр, талай қазақ баласы.
- English translation: Many Kazakh children study on the Internet.
- Brief description of the context that will explain to readers its usage: The meaning of the proverb is related to the situation with COVID-19 in the country, where all students now go to online education. (This statement refers to the situation with COVID-19 in the country, when all students have switched to online education).
- Language mechanism(s) used in creating this anti-proverb: Reception of "phonetic mimicry," sound assimilation of a word or its transformed version to other words. The technique is based on a partial morpho-phonetic transformation of the component, leading to a complete change in the semantics of the component and the entire proverb.
- URL: https://atyrautv.kz/kz/news/society/internette-okyp-zhur-talai-kazak-balasy

63. *Traditional proverb:* Ит жоқта шошқа үреді қораға, би жоқта құл жүреді жораға.
- English translation: Honey is not for the ass's mouth.
- Meaning, literal and/or figurative: The main point of this proverb is in the second line. In fact, a pig barks when there is no dog. If there is no real judge, anyone can be judge, even a slave. The guard of the peace of the barn is a dog, the guardian of the peace of the country is a bi (governor). The meaning of "a dog" is used in a good sense as guard. A pig is compared with a slave without a name is like a pig. "Slave" refers to an unholy person who has no freedom at first, who is at the door of a person, but a person who does not speak a fair decision.

Anti-proverb #1: Ит жоқта шошқа үреді.
- English translation: A pig barks when there is no dog.

- Brief description of the context that will explain to readers its usage: Since the words "bi" and "slave" are not often used today, this proverb is abbreviated as "a pig barks when there is no dog."
- URL: https://tengrinews.kz/kazakhstan_news/nege-makal-mateldn-jartyisyin-gana-aytyip-jurmz-386191/

Anti-proverb #2: Ит жоқта — шошқа, сеть жоқта — сотка үреді.
  - Brief description of the context that will explain to readers its usage: A pig barks when there is no dog, a mobile barks when there is no Internet.
  - Language mechanism(s) used in creating this anti-proverb: The final elements of a multicomponent unit are reduced. The reduction of the component composition is called ellipsis.
  - URL: https://interesnoe.me/view/content/1

64. *Traditional proverb: Көршің соқыр болса бір көзіңді қысып жүр.*
  - English translation: A real friend is one who walks in when the rest of the world walks out.
  - Meaning, literal and/or figurative: Do not take advantage of your neighbor or your spouse when you have power.
  - English equivalent if there is one: *Treat people as you would like to be treated.*

Anti-proverb: Жолдасың соқыр болса, сен де бір көзіңді қысып жүр.
  - Brief description of the context that will explain to readers its usage: (Literally) If your friend is blind, then close one eye. The main thing is spiritual blindness. We also call it the "eye of the chest." In general, a person who thinks only about material things, he does not pay much attention to spiritual matters. The spiritual issues we are talking about are now a world. Only people with open eyes pay attention to the world.
  - Language mechanisms used in creating anti-proverbs: substituting one or more words, the proverb component with a stylistical synonym.
  - URL: https://kozhalar.kz/20208291-mani-ozgergen-maqaldar-3-

65. *Traditional proverb: Күлме досқа келер басқа.*
  - English translation: He who hatches mischief, is caught by mischief.
  - Meaning, literal and/or figurative: From this proverb you will learn that good is a lofty concept, and evil clings to you when you step on it. It means you can't fly high by lowering others.
  - English equivalent if there is one: *Don't laugh at someone else's misfortune.*

Anti-proverb: Күлме DDOS-қа, келер басқа.
- Brief description of the context that will explain to readers its usage: DDoS stands for Distributed Denial of Service, a method where cyber criminals flood a network with so much malicious traffic that it cannot operate or communicate as it normally would. This causes the site's normal traffic, also known as legitimate packets, to come to a halt.
- Language mechanisms used in creating anti-proverbs: Reception of "phonetic mimicry," sound assimilation of a word or its transformed version to other words. The technique is based on a partial morpho-phonetic transformation of the component, leading to a complete change in the semantics of the component and the entire proverb.
- URL: https://surak.baribar.kz/618367/

66. *Traditional Proverb: Күйесіз қазан жоқ, қайғысыз адам жоқ.*
- English translation: There is no kazan without soot, there is no man without grief.
- Meaning, literal and/or figurative: There is almost no one in this life who has not lost a loved one. But you don't have to worry about it all your life. The essence of the proverb is that there is no person in life without pain and sorrow.
- English equivalent if there is one: Trouble is the common denominator of living - Soren Kirkegaard. *Yet man is born unto trouble, as the sparks fly upward.* Job 5:7

Anti-proverb #1: Жемісін жүрген адам жоқ.
- Brief description of the context that will explain to readers its usage: A proverb about everyday life. It tells everyone that they have problems.
- Language mechanisms used in creating anti-proverbs: Change in the component composition of proverbs, as a rule, affects both the lexical and grammatical levels of the utterance. Reduction of the component composition.
- URL: https://kozhalar.kz/20208291-mani-ozgergen-maqaldar-3-

Anti-proverb # 2: Оңып жатқан Оспан жоқ.
- Brief description of the context that will explain to readers its usage: It means that in everyday life there is no one who is carefree and happy.
- Language mechanisms used in creating anti-proverbs: Change in the component composition of proverbs, as a rule, affects both the lexical and grammatical levels of the utterance. Reduction of the component composition.

- URL: https://kozhalar.kz/20208291-mani-ozgergen-maqaldar-3-
67. *Traditional Proverb: Күйеу—жүз жылдық, құда—мың жылдық.*
  - English translation: Husband is for 100 years, in-laws for 1,000 years.
  - Meaning, literal and/or figurative: It is one of the traditions of the Kazakh people that has a special place in weddings. Such a tradition between two families is called "kudalykh" in the Kazakh language. After that, the intimacy and respect between the two young families will last for a long time.

Anti-proverb: Күйеудің өзі—жүз жылдық, ал әуресі—мың жылдық.
  - English translation: The husband is for 100 years, and its concerns are for a thousand years.
  - Brief description of the context that will explain to readers its usage: The first formal kudalykh step is taken when the young couple get married with the prior consent of the parents of both families or by the engagement of the bride and groom. After that, according to the ceremony of marriage, exchange of jewelry, presenting earrings, wedding traditions, etc. are performed. It is followed by endless traditions. This means that it will be passed onto future generations, so the marriage will last for centuries.
  - Language mechanism(s) used in creating this anti-proverb: This is a stylistically modified and invariant version of the proverb. It is obvious that such stylistic changes give the sentence simplicity, accuracy, and emotional character.
  - URL: (Zhas Alash, 19.01.2010), Caravan news—https://kaz.cara van.kz/zhangalyqtar/
68. *Traditional Proverb: Қара қытай қаптаса, сары орыс әкеңдей көрінеді.*
  - English translation: When the black Chinese come, the red-haired Russian seems like a father.
  - Meaning, literal and/or figurative: What is the origin of the saying, " When black Chinese come, the red-haired Russian seems like a father"? Kazakhs are a nation that lives for generations. Many people are envious of the vast lands and riches of the country. Therefore, the main issue is to strengthen the borders and withstand external demographic pressures.
  - English equivalent, if there is one: When you have neighbors as Chinese, Russians are like your parents. It means to be a neighbor of Russia is better than to have a neighbor of China (It was also told by

ancestors. They had predictions that the Chinese would govern the land of the earth in future).

Anti-proverb #1: Қара қытай қаптаса, сары орыс нағашыңдай болады.

- Brief description of the context that will explain to readers its usage: (literally) When black Chinese come, the Russians seem like a relative from the mother's side. Kazakhs are patrilineal, but there is a special relationship and intimacy with the mother's side of the family. But Kazakh people prefer to be close to their father's side.
- Although the current level of relations between China and Kazakhstan is at a high level, there is an opinion that if my grandfather were Chinese, it would be the end of the world. The meaning of the proverb "If a black Chinese captures the country, a yellow Russian will be like your uncle" also describes the massive influx of Chinese into the country at this time. The fact that the Chinese population is so large and dispersed throughout the world. This proverb appeared because ancestors warned it is better to be closer to the people neighboring Russia than the Chinese people.
- Language mechanism used in creating this anti-proverb: Replacing proverb components with stylistic synonyms.
- URL: https://www.inform.kz/kz/nazarbaev-kytaymen-karym-katynas-turaly-tarih-biz

Anti-proverb #2: Қара қытай қаптаса сары орысқа жылап көрісерсің.

- Brief description of the context that will explain to readers its usage: (literally) When black Chinese come, you will meet red-haired Russians with hugs. The article says that Kazakhstan's proximity to China, the country's vast oil reserves and vast natural resources, and the neighboring country's need for energy resources could hurt the country's future.
- Language mechanism used in creating this anti-proverb: Change in the component composition of proverbs, as a rule, affects both the lexical and grammatical levels of the utterance. Expansion of the component composition.
- URL: https://alashainasy.kz/shymkent/tauelszdk-kazakka-ne-berd-170750/

69. *Traditional proverb: Қарға қарғаның көзін шұқымайды.*

- English translation: A raven will not peck out a raven's eyes.
- Meaning, literal and/or figurative: This is due to the nature of the bird—the habit of not harming each other. The meaning of the proverb is to hide the crime, guilt, shortcomings, etc. committed by the relatives, friends, etc. This means that even if one knows or sees

bad habits or criminal things, he will not go to tell on them, even if it is necessary that they need to be accused and punished. If possible, they try to cover up their actions. This is a concept that refers to the concealment of negative social phenomena in society, among people (kinship, citizenship, clan, corruption, etc.).
- English equivalent if there is one: *Snitches get stitches*

Anti-proverb: Қарғаның көзін қарға шұқиды екен.
- English translation: A raven will peck out a raven's eyes.
- Brief description of the context that will explain to readers its usage: To make entrepreneurship as a basis of our economy is one of the main tasks of our country from the moment of gaining independence. Adapting to the market economy and satisfying the needs of the population has become an economically reliable strategy of the state.
- Language mechanism used in creating this anti-proverb: Change in the component composition of proverbs, as a rule, affects both the lexical and grammatical levels of the utterance. Expansion of the component composition.
- URL: https://abai.kz/post/3298

70. *Traditional proverb: Қатын қайраттанса, қазан қайнатады.*
- English translation: When the wife gets power, the cooking pot boils.
- Meaning, literal and/or figurative: The essence of the proverb is the place of the Kazakh woman in the feudal patriarchal society.
- English equivalent, if there is one: *She has the power to build him up or tear him down.*

Anti-proverb: Қатын қайраттанса отбасының ғана емес, отанның да ойранын шығарады.
- English translation: When a woman is angry, she destroys not only her family but also her homeland.
- Brief description of the context that will explain to readers its usage: Anti-proverb means that a modern woman can do anything now.
- Language mechanism used in creating this anti-proverb: Change in the component composition of proverbs, as a rule, affects both the lexical and grammatical levels of the utterance. Expansion of the component composition.
- URL: https://www.facebook.com

71. *Traditional proverb: Қыздың қырық шырағы бар.*
- English translation: The girl has forty souls (lives).

- Meaning, literal and/or figurative: As a woman grows older, we often notice that a woman's fate is complex. It means that a woman has a lot of responsibilities both in life and at home.
- English equivalent: *Well-behaved women seldom make history.*

Anti-proverb: Қыздың қырық сайты бар.

- Brief description of the context that will explain to readers its usage: The girl has forty websites.
- Language mechanism used in creating this anti-proverb: Replacing proverb components with contextual synonyms.
- URL: https://vk.com/wall-101941802_449

72. *Traditional proverb: Қыз кезінде бәрі жақсы, жаман қатын қайдан шығады?*
- English translation: Every young girl is good, but where do the bad women come from?
- Meaning, literal and/or figurative: When a couple meets, the girl's character is different in the beginning. However, some girls change their behavior after marriage due to various factors.
- English equivalent: You can't turn a bad girl good, but once good girls go bad, she's gone forever.

Anti-Proverb #1: Өлген кезінде бәрі жақсы, жаман адам қайдан шығады?
- Brief description of the context that will explain to readers its usage: Every dead person is good, but where do the bad people come from?
- Language mechanism used in creating this anti-proverb: New lexical content of the same syntactic structure (complete).
- URL: http://www.halyk-azeti.kz/index.php?option=com_content&view=article&id=5797:2016-06-30-04-58-40&catid=5:2011-11-18-09-02-24&Itemid=5&month=7&year=2016

Anti-Proverb #2: Идея кезде бәрі жақсы, жаман проект қайдан шығады?!
- Brief description of the context that will explain to readers its usage: All ideas are good, where do bad projects come from?!
- Language mechanism used in creating this anti-proverb: Expansion of the lexical meaning of the composition.
- URL: https://surak.baribar.kz/618367/

73. *Traditional Proverb: Қойшы көп болса, қой арам өледі.*
- English translation: When there are a lot of shepherds, the sheep begin to die.
- Meaning, literal and/or figurative: It means that the more people involved / in charge, the less work gets done.
- English equivalent: *Too many cooks spoil the broth.*

Anti-Proverb: Қой бағушы көп болса, қой арам өледі.
- Brief description of the context that will explain to readers its usage: When there are many shepherds, the sheep will die.
- Language mechanism used in creating this anti-proverb: Replacing proverb components with stylistic synonyms.
- URL: https://tengrinews.kz/kazakhstan_news/nege-makal-mateldn-jartyisyin-gana-aytyip-jurmz-386191/

74. *Traditional Proverb:* Қыз өссе—елдің көркі, гүл өссе—жердің көркі.
- English translation: A ripe flower is the beauty of nature; a young maiden is the people's beauty.
- Meaning, literal and/or figurative: The essence of the proverb praises the girl's tenderness, charm, intelligence, decency and modesty, her value.
- English equivalent: *Change always starts with a girl.*

Anti-proverb: Қыз өссе—елдің көркі, гүл өссе—әкімшіліктің көркі.
- Brief description of the context that will explain to readers its usage: A ripe flower is the beauty of city administration; a young maiden is the people's beauty.
- Language mechanism used in creating this anti-proverb: Replacing proverb components with contextual synonyms.
- URL: https://vk.com/wall-101941802_449

75. *Traditional Proverb:* Қызым саған айтамын, келінім, сен тыңда.
- English translation: Daughter-in-law, listen, while I am telling you, my daughter
- Meaning, literal and/or figurative: The proverb says that the mother-in-law gives advice to the bride, who comes to a new family to serve them because she is someone's daughter, and that this is a national example of Kazakh upbringing.
- Equivalent, if there is one: Oh, daughter I'm telling you. Oh, daughter-in-law, listen to it! (Indian proverb)

Anti-proverb #1 Келінім саған айтам, қызым сен тыңда.
- Brief description of the context that will explain to readers its usage: According to the proverb, the girl's mother or sister-in-law often gives such advice to the bride indirectly, rather than immediately expressing her directly.
- Language mechanism(s) used in creating this anti-proverb: Replacing proverb components with stylistic synonyms.
- URL: https://www.wikiwand.com/

Anti-proverb #2 Қызым саған айтам, сен ешкімге айтпа.

- Brief description of the context that will explain to readers its usage: Literally, I tell my daughter a secret, don't tell it to anyone.
- Language mechanism(s) used in creating this anti-proverb: Expansion of the component composition.
- URL: https://vk.com/wall-101941802_449

76. *Traditional Proverb: Қырық жыл қырғын болса да, ажалды өлер.*
- English translation: Even though there have been plenty of battles, death comes when it is time.
- Meaning, literal and/or figurative: It means an immortal person does not die if God lets him to live, but when it is time for death anyone can stay alive. It means we live the life God has given us.
- English equivalent if there is one: Death waits for no one.

Anti-proverb: Қырық жыл қырғын болса да, ажалсыз адам тірі қалар.
- Brief description of the context that will explain to readers its usage: Literally it means the immortal person will survive, even there are forty years of genocide.
- Language mechanism(s) used in creating this anti-proverb: Expansion of the component composition.
- URL: M. Magauin. Qiyadagy kystau, P. 37.

77. *Traditional proverb: Құм жиылып тас болмас, құл жиылып бас болмас.*
- English translation: No matter how much sand there is, it isn't a stone, a slave is never rich.
- Meaning, literal and/or figurative: The original meaning was expressed mainly in terms of social status, that is, everything and everyone has its place.
- English equivalent, if there is one: *Pigs are pigs; Once a priest, always a priest.*

Anti-proverb: Құм жиылып тас болды, құл жиылып бас болды.
- Brief description of the context that will explain to readers its usage: Literally it means the sand becomes a stone when it is piled up and the slave will become a leader when they are united.
- Language mechanism(s) used in creating this anti-proverb: Change in the component composition of proverbs, as a rule, affects both the lexical and grammatical levels of the utterance. Expansion of the component composition.
- URL: https://emle.kz/articles/get/109

78. *Traditional Proverb: Мал өсірсең—қой өсір, өнімі оның көл-көсір.*
- English translation: If you raise livestock, raise sheep, it is profitable.

- Meaning, literal and/or figurative: This means that sheep multiply rapidly and give more production.
- English equivalent, if there is one: You care for your livestock, and they provide you with offspring.

Anti-Proverb: Ұл өсірме, қыз өсір, қалыңмалы оның көл-көсір.

- Brief description of the context that will explain to readers its usage: Literally it means there are benefits to raising a boy and raising a girl. You get a lot of money when you bring up a girl, which means that in modern Kazakh society the tradition of bridesmaids, the revival of the tradition of "kalyn mal" (bridewealth) is reflected in this proverb. However, this does not mean that everyone will be rich because of "kalyn mal."
- Language mechanism(s) used in creating this anti-proverb: The form of the new proverb is grammatically and lexically modified, for example, the replacement of two words, and its meaning is the revival of traditions in modern Kazakhstani society, which show the importance of the tradition of daughter's farewell, welcoming the bride, and "money given for bride." Hence, we understand the pragmatic function of modern proverbs as an irreplaceable literary tool in describing the life of a nation.
- URL: https://halyqline.kz/halyk-bet/oipyrmai/maqal-soezding-saqaly/

79. *Traditional proverb:* Мен жазбаймын өлеңді ермек үшін (Абай).
- English translation: I don't write poetry for pleasure
- Meaning, literal and/or figurative: Abai said that he wrote the song not just for fun, but for a special purpose.
- English equivalent if there is one: "Poetry is not an expression of the party line. It's that time of night, lying in bed, thinking what you really think, making the private world public, that's what the poet does." Allen Ginsburg

Anti-proverb: Мен жазбаймын посттарды ермек үшін

- Brief description of the context that will explain to readers its usage: Literally it means I don't write posts for pleasure
- Language mechanism used in creating this anti-proverb: Replacing proverb components with stylistic synonyms.
- URL: https://interesnoe.me/view/content/1

80. *Traditional proverb*: Не ексең, соны орасың, жаман тұқымнан жақсы өнім күтпе.
   - English translation: You reap what you sow, Do not expect a good harvest from a bad seed.
   - Meaning, literal and/or figurative: The proverb says that the more a person works, the more he earns, the more benefits he receives.
   - English equivalent if there is one: As you sow so shall you reap. A tree is known by its fruit. As you have made your bed, so you must lie on it.

Anti-proverb: "Не сепсең, соны орасың", "жаман тұқымнан жақсы өнім күтпе",-деп бекерден-бекер айтылмаған.
   - Brief description of the context that will explain to readers its usage: Literally it means, no wonder they say: "What you sow, so you reap," "Do not expect a good harvest from a bad seed."
   - Language mechanism(s) used in creating this anti-proverb: This anti-proverb is created by contamination, the formation of a new stable phrase because of the crossing of two different proverbs or expressions, and this phenomenon of contamination is often used by authors to create a comic effect or a pun.
   - URL: The newspaper: Zhetisu, 12 October 2013.

81. *Traditional proverb*: Отыз тістен шыққан сөз отыз рулы ерге тарайды.
   - English translation: A word comes out of thirty teeth and enters thirty tribes.
   - Meaning, literal and/or figurative: The spoken word is like a bullet. That is, an opinion about something or a situation, whether positive or negative, cannot be taken back, and it quickly spreads among the people.
   - English equivalent if there is one: A word spoken is past recalling. Bad news has wings. Bad news travels fast.

Anti-proverb: Он саусақтан шыққан пост он рулы елге тарайды.
   - Brief description of the context that will explain to readers its usage: The post comes out of thirty teeth and enters into thirty tribes.
   - Language mechanism(s) used in creating this anti-proverb: Replacing proverb components with stylistic synonyms.
   - URL: https://interesnoe.me/view/content/1

82. *Traditional proverb*: Өзін аямаған басқаны да аямайды.
   - English translation: Who does not regret himself will not regret others.

- Meaning, literal and/or figurative: The proverb means to suffer for the sake of others, or to fight selflessly for the protection of one's homeland.
- English equivalent, if there is one: In taking revenge, a man is but even with his enemy, but in passing it over, he is superior (Francis Bacon).

Anti-proverb: Өзін-өзі аямаған басқаның бетін шиедей қылады.

- Brief description of the context that will explain to readers its usage: If we fight against people without fear and without feeling sorry for ourselves, others will be afraid of us. If Kazakhs who do not speak Kazakh language will not be hired to official positions, all of them will speak Kazakh within a year. We need to impose strict requirements on officials who ignore the national language. Seeing that Kazakhs do not feel sorry for Kazakhs, the representatives of other nationalities also will try to learn the Kazakh language voluntarily.
- Language mechanism(s) used in creating this anti-proverb: Replacing proverb components with stylistic synonym, do not spare "аямайды" is replaced with "бетін шиедей қылады" scratching face until bleeding.
- URL: https://abai.kz/post/6550

83. *Traditional proverb: Өзімдікі дегенде өгіз қара күшім бар, өзгенікі дегенде адам таппас ісім бар.*
  - English translation: things that a person does or chooses to do for himself, his family, others do not seem burdensome, tiresome.
  - Meaning, literal and/or figurative: According to the proverb, if a person works for himself, he does not feel sorry for himself, he does not regret the effort he did for himself.
  - English equivalent if there is one: A burden of one's own choice is not felt.

Anti-proverb #1: Өзімдікі дегенде өгіз қара күшім бар, кісінікі дегенде анау-мынау ісім бар.

- Brief description of the context that will explain to readers its usage: The proverb is about people who do their business with diligence, and when it is necessary to help others, they make excuses.
- Language mechanism(s) used in creating this anti-proverb: Change in the component composition of proverbs, as a rule, affects both the lexical and grammatical levels of the utterance. Expansion of the component composition.
- URL: http://toibastar.kz/makal/

Anti-proverb #2: Өзімдікі дегенде өгіз қара күшім бар, кісінікі дегенде кішкентай ғана күшім бар.
  - Brief description of the context that will explain to readers its usage: So, they say about the hard work that you do for yourself. For example: building a house, raising children, caring for old parents. And although this work is not easy, it is still less burdensome for a person than work for someone—for an employer or for the state.
  - Language mechanism(s) used in creating this anti-proverb: Change in the component composition of proverbs, as a rule, affects both the lexical and grammatical levels of the utterance. Expansion of the component composition.
  - URL: http://88.204.166.7/kz/news/view/oten_ahmet_tozbas_u lgi_sarkilmas_mektep__21545

84. *Traditional proverb: Өнерді үйрен де, жирен!*
  - English translation: Learn the art, master the skill, then give it up.
  - Meaning, literal and/or figurative: This proverb obliges a person to learn art, saying that first learn, know, and then you will know whether you hate it or not.
  - English equivalent if there is one: Learning is a treasure that will follow its owner everywhere.

Anti-proverb: Жемқордан—үйрен, жей алмайтыннан—жирен.
  - English translation: Learn from the corrupt person and loathe people, who can't corrupt.
  - Brief description of the context that will explain to readers its usage: The issue of corruption in society is criticized in the proverb.
  - Language mechanism(s) used in creating this anti-proverb: The speech figure oxymoron is used to create this new phrase, which is based on a logical contradiction.
  - URL: https://qazaqadebieti.kz/12415/mit-z-lharova-shta-an

85. *Traditional proverb: Өтіріктің құйрығы бір-ақ біртұтам.*
  - English translation: The tail of a lie is half a foot; you can't get far on a lie.
  - Meaning, literal and/or figurative: The use of the concept of unity here shows that the "life" of deception is too short through allegorical, metaphorical meanings.
  - English equivalent if there is one: *Lies have short legs.*

Anti-proverb: Қазақ айласының құйрығы бір-ақ біртұтам.
  - Brief description of the context that will explain to readers its usage: The tail of a Kazakh lie is too short!

- Language mechanism(s) used in creating this anti-proverb: New lexical content of the same syntactic structure (partial).
- URL: https://pps.kaznu.kz/ru/Main/FileShow2/138513/95/137/16589

86. *Traditional proverb: Сақалын сатқан кәріден, еңбегін сатқан бала артық. Күріш арқасында күрмек су ішер.*
   - English translation: A young man who sells his labor is better than an old man who speculates with his beard. When the rice is watered, the water weed next to the rice gets drunk.
   - Meaning, literal and/or figurative: Abai's proverb "Better is an old man who sells his beard than a child who sells his labor" promotes honest work, criticizes the shortcomings of society, tries to influence the way of life to good for future generations, and the second part is "Rice drinks water because of rice."
   - English equivalent if there is one: Hard work brings prosperity; playing around brings poverty. No man should live by another's labor.

Anti-proverb: Қой, балам, масыл болып, сақалымды сатып, күріш арасына шыққан күрмек секілді болмайын, отарымды басқа біреуге өткізейін.
   - Brief description of the context that will explain to readers its usage: Stop, my son! Instead of selling my beard and being an idle man, I would better pass my deals to another person.
   - Language mechanisms used in creating anti-proverbs: an anti-proverb is created from the intertwining of two proverbs.
   - URL: https://emirsaba.org/maalalar-bayandamalar-jinafi-v2.html?page=41

87. *Traditional proverb: Соқыр тауыққа бәрі бидай.*
   - English translation: To a blind chicken, everything seems like wheat.
   - Meaning, literal and/or figurative: The meaning of the proverb is to describe a person who does not know and does not want to know, whether he is good or bad, honest, or dishonest. Often it is the person who is unaware of a particular situation who makes a mistake.
   - English equivalent if there is one: Blind men can judge no colors.

Anti-proverb: Соқыр тауыққа линза тауып берейік.
   - Brief description of the context that will explain to readers its usage: Let's find a lens for a blind chicken.
   - Language mechanisms used in creating anti-proverbs: Extension of the syntactic structure.

- URL: https://interesnoe.me/view/content/1

88. *Traditional proverb: Судың да сұрауы бар.*
   - English translation: There is also a price for water.
   - Meaning, literal and/or figurative: The world that a person accumulates in his life is a useless thing that is left behind in vain in the end.
   - English equivalent if there is one: Water is unappreciated—until the well runs dry.

Anti-proverb: Жолдың да сұрауы бар.
   - Brief description of the context that will explain to readers its usage: There is also a demand for a road? It means road repair is very important. Because the road serves passengers and people.
   - Language mechanisms used in creating anti-proverb: Replacing proverb component with stylistic synonym.
   - URL: https://24.kz/kz/zha-aly-tar/o-am/item/402280-zholdy-das-rauy-bar

89. *Traditional proverb: Сыйға—сый, сырға—бал.*
   - English translation: Gift for a gift, honey for a secret.
   - Meaning, literal and/or figurative: According to the proverb: if you reveal your "private" secret to your friend, he will not spare you all the treasures he has.
   - English equivalent if there is one: *Every man has his price.*

Anti-proverb: Сыйға – сый, сыраға – бал.
   - Brief description of the context that will explain to readers its usage: It is an unwritten law to give a gift, to return a good deed for a good deed.
   - Language mechanisms used in creating anti-proverb: Replacing proverb component with contextual synonym.
   - URL: https://egemen.kz/article/178243-naqypbek-saduaqasov-maqaldynh-bari-mandi-emes

90. *Traditional proverb: Талаптыға нұр жауар.*
   - English translation: Light shines for the seeker.
   - Meaning, literal and/or figurative: Hard work pays off.
   - English equivalent if there is one: The gifted person has perspectives.

Anti-proverb: Талаптыдан теңге артық.
   - Brief description of the context that will explain to readers its usage: Money is better than an inquisitive one.
   - Language mechanism(s) used in creating this anti-proverb: Substitution of the lexical structure of proverbs.
   - URL: https://egemen.kz/article/168345-soz-soyyl-%E2%84%9659

91. *Traditional proverb:* Тоқал ешкі мүйіз сұраймын деп, сақалынан айрылыпты.
   · English translation: A nanny goat lost her beard because she wanted goat horns.
   · Meaning, literal and/or figurative: He who begs for more may lose everything.
   · English equivalent, if there is one: The camel going to seek horns, lost his ears. Looking for the stones you may lose the diamond.

Anti-proverb #1 Тоқал ешкі мүйіз сұраймын деп құлағынан айрылыпты.
   · Brief description of the context that will explain to readers its usage: The goat without horn lost his ear to ask for the horns
   · Language mechanism(s) used in creating this anti-proverb: Replacing proverb component with stylistic synonym.
   · URL: https://massaget.kz/layfstayl/ezutartar/4760/

Anti-proverb #2 Тоқал ешкі мүйіз сұраймын деп барынан айрылыпты.
   · English translation: The goat without horns lost everything when she asked for horns.
   · Brief description of the context that will explain to readers its usage: The goat without horns lost everything when asked the horns. There is a lot of food and clothes for the people in the country. As the whole country is lending a hand, don't be so greedy.
   · Language mechanism(s) used in creating this anti-proverb: Replacing proverb component with stylistic synonym.
   · URL: https://sn.kz/sn-adebiet-zhane-oner/5627

92. *Traditional proverb:* Туған жердің жуасы да тәтті.
   · English translation: And onions are sweet as honey if they grow in your homeland.
   · Meaning, literal and/or figurative: The birthplace of all peoples is a sacred place in human life. It is this place that connects people with the country, past and future. That is why it is said that a sense of patriotism awakens in a person even from childhood.
   · English equivalent, if there is one: An onion can be as sweet as honey if it grows in your Motherland.

Anti-proverb: Туған жердің түтіні де тәтті . . . .
   · Brief description of the context that will explain to readers its usage: The proverb has a meaning "what you find elsewhere is not comparable to what you find in your homeland." Everyone has such a mysterious gravitational pull of the Motherland. And if you want to live a happy life in your homeland, appreciate its independence.

Protect your country, your land, and only then your happiness will last a long time.
- Language mechanisms used in creating anti-proverb: Replacing proverb component with stylistic synonym.
- URL: https://massaget.kz/blogs/26332/

93. *Traditional proverb: Туған жердің тасы да болысады.*
- English translation: In the native land the stones intercede.
- Meaning, literal and/or figurative: According to the proverb, a person feels better in his homeland, works better at home or in a familiar environment than in a strange place.
- English equivalent if there is one: There's no place like home.

Anti-proverb: Туған жердің тасы да ыстық.
- Brief description of the context that will explain to readers its usage: The meaning of the proverb is that there is no place like the motherland, even its every stone is precious.
- Language mechanism(s) used in creating this anti-proverb: Substitution of the lexical structure of proverbs.
- URL: https://kzref.org/janta-osimdigi-turali-jalpi-sipattama.html

94. *Traditional proverb: Сырын білмеген аттың сыртынан жүрме.*
- English translation: Don't ride a horse if you don't know its secret.
- Meaning, literal and/or figurative: The inner meaning of the proverb is that if you are very close with someone who you don't not know the secret to, you might be in an awkward situation.
- English equivalent if there is one: Don't judge a book by its cover.

Anti-proverb: Сырын білмеген қатынның қасына жатпа.
- Brief description of the context that will explain to readers its usage: Literally, it means don't lie next to a woman if you don't know her secret.
- Language mechanisms used in creating anti-proverb: New lexical content of the same syntactic structure (complete).
- URL: https://old2.aikyn.kz/2018/03/08/45538.html

95. *Traditional proverb: Үйіңде қартың болса, жазулы тұрған хатпен тең.*
- English translation: If you have an elderly person at home, it is like a letter.
- Meaning, literal and/or figurative: It is known that the Kazakh people consider respect for the elders as the basis of education and have a special respect for the preparation of the elder's equipment and

things for them and serve for them. The meaning of the proverb is that if the house has an older person, the house has a treasure.

· English equivalent if there is one: Wisdom comes at an old age to replace the mind. When the elderly die, a library is lost, and volumes of wisdom and knowledge are gone.

Anti-proverb: Интернетің бар болса, жазулы тұрған хатпен тең.

· Brief description of the context that will explain to readers its usage: If you have an internet, it is like a written document (letter).

· Language mechanism(s) used in creating this anti-proverb: Substitution of the lexical structure of a proverb.

· URL: https://interesnoe.me/view/content/1

96. *Traditional proverb: Үндемеген үйдей пәледен құтылады*

· English translation: Who will remain silent, he will pass the big trouble.

· Meaning, literal and/or figurative: The proverb's advice is that in some cases it is better to remain silent than to say something without thinking.

· English equivalent, if there is one: Speech is silver, but silence is golden.

Anti-proverb #1: Үйде отырған үйдей пәледен құтылады.

· Brief description of the context that will explain to readers its usage: During the covid-19 it is safe to stay at home. A person will be saved from troubles if he stays at home.

· Language mechanisms used in creating anti-proverb: New lexical content of the same syntactic structure (partial).

· URL: https://serpyn.kz/kogam

Anti-proverb #2: "Үндемеген үйдей пәледен құтылады" деуші еді, бүгінде үндемейтіндер ең ақылды, кемеңгер адам болып саналады.

· Brief description of the context that will explain to readers its usage: They say that who will remain silent, he will pass the big trouble, those who remain silent today are considered the smartest and wisest.

· Language mechanisms used in creating anti-proverb: A stylistic device based on a play on words in a metaphorical and literal sense is called wellerism. The anti-proverb is created by wellerism.

· URL: http://mkarasartov.blogspot.com/2013/12/blog-post.html

97. *Traditional proverb: Ішің ауырса, тамағыңды тый, көзің ауырса, қолыңды тый.*

· English translation: If your stomach hurts, stop eating if your eyes hurt, stop your hands.

- Meaning, literal and/or figurative: Your eyes are your two sides, you know how important they are when you feel when your eyes are sick, damaged or there is something that hurts your eyes. In this regard, our people say, "If your stomach hurts, keep your mouth shut, if your eyes hurt, restrain your hands."
- English equivalent if there is one: Adapt the remedy to the disease.

Anti-proverb: Ішің ауырса аузыңды тый.

- Brief description of the context that will explain to readers its usage: If you have a stomachache, stop eating. In the modern world it is during the covid-19 it is safe to stay at home.
- Language mechanism(s) used in creating this anti-proverb: Reduction of the component composition of the proverb—ellipsis.
- URL: bilim-all.kz/quote/3738

98. *Traditional proverb: Шақырған жерден қалма, шақырмаған жерге барма.*
   - English translation: Don't refuse to go where you are invited, don't go where you are not invited
   - Meaning, literal and/or figurative: You should not refuse an invitation. And if you do not want to be a guest of honor, you should not go to an uninvited place.
   - *English equivalent if there is one: The place of an uninvited guest is behind the door. (Yugoslavian proverb)*

Anti-proverb: Шақырылмаған қонақ келмейді.

   - Brief description of the context that will explain to readers its usage: The guests do not come if they are not invited.
   - Language mechanism(s) used in creating this anti-proverb: Reduction of the component composition of the proverb—ellipsis.
   - URL: https://www.facebook.com/MadeInqaZ/posts/65808180 7732034/

99. *Traditional proverb: Шапқан озар, жатқан қалар.*
   - English translation: The runner will overtake, the lying one will lag behind
   - Meaning, literal and/or figurative: Everyone is an owner of his future. At the same time, the proverb says that a person who works and is strong will reach heights, and a person who is lazy and weak will not reach his goals.
   - English equivalent if there is one: All Work and No Play (Makes Jack a Dull Boy). The early bird catches the worm.

Anti-proverb: Шапқан озар, жатқан тозар.
- · Brief description of the context that will explain to readers its usage: Who races, will be a winner, who is lazy will be torn and worn.
- · Language mechanism(s) used in creating this anti-proverb: Replacing proverb components with stylistic synonyms.
- · URL: https://portal.bilimal.kz/records/view?id=4445

100. *Traditional proverb: Шешесін көріп, қызын ал, аяғын көріп асын іш.*
- · English translation: Marry the girl after knowing her mother, eat her meals after looking at her dish.
- · Meaning, literal and/or figurative: It means whatever the mother tells her daughter, she does well. Many parents want their children to marry well-mannered, well-educated girls.
- · English equivalent, if there is one: Like mother, like daughter.

Anti-proverb #1: Инстаграмына қарап қызын ал.
- · Brief description of the context that will explain to readers its usage: Marry the girls after looking at her Instagram.
- · Language mechanism(s) used in creating this anti-proverb: New lexical content of the same syntactic structure (complete).
- · URL: https://www.youtube.com/watch?v=VS4YbMrXY-o&list=RDCMUCOBmXp_2O09zqNR5qv2Qr-A

Anti-proverb #2: "Шешесіне қарап қызын ал" деуші еді, бүгінде жігіттер қыздарының мінген көлігі мен тұратын көшесіне қарайтын болды.
- · Brief description of the context that will explain to readers its usage: Marry the girl after knowing her mother, they say, today guys are looking at her car and the street where the girls live.
- · Language mechanism(s) used in creating this anti-proverb: A stylistic device based on a play on words in a metaphorical and literal sense is called wellerism. The anti-proverb is created by wellerism.
- · URL: http://mkarasartov.blogspot.com/2013/12/blog-post.html

Notes on Contributors

AASLAND ERIK, Affiliate Assistant Professor of Anthropology, Fuller School of Intercultural Studies, Pasadena, California, the USA. Email: e_aasland@fuller.edu

ABDIGAPBAROVA ZHANAR, Candidate of Philological Sciences, Assistant Professor of the Department of the Kazakh language and Turkic studies, Nazarbayev University, Kazakhstan. Email: zhabdigapar@nu.edu.kz

ABDIMAULEN GULMIRA, Ph.D. Student, L.N.Gumilyov Eurasian National University, Nur-Sultan, Kazakhstan. Email: abdimaulen.gulmira@yandex.ru

AMALBEKOVA AIDANA, Master of Education, L.N. Gumilyov Eurasian National University, Nur-Sultan, Kazakhstan. Email: aidana.amalbekova@alumni.nu.edu.kz

ARINOVA BAKHYT, Candidate of Pedagogical Sciences, Associate Professor, Al-Farabi Kazakh National University, Almaty, Kazakhstan. Email: baxit-a@mail.ru

BEKKOZHANOVA GULNAR, Candidate of Philological Sciences, Associate Professor, Al-Farabi Kazakh National University, Almaty, Kazakhstan. Email: almaty.gulnar@mail.ru

BURANKULOVA ELMIRA, Ph.D. Student, K.Zhubanov Aktobe Regional University, Kazakhstan. Email: elmira.burankulova@inbox.ru

DUISENOVA KARYLGA, Master of Pedagogy, Zhubanov Aktobe Regional University Confucius Institute, Kazakhstan. Email: dkarylga@mail.ru

GUVEN FUNDA, Ph.D., Assistant Professor of the Department of the Kazakh language and Turkic studies, Nazarbayev University, Kazakhstan. Email: funda.guven@nu.edu.kz

KURMANBAYEVA AIZHAN, Ph.D. Student, Researcher of Auezov House, Institute of Literature and Art named after M.O. Auezov, Almaty, Kazakhstan. Email: aizhankurmanbai@gmail.com

NURGALIYEVA DOLORES, Candidate of Pedagogical Sciences, Assistant Professor of the Al-Farabi Kazakh National University, Almaty, Kazakhstan. Email: nurdolores@mail.ru

OMARBEKOVA GULNARA, Candidate of Philological Sciences, Associate Professor of the Department of the Kazakh language and Turkic studies, Nazarbayev University, Kazakhstan. Email: gulnara.omarbekova@nu.edu.kz

ORAZALIYEVA ELMIRA, Doctor of Philological Sciences, Associate Professor of the Department of the Kazakh Language and Turkic Studies, Nazarbayev University, Kazakhstan. Email: elmira.orazaliyeva@nu.edu.kz

ORAZBAYEVA FAUZIYA, Doctor of Philological Sciences, Professor, Director of the scientific and practical center "Latyn" at the Kazakh National Pedagogical University named after Abai, Almaty, Kazakhstan. Email: O_Fauziya@mail.ru

OSPANOVA GULMARIYA, Ph.D. Student, Al-Farabi Kazakh National University, Almaty, Kazakhstan. Email: Maryama140870@gmail.com

PIRALI GULZIA, Doctor of Philological Sciences, Chief Researcher of Auezov House, Institute of Literature and Art named after M.O. Auezov, Almaty, Kazakhstan. Email: Piralieva58@mail.ru

SHAKHANOVA ROZALINDA, Doctor of Pedagogical Sciences, Professor, Abay Kazakh National Pedagogical University, Almaty, Kazakhstan. Email: r.shakhanova@mail.ru

SHOKYM GULZHAN, Doctor of Philological Sciences, Professor, K. Zhubanov Aktobe Regional University, Kazakhstan. Email: shokum@mail.ru

TOLEGEN AIZHULDYZ, Master of Education, L.N. Gumilyov Eurasian National University, Nur-Sultan, Kazakhstan. Email: taizhuldyz@mail.ru

ZHANABEKOVA AIMAN, Doctor of Philological Sciences, Institute of Linguistics named after A. Baitursynuly, Almaty, Kazakhstan. Email: aiman_miras@mail.ru

ZHUSSUPOVA ROZA, Candidate of Pedagogical Sciences, Associate Professor in the Department of Theory and Practice of Foreign Languages, L.N. Gumilyov Eurasian National University, Nur-Sultan, Kazakhstan. Email: rozazhusupova@rambler.ru

Index

Alan Dundes, *Founding Editor*

Wolfgang Mieder, *General Editor*

This series includes theoretical studies of any genre or aspect of folklore. The series welcomes individually authored and collaboratively authored books, monographs, collections of data, bibliographies, and Festschriften. The emphasis will be on analytic and methodological innovations in the consideration of myth, folktale, legend, superstition, proverb, riddle, folksong, festival, game or any other form of folklore as well as any of the interpretative approaches to folklore topics.

Inquiries or manuscripts in English should be submitted to

Wolfgang.Mieder@uvm.edu

To order books, please contact our Customer Service Department:

peterlang@presswarehouse.com (within the U.S.)
orders@peterlang.com (outside the U.S.)

Or browse online by series: www.peterlang.com

Printed in Great Britain
by Amazon

29725416R00141